morning glories

volume five

tests

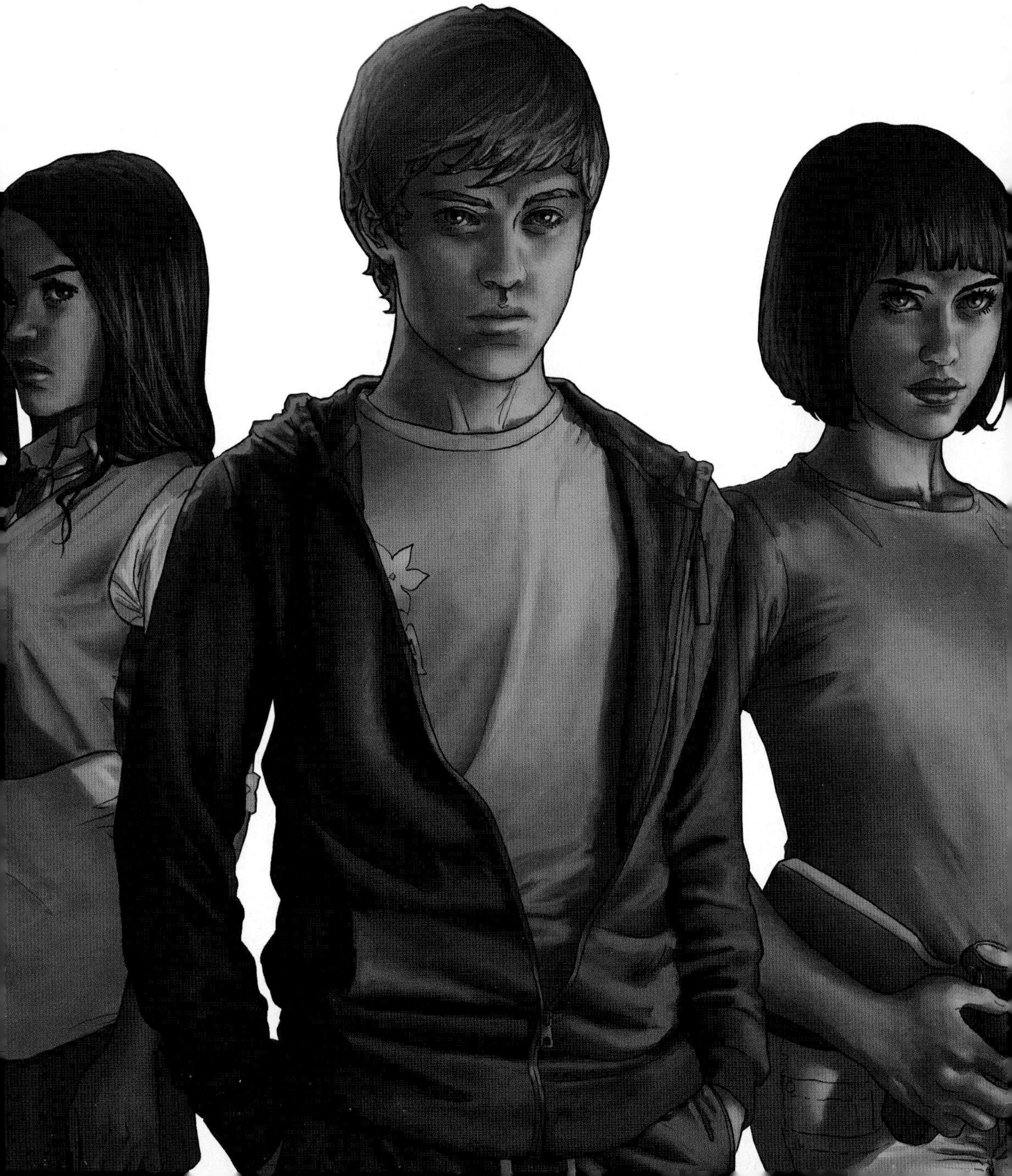

WORDS
NICK SPENCER

ART
JOE EISMA

RODIN ESQUEJO
COVERS

ALEX SOLLAZZO - PAUL LITTLE - MICHAEL SPICER
COLORS

JOHNNY LOWE - TIM DANIEL
LETTERS   DESIGN

IMAGE COMICS, INC.
Robert Kirkman - chief operating officer
Erik Larsen - chief financial officer
Todd McFarlane - president
Marc Silvestri - chief executive officer
Jim Valentino - vice-president

Eric Stephenson - publisher
Ron Richards - director of business development
Jennifer de Guzman - pr & marketing director
Branwyn Bigglestone - accounts manager
Emily Miller - accounting assistant
Jamie Parreno - marketing assistant
Emilio Bautista - sales assistant
Susie Giroux - administrative assistant
Kevin Yuen - digital rights coordinator
Tyler Shainline - events coordinator
David Brothers - content manager
Jonathan Chan - production manager
Drew Gill - art director
Jana Cook - print manager
Monica Garcia - senior production artist
Vincent Kukua - production artist
Jenna Savage - production artist
www.imagecomics.com

twentysix

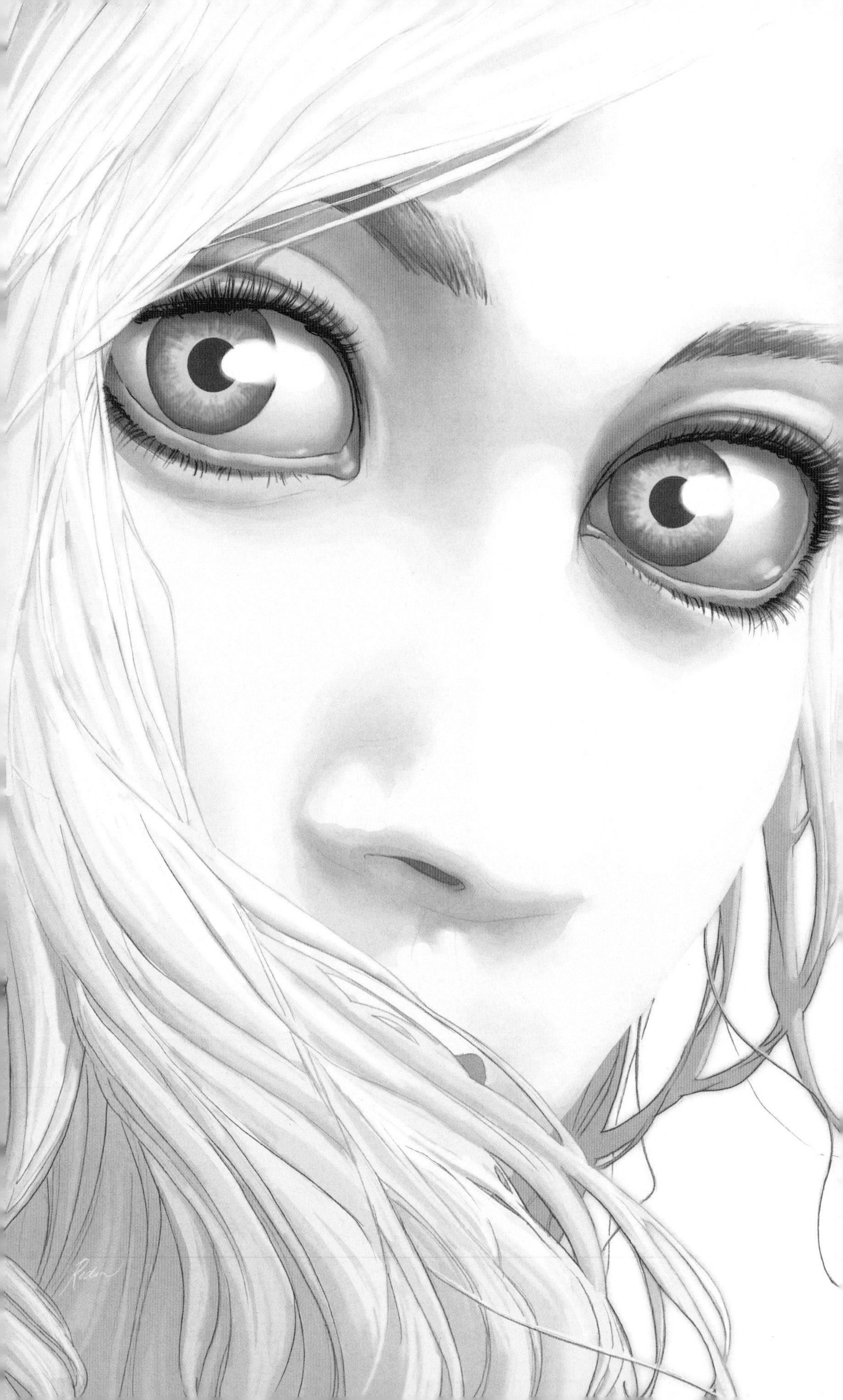

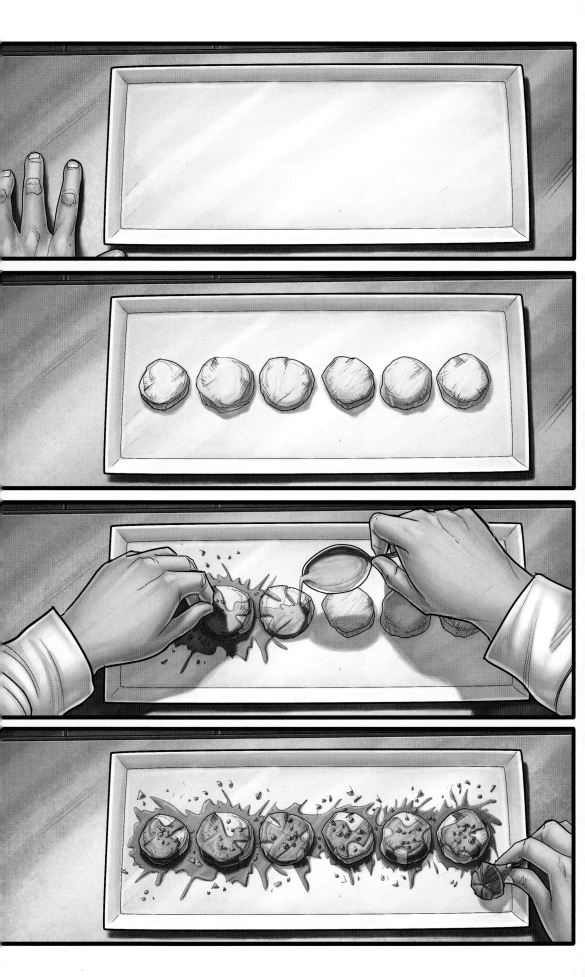

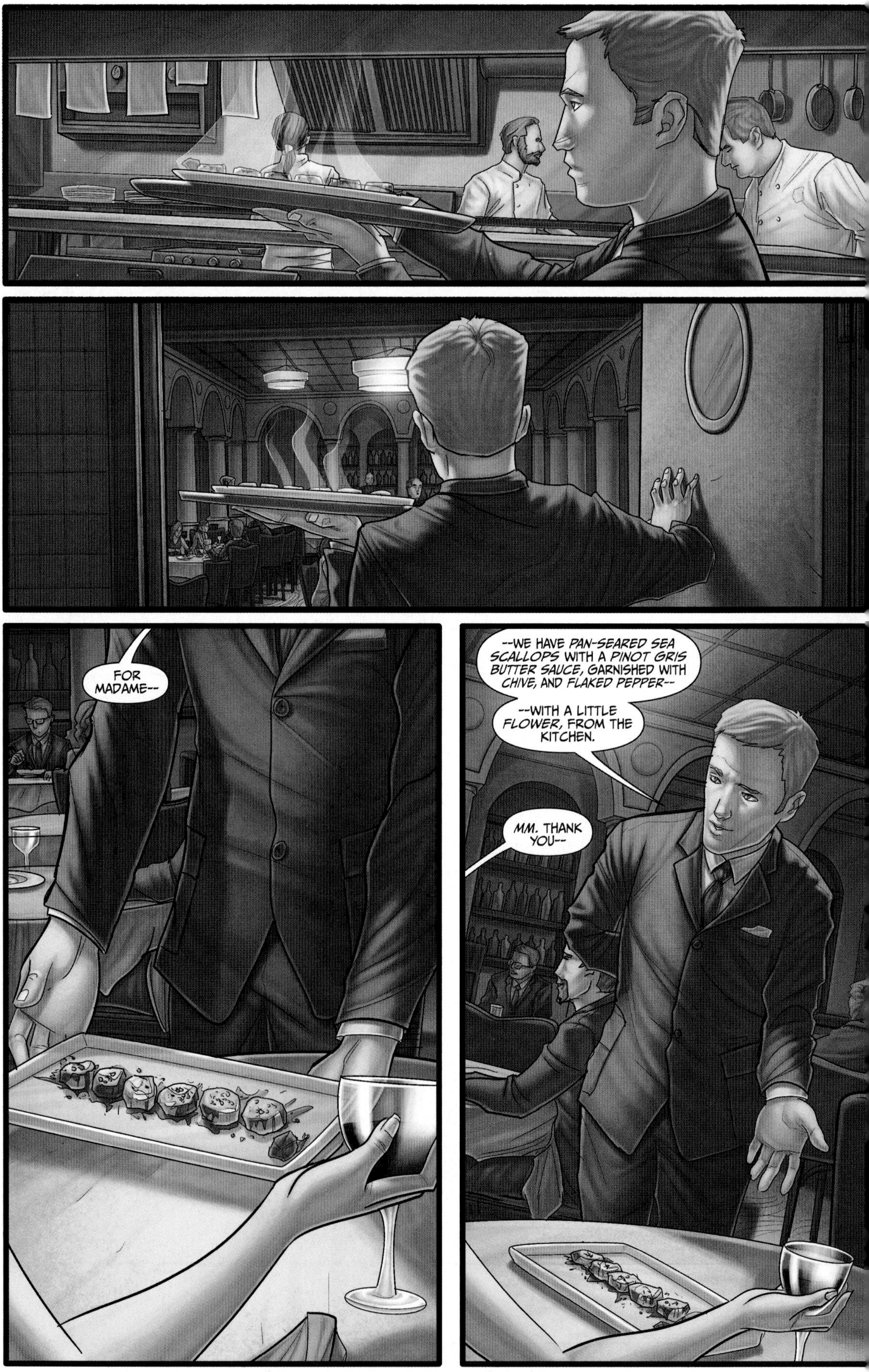
FOR MADAME--
--WE HAVE PAN-SEARED SEA SCALLOPS WITH A PINOT GRIS BUTTER SAUCE, GARNISHED WITH CHIVE, AND FLAKED PEPPER--
--WITH A LITTLE FLOWER, FROM THE KITCHEN.
MM. THANK YOU--

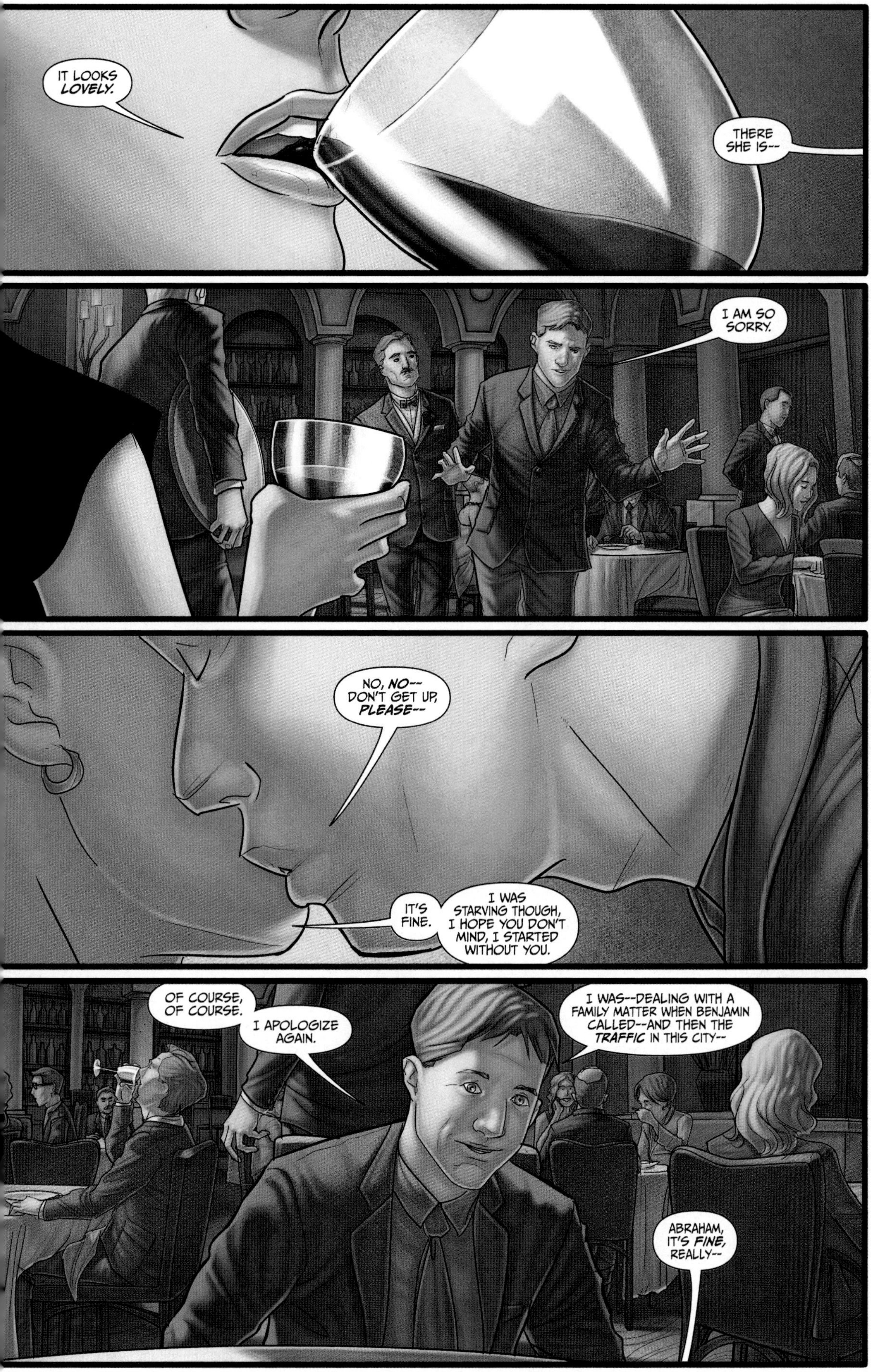
IT LOOKS LOVELY.
THERE SHE IS--
I AM SO SORRY.
NO, NO-- DON'T GET UP, PLEASE--
IT'S FINE.
I WAS STARVING THOUGH, I HOPE YOU DON'T MIND, I STARTED WITHOUT YOU.
OF COURSE, OF COURSE.
I APOLOGIZE AGAIN.
I WAS--DEALING WITH A FAMILY MATTER WHEN BENJAMIN CALLED--AND THEN THE TRAFFIC IN THIS CITY--
ABRAHAM, IT'S FINE, REALLY--

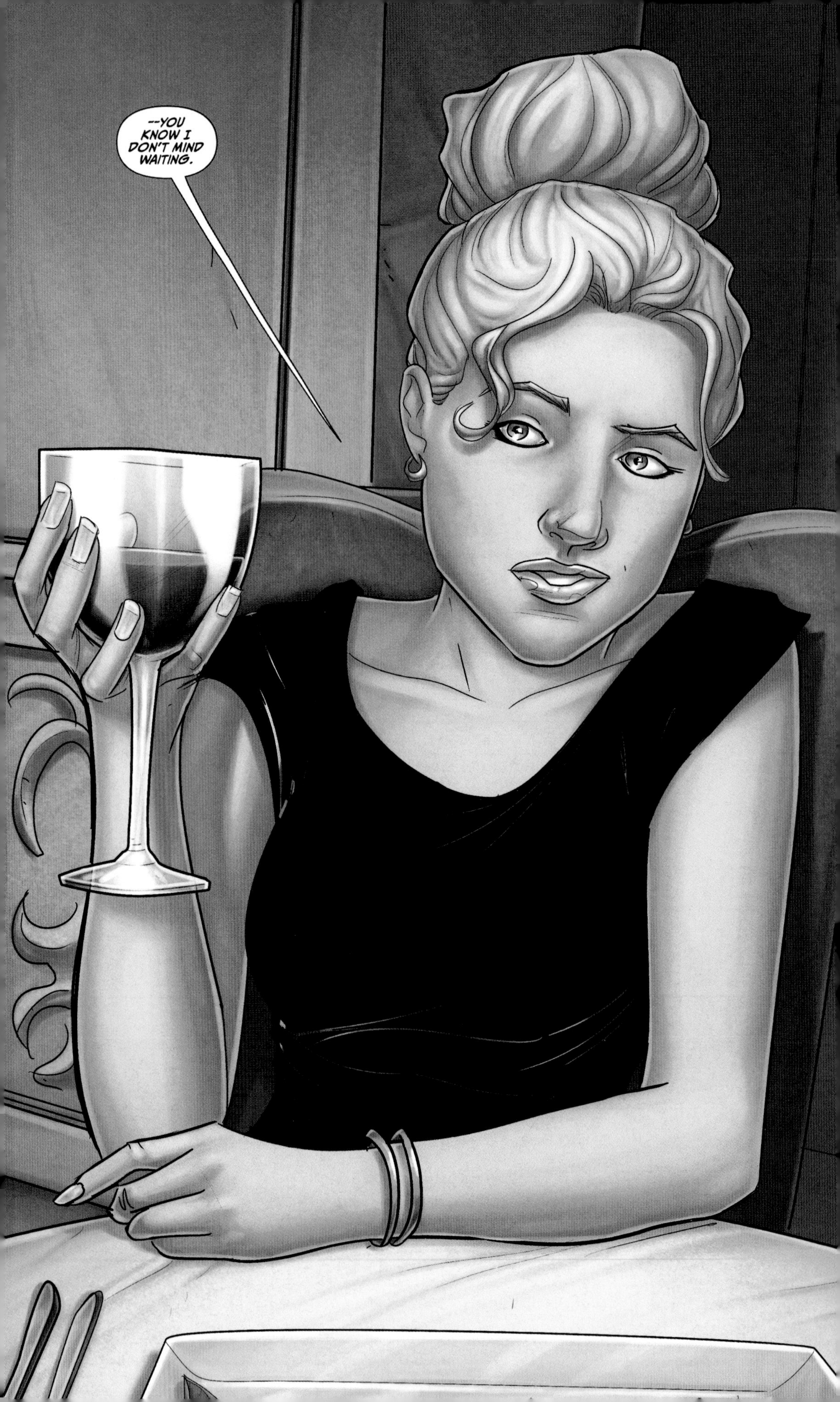
--YOU KNOW I DON'T MIND WAITING.

morning

glories
seasontwo

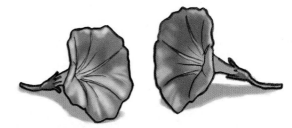

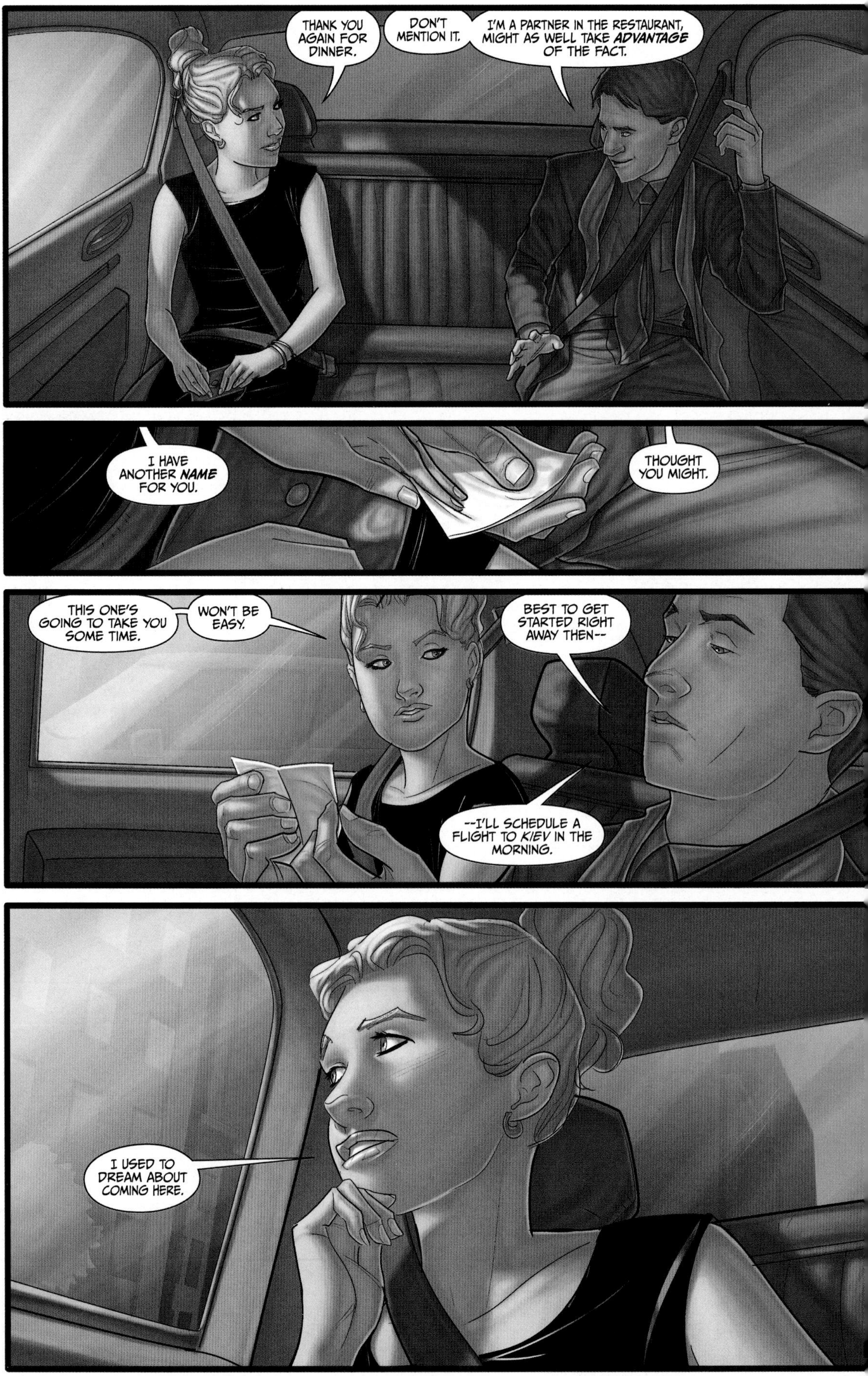
THANK YOU AGAIN FOR DINNER.
DON'T MENTION IT.
I'M A PARTNER IN THE RESTAURANT, MIGHT AS WELL TAKE *ADVANTAGE* OF THE FACT.
I HAVE ANOTHER *NAME* FOR YOU.
THOUGHT YOU MIGHT.
THIS ONE'S GOING TO TAKE YOU SOME TIME.
WON'T BE EASY.
BEST TO GET STARTED RIGHT AWAY THEN--
--I'LL SCHEDULE A FLIGHT TO *KIEV* IN THE MORNING.
I USED TO DREAM ABOUT COMING HERE.

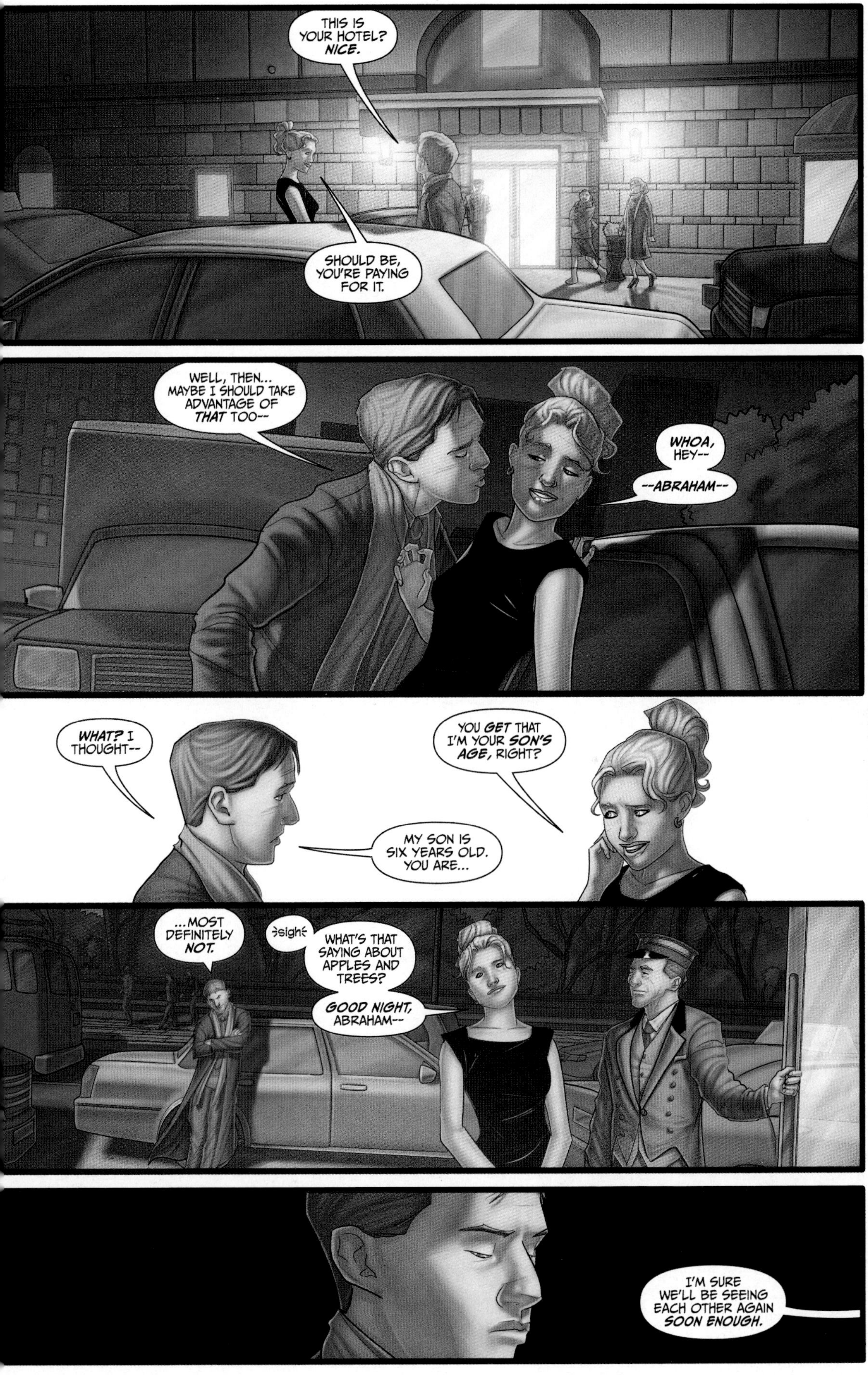
THIS IS YOUR HOTEL? NICE.
SHOULD BE, YOU'RE PAYING FOR IT.
WELL, THEN... MAYBE I SHOULD TAKE ADVANTAGE OF THAT TOO--
WHOA, HEY--
--ABRAHAM--
WHAT? I THOUGHT--
YOU GET THAT I'M YOUR SON'S AGE, RIGHT?
MY SON IS SIX YEARS OLD. YOU ARE...
...MOST DEFINITELY NOT.
sigh
WHAT'S THAT SAYING ABOUT APPLES AND TREES?
GOOD NIGHT, ABRAHAM--
I'M SURE WE'LL BE SEEING EACH OTHER AGAIN SOON ENOUGH.

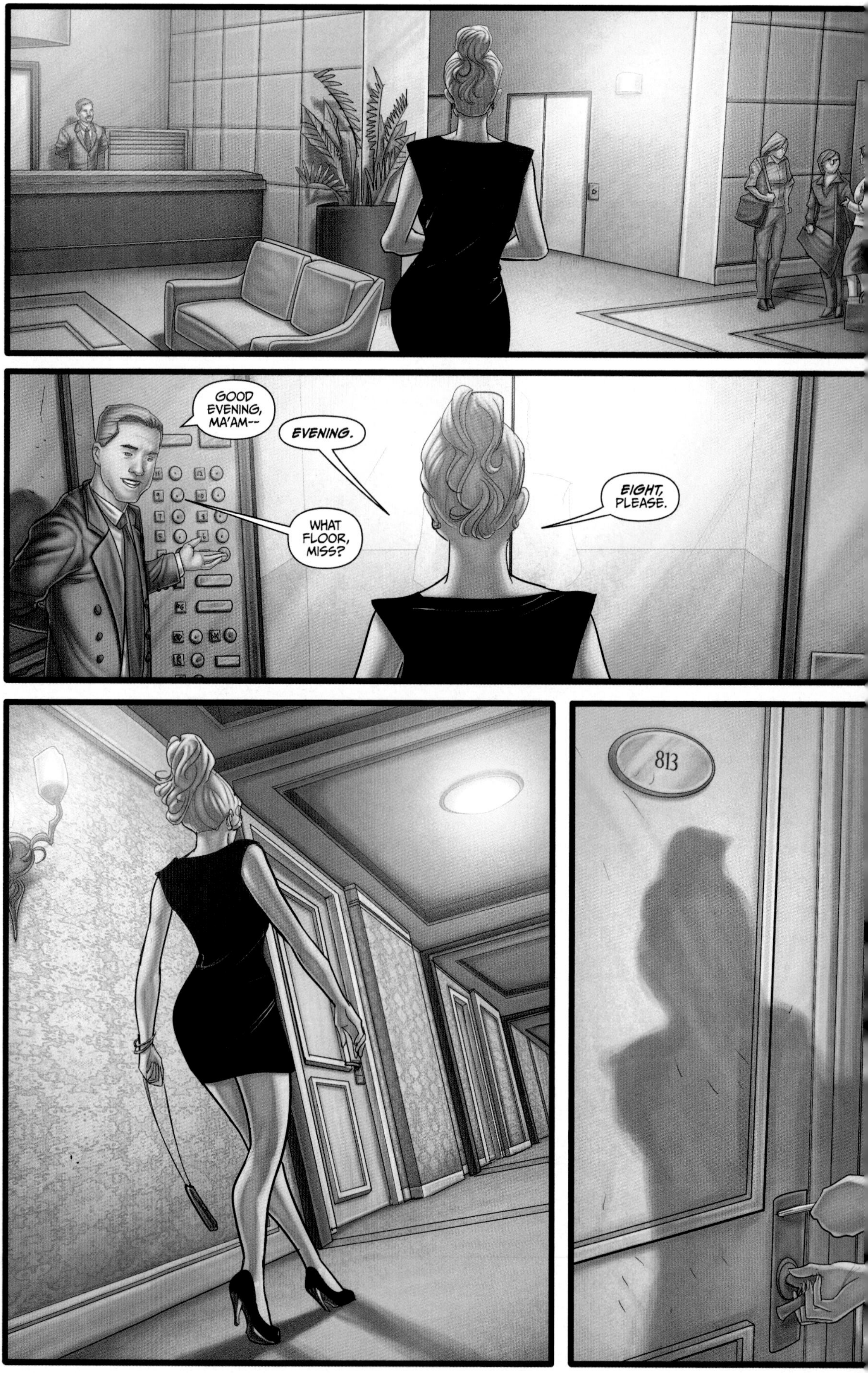
GOOD EVENING, MA'AM--
EVENING.
WHAT FLOOR, MISS?
EIGHT, PLEASE.
813

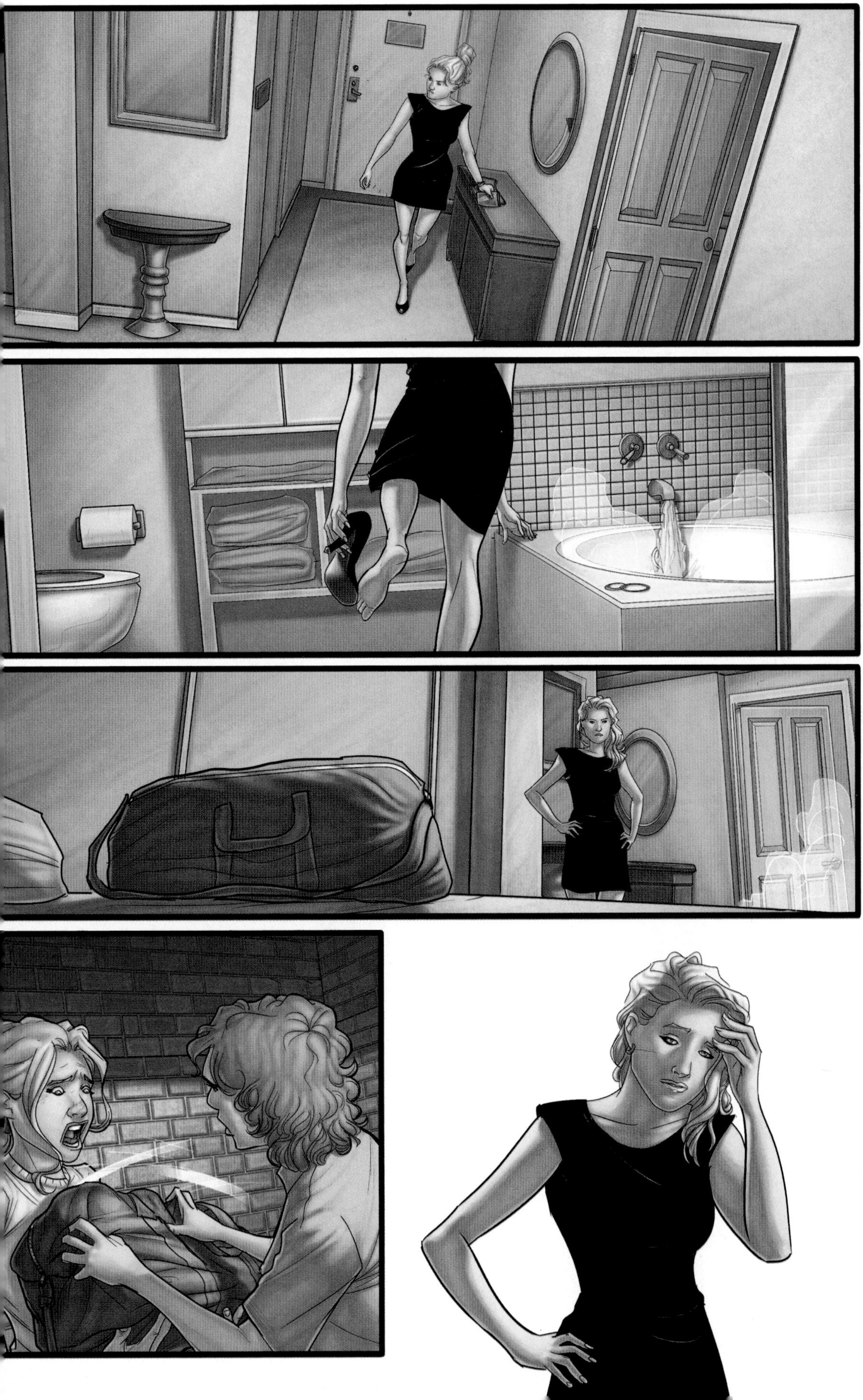

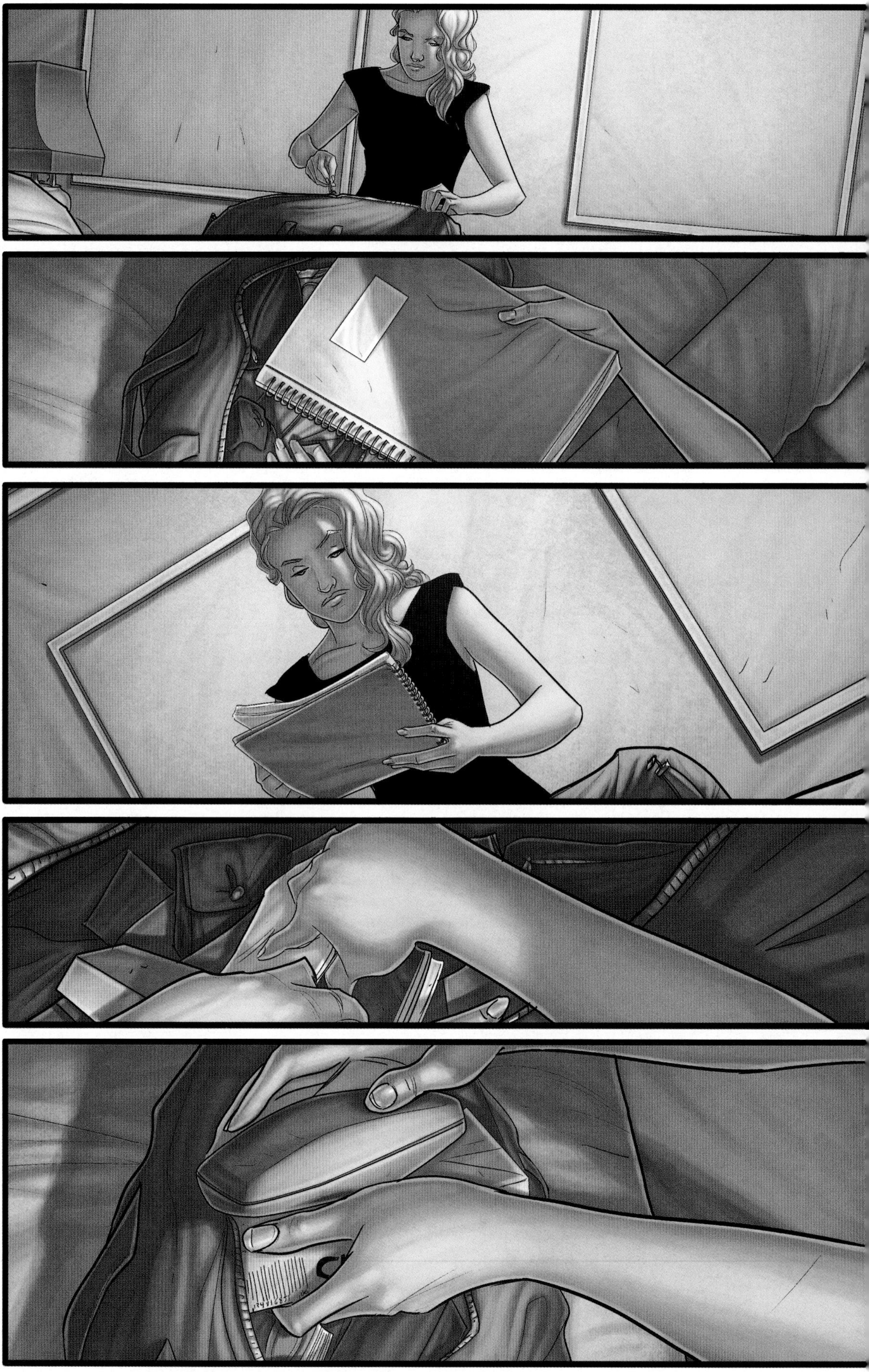

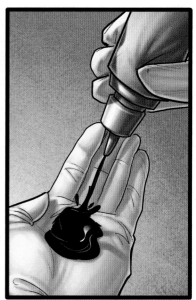

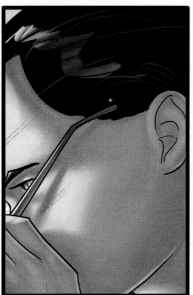

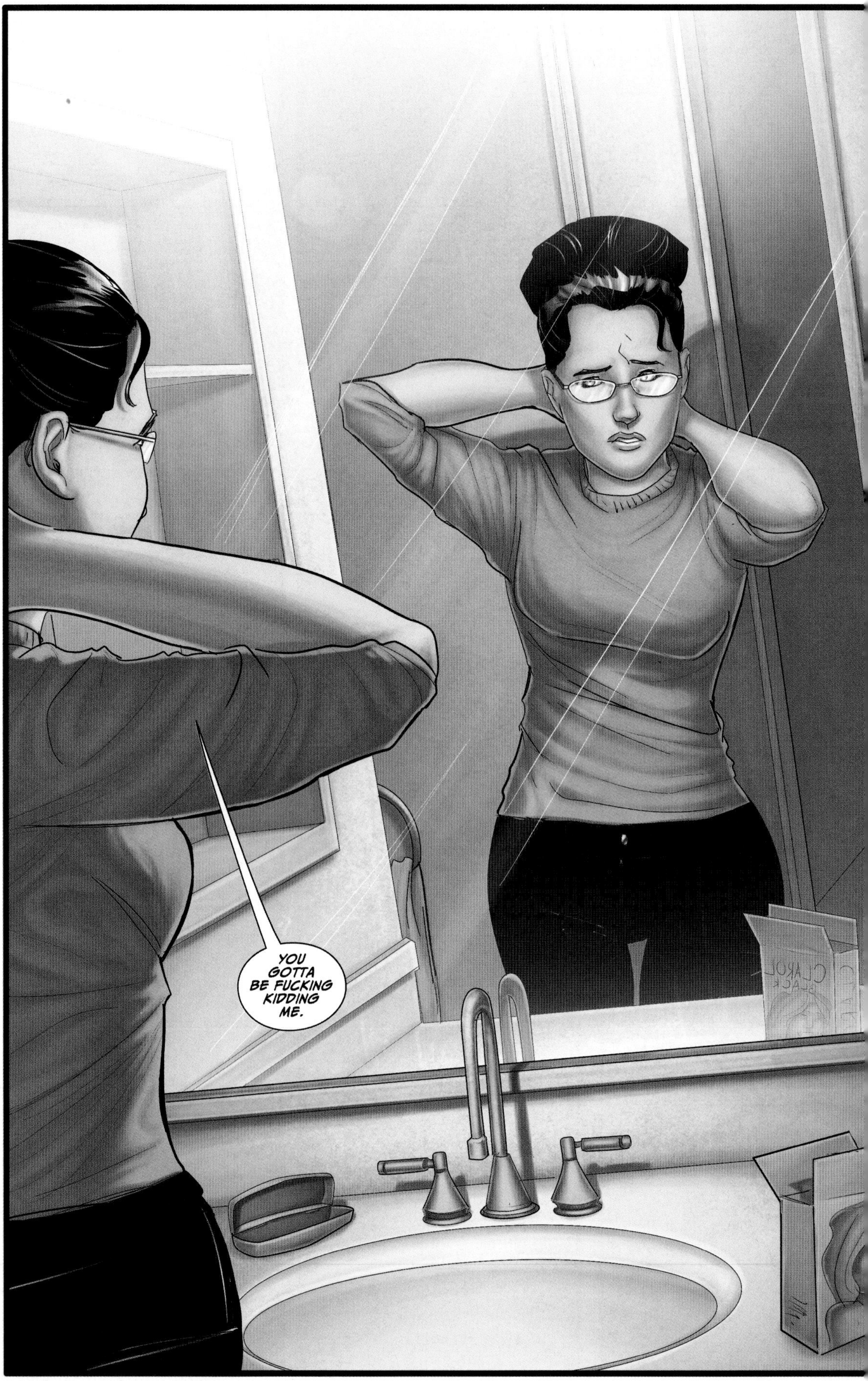
YOU GOTTA BE FUCKING KIDDING ME.

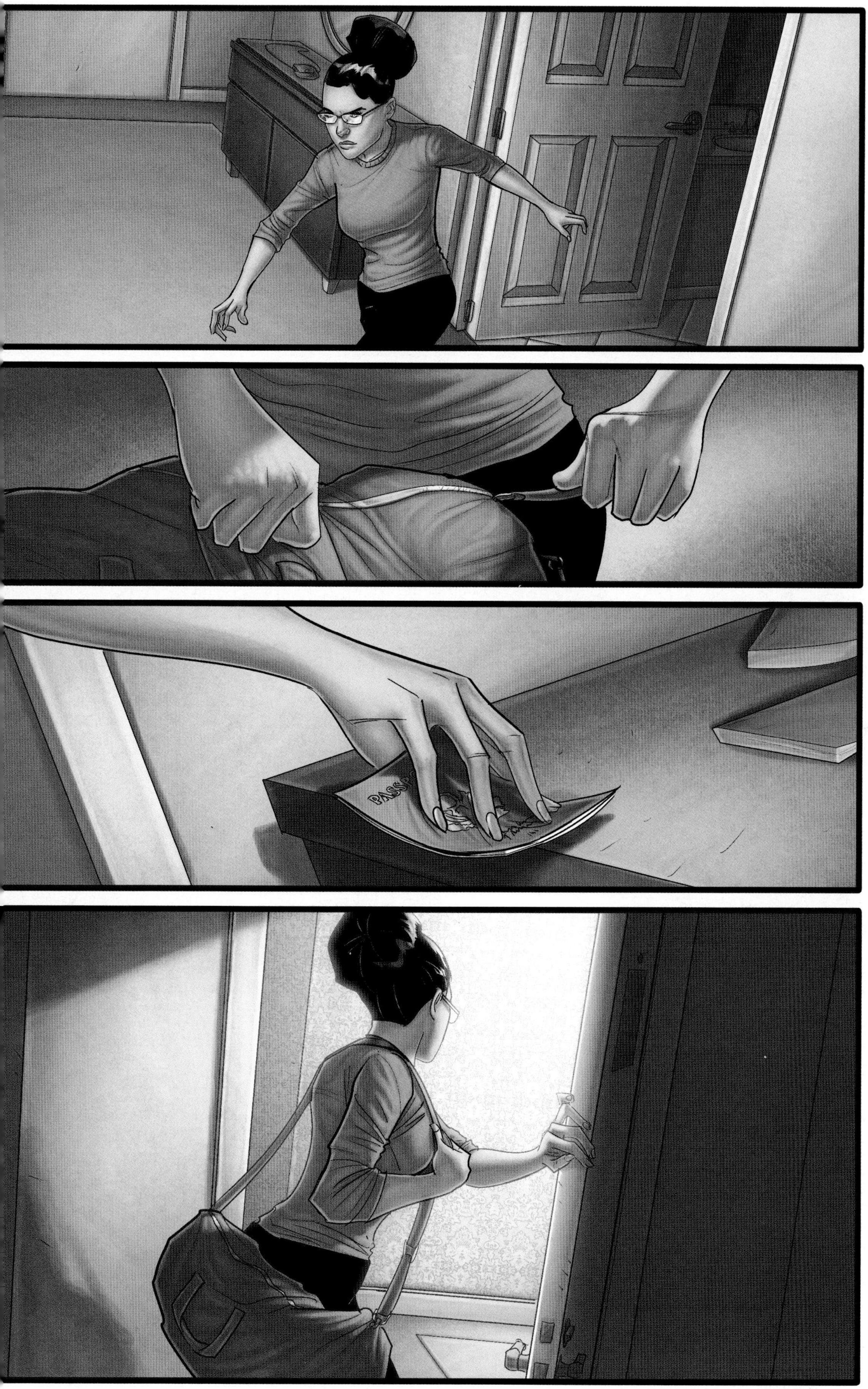

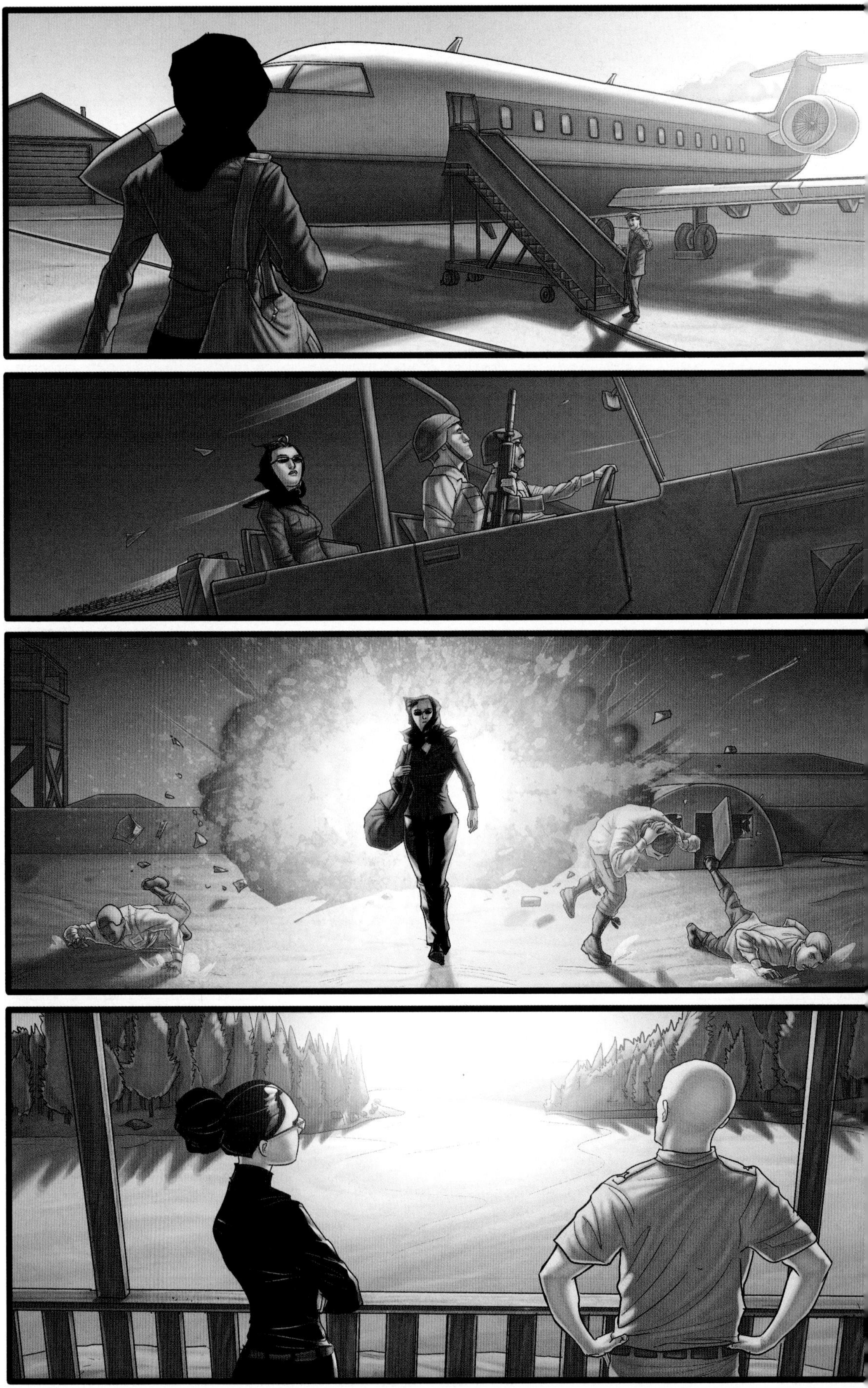

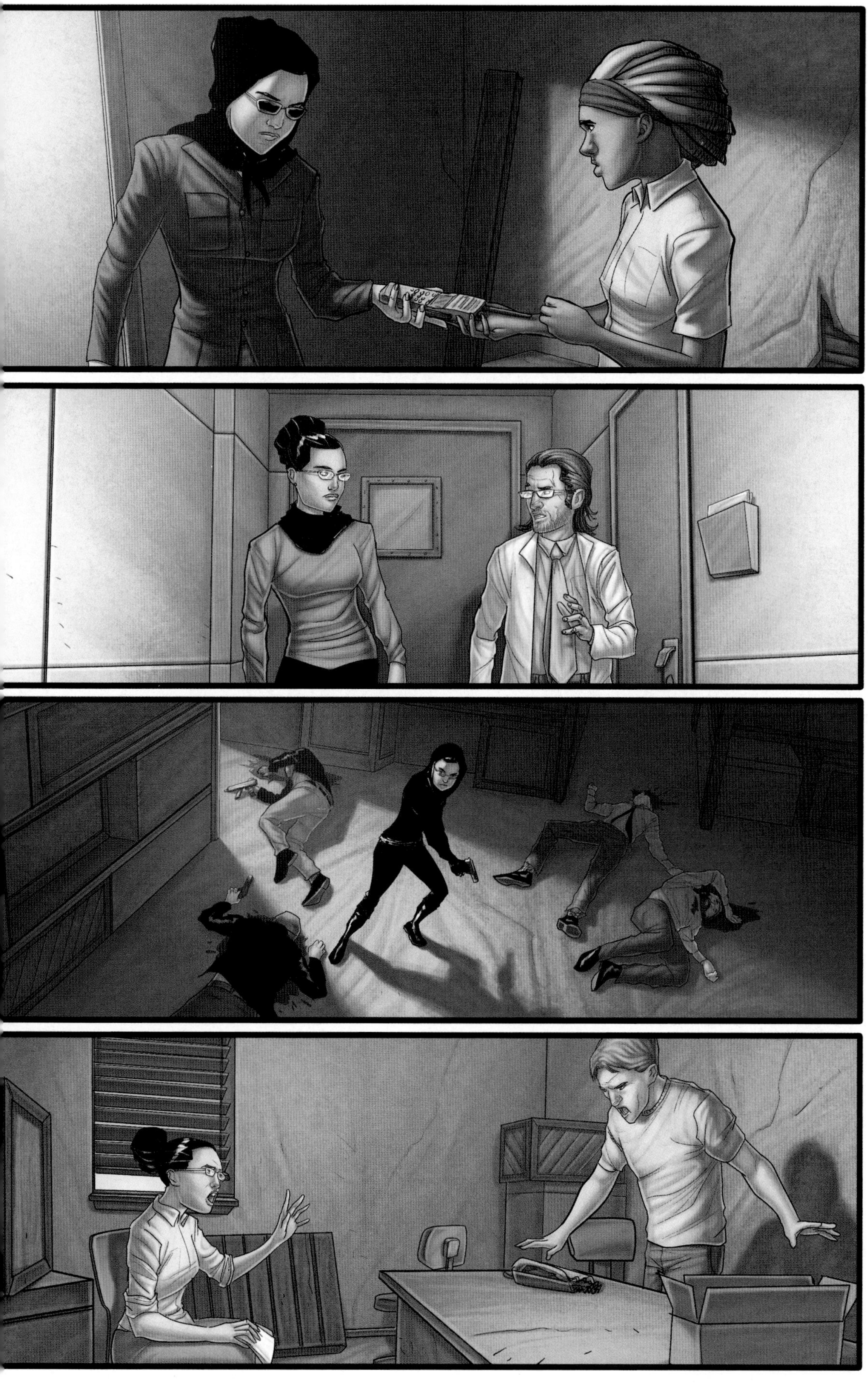

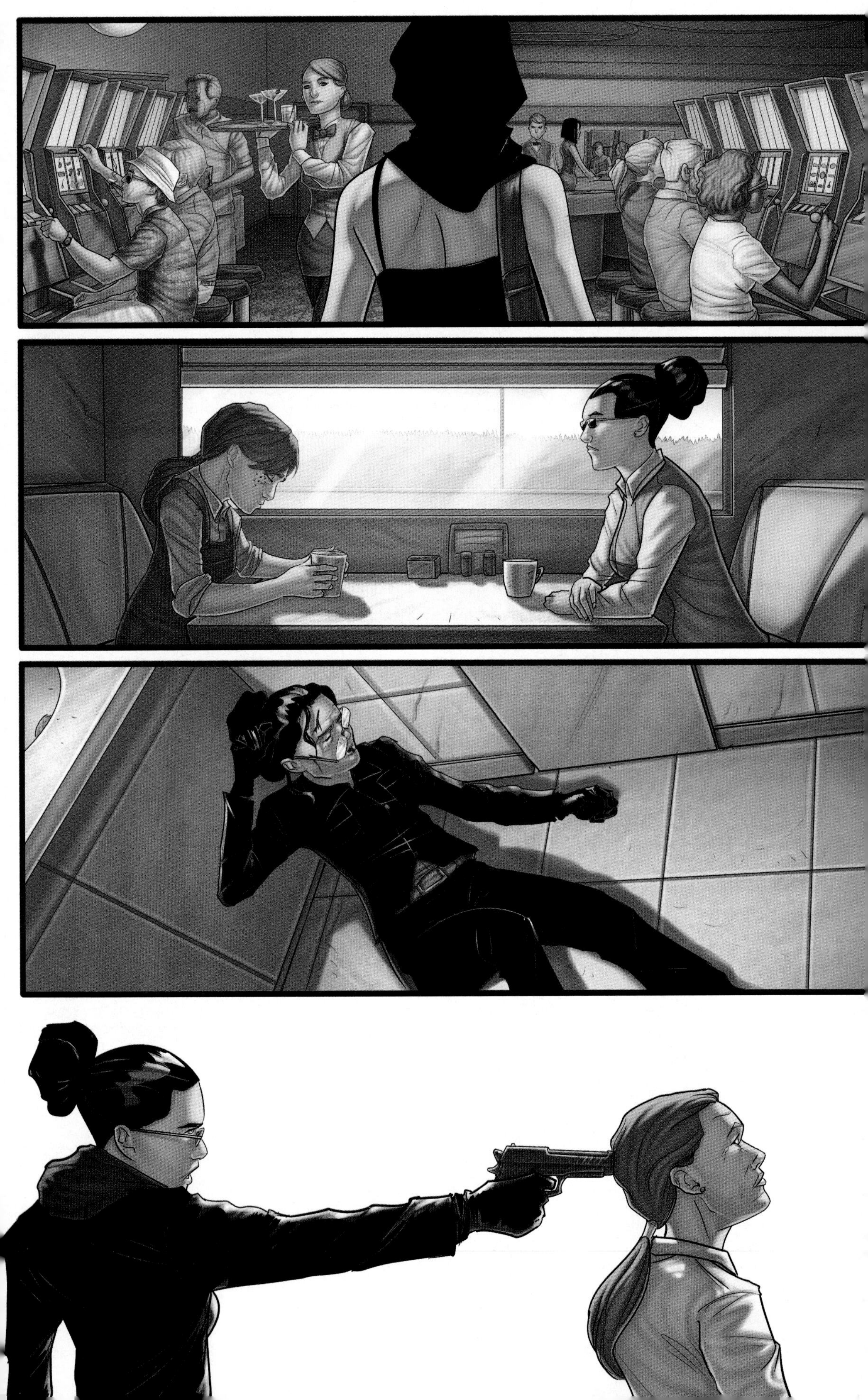

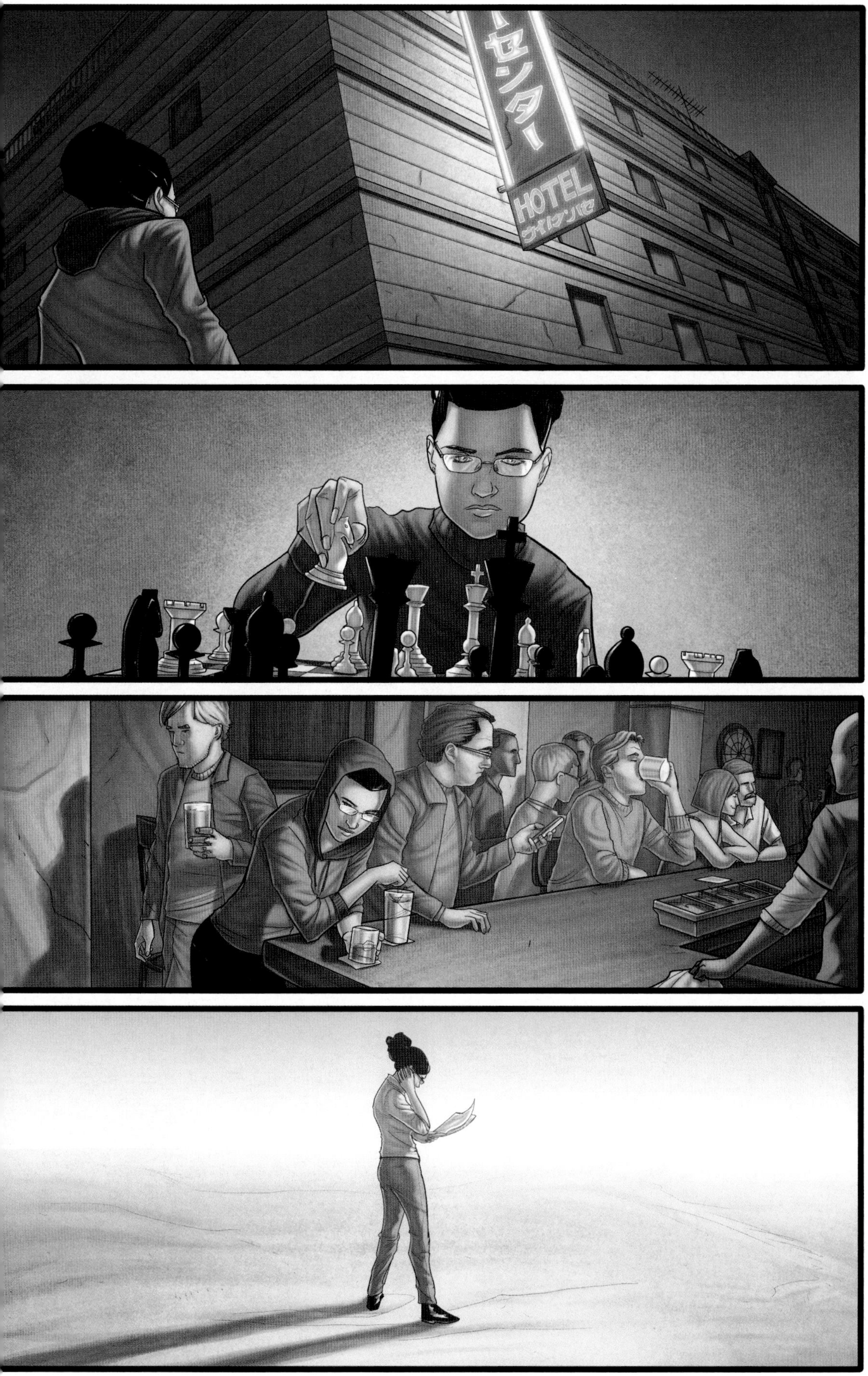
センター
HOTEL

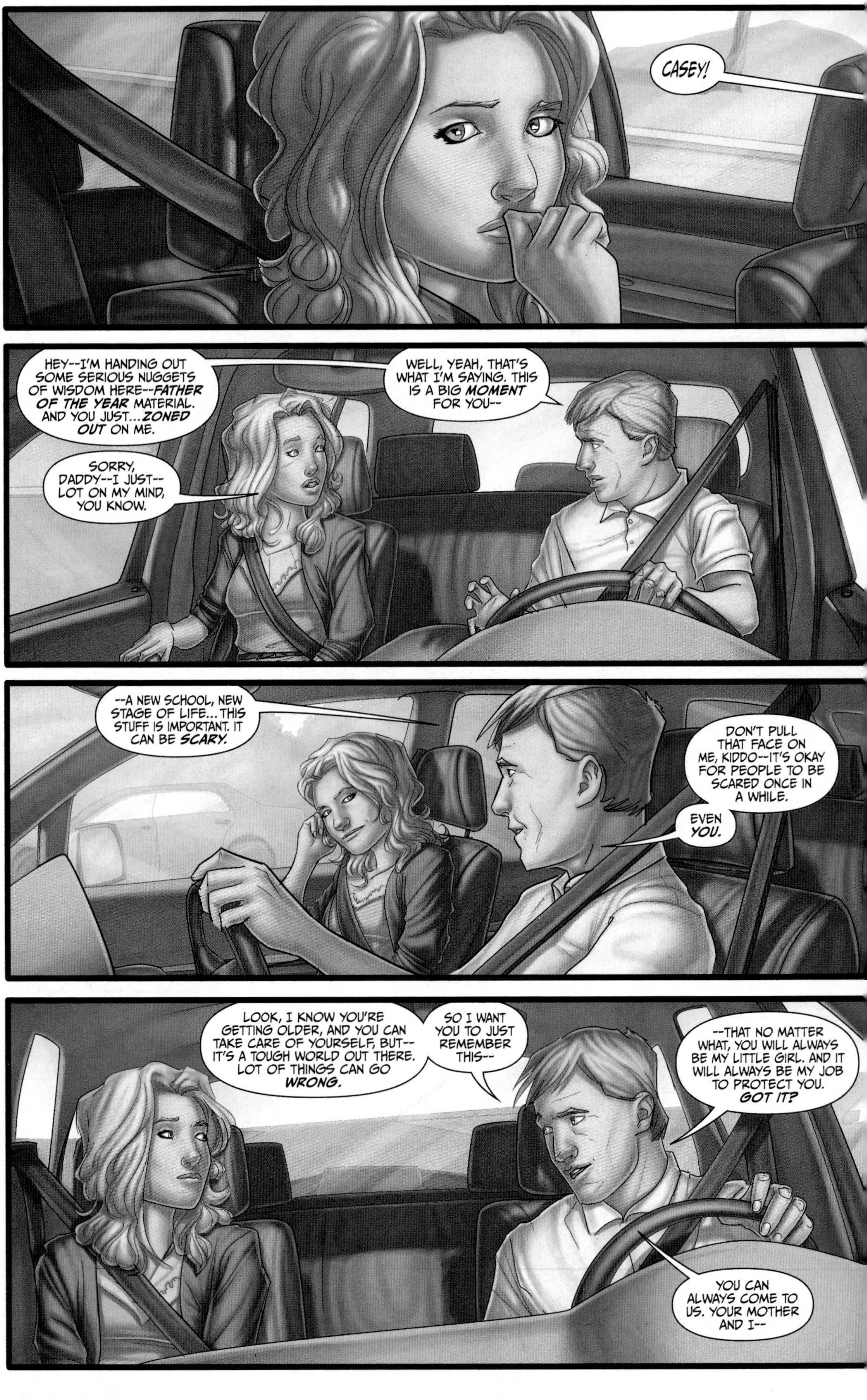
CASEY!
HEY--I'M HANDING OUT SOME SERIOUS NUGGETS OF WISDOM HERE--FATHER OF THE YEAR MATERIAL. AND YOU JUST...ZONED OUT ON ME.
WELL, YEAH, THAT'S WHAT I'M SAYING. THIS IS A BIG MOMENT FOR YOU--
SORRY, DADDY--I JUST--LOT ON MY MIND, YOU KNOW.
--A NEW SCHOOL, NEW STAGE OF LIFE... THIS STUFF IS IMPORTANT. IT CAN BE SCARY.
DON'T PULL THAT FACE ON ME, KIDDO--IT'S OKAY FOR PEOPLE TO BE SCARED ONCE IN A WHILE.
EVEN YOU.
LOOK, I KNOW YOU'RE GETTING OLDER, AND YOU CAN TAKE CARE OF YOURSELF, BUT--IT'S A TOUGH WORLD OUT THERE. LOT OF THINGS CAN GO WRONG.
SO I WANT YOU TO JUST REMEMBER THIS--
--THAT NO MATTER WHAT, YOU WILL ALWAYS BE MY LITTLE GIRL. AND IT WILL ALWAYS BE MY JOB TO PROTECT YOU. GOT IT?
YOU CAN ALWAYS COME TO US. YOUR MOTHER AND I--

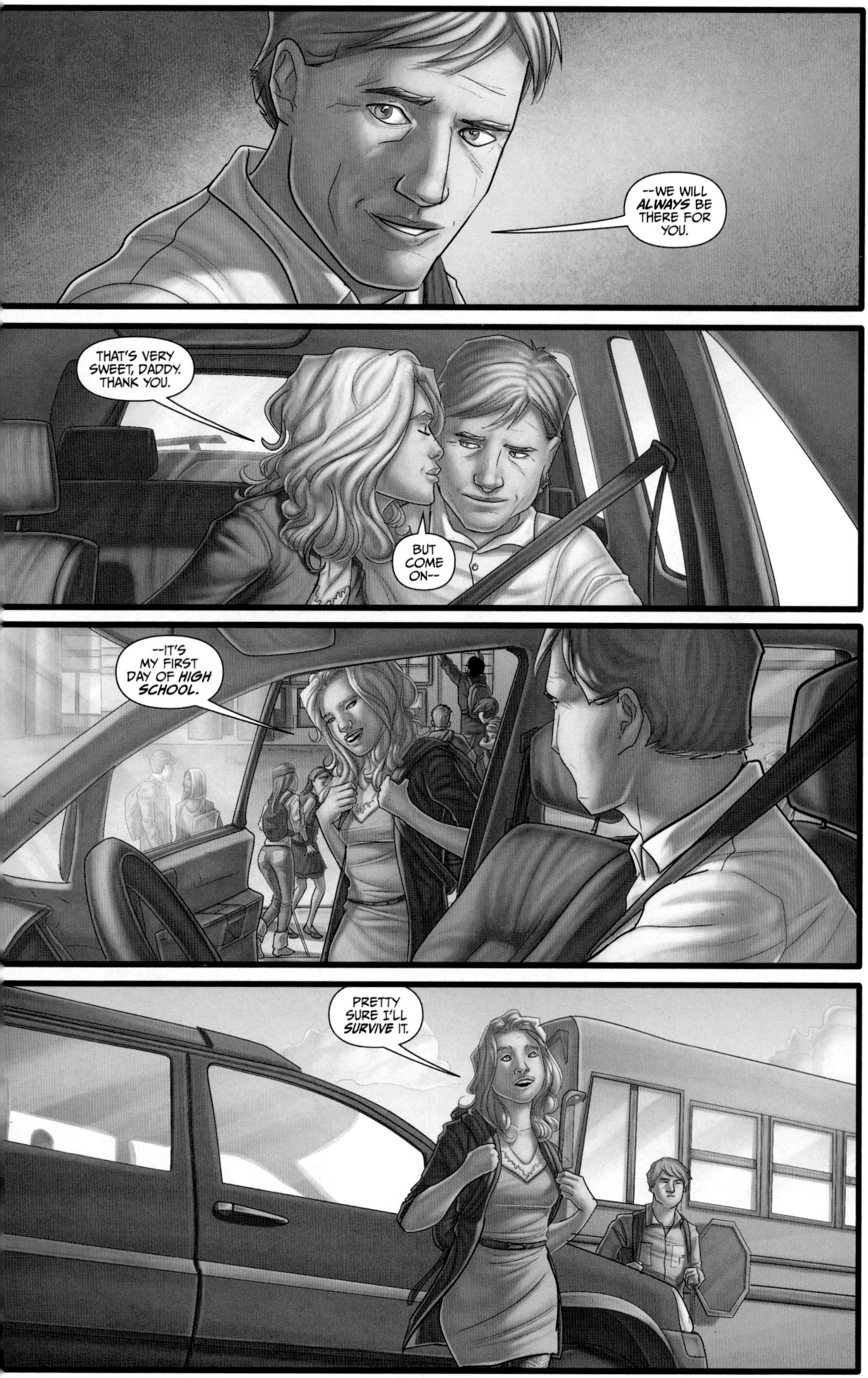

--WE WILL ALWAYS BE THERE FOR YOU.
THAT'S VERY SWEET, DADDY. THANK YOU.
BUT COME ON--
--IT'S MY FIRST DAY OF HIGH SCHOOL.
PRETTY SURE I'LL SURVIVE IT.

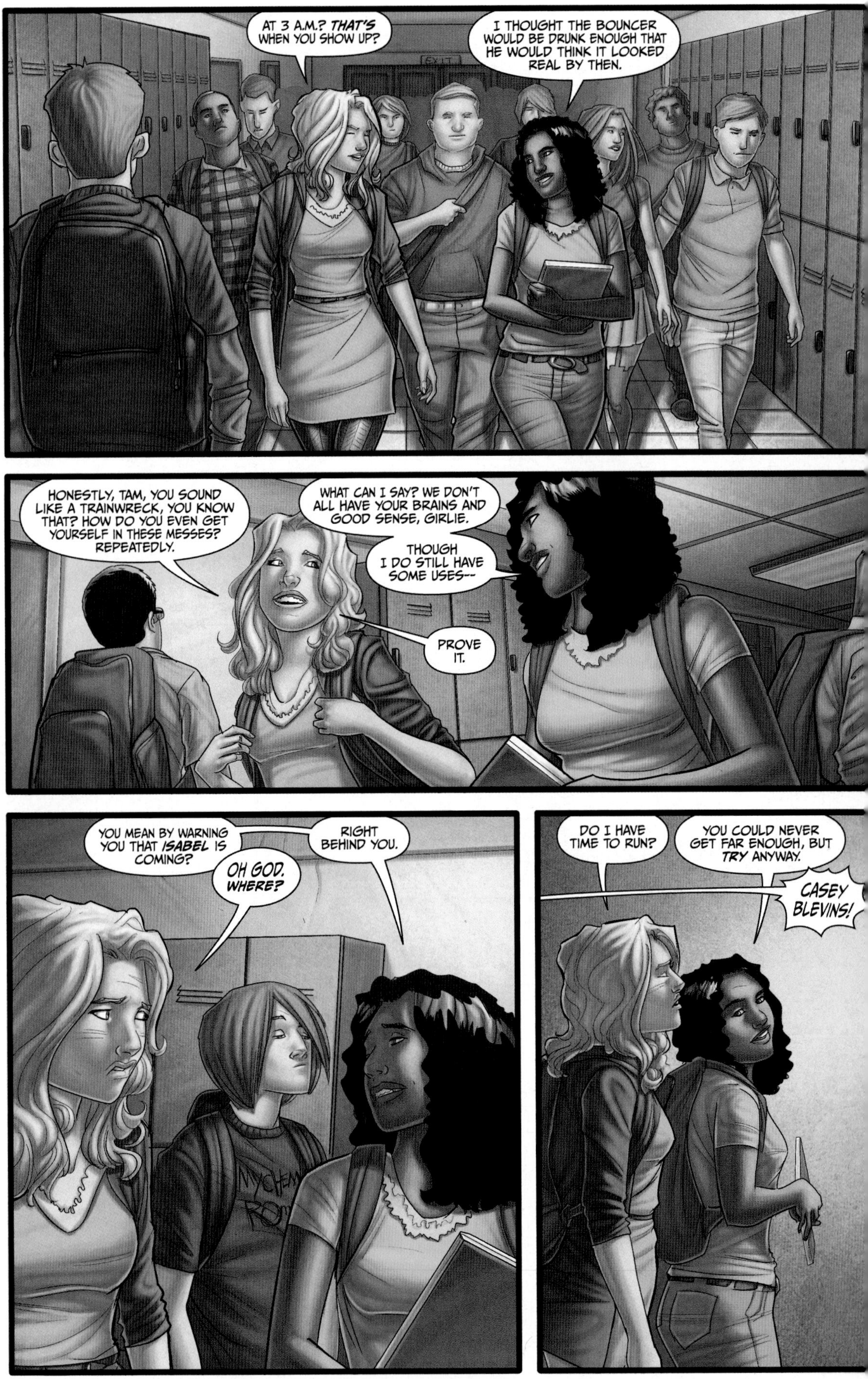
AT 3 A.M.? *THAT'S* WHEN YOU SHOW UP?
I THOUGHT THE BOUNCER WOULD BE DRUNK ENOUGH THAT HE WOULD THINK IT LOOKED REAL BY THEN.
EXIT
HONESTLY, TAM, YOU SOUND LIKE A TRAINWRECK, YOU KNOW THAT? HOW DO YOU EVEN GET YOURSELF IN THESE MESSES? REPEATEDLY.
WHAT CAN I SAY? WE DON'T ALL HAVE YOUR BRAINS AND GOOD SENSE, GIRLIE.
THOUGH I DO STILL HAVE SOME USES--
PROVE IT.
YOU MEAN BY WARNING YOU THAT *ISABEL* IS COMING?
RIGHT BEHIND YOU.
OH GOD. WHERE?
DO I HAVE TIME TO RUN?
YOU COULD NEVER GET FAR ENOUGH, BUT *TRY* ANYWAY.
CASEY BLEVINS!

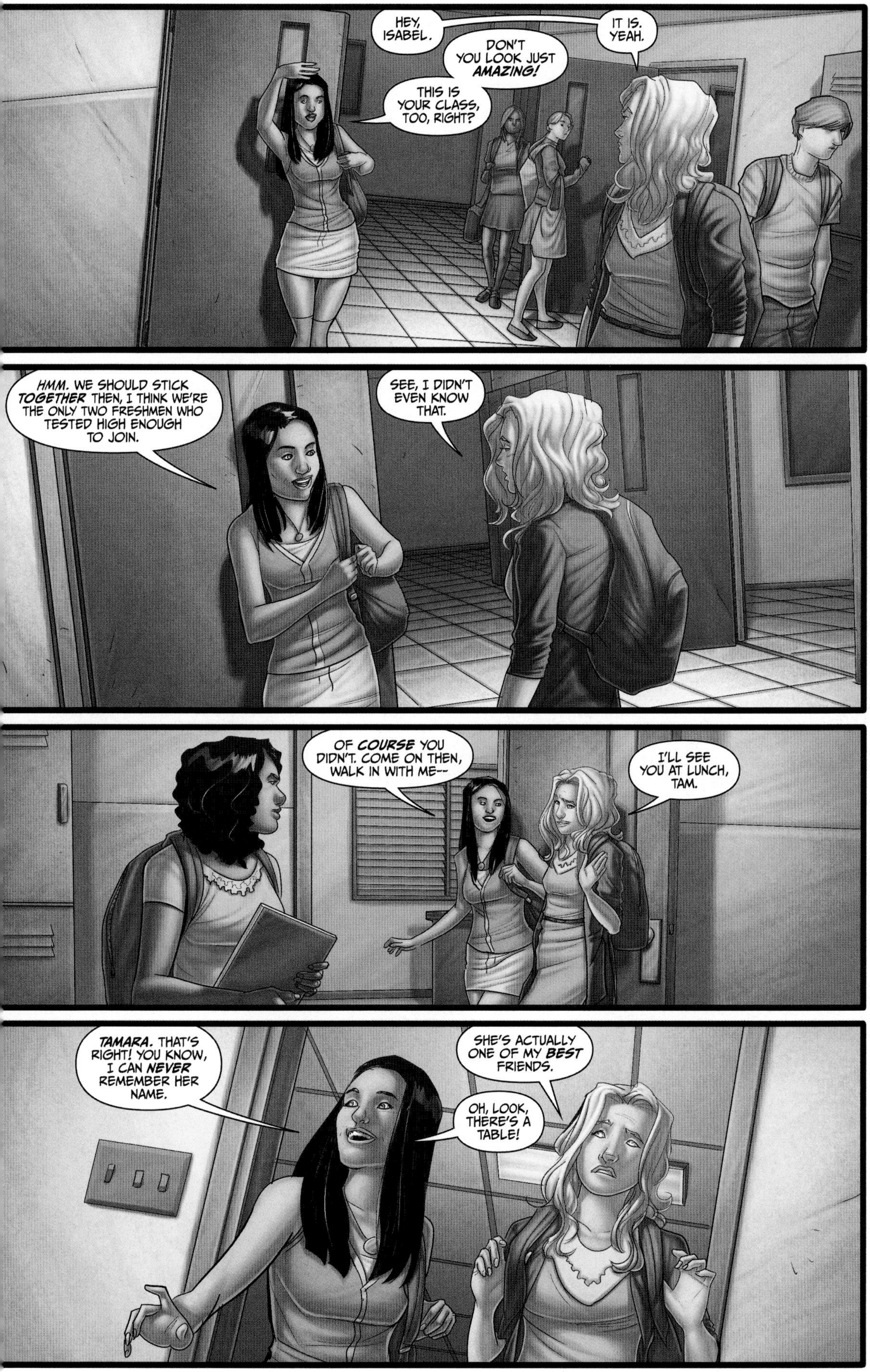
HEY, ISABEL.
IT IS. YEAH.
DON'T YOU LOOK JUST AMAZING!
THIS IS YOUR CLASS, TOO, RIGHT?
HMM. WE SHOULD STICK TOGETHER THEN, I THINK WE'RE THE ONLY TWO FRESHMEN WHO TESTED HIGH ENOUGH TO JOIN.
SEE, I DIDN'T EVEN KNOW THAT.
OF COURSE YOU DIDN'T. COME ON THEN, WALK IN WITH ME--
I'LL SEE YOU AT LUNCH, TAM.
TAMARA. THAT'S RIGHT! YOU KNOW, I CAN NEVER REMEMBER HER NAME.
SHE'S ACTUALLY ONE OF MY BEST FRIENDS.
OH, LOOK, THERE'S A TABLE!

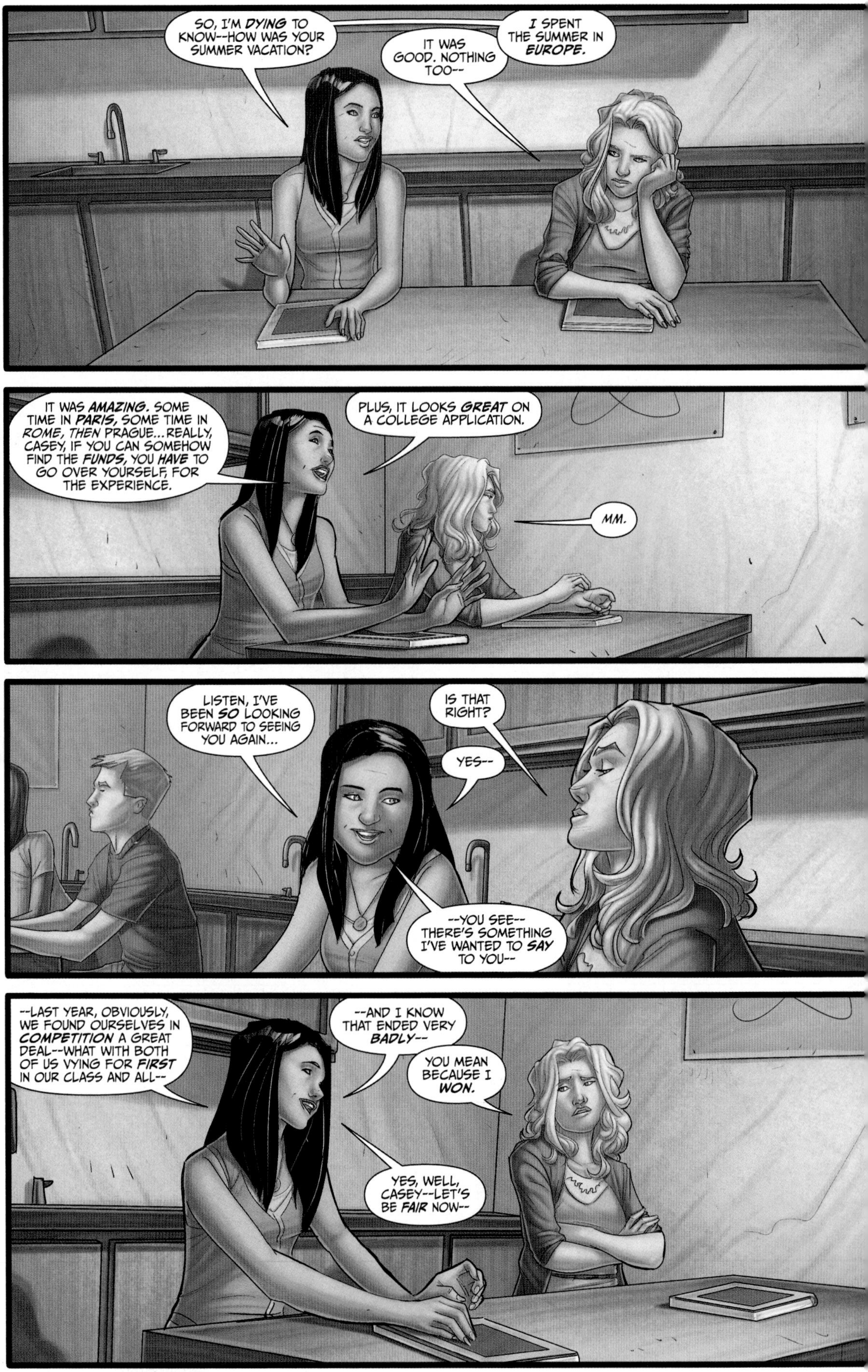
SO, I'M DYING TO KNOW--HOW WAS YOUR SUMMER VACATION?
IT WAS GOOD. NOTHING TOO--
I SPENT THE SUMMER IN EUROPE.
IT WAS AMAZING. SOME TIME IN PARIS, SOME TIME IN ROME, THEN PRAGUE... REALLY, CASEY, IF YOU CAN SOMEHOW FIND THE FUNDS, YOU HAVE TO GO OVER YOURSELF, FOR THE EXPERIENCE.
PLUS, IT LOOKS GREAT ON A COLLEGE APPLICATION.
MM.
LISTEN, I'VE BEEN SO LOOKING FORWARD TO SEEING YOU AGAIN...
IS THAT RIGHT?
YES--
--YOU SEE--THERE'S SOMETHING I'VE WANTED TO SAY TO YOU--
--LAST YEAR, OBVIOUSLY, WE FOUND OURSELVES IN COMPETITION A GREAT DEAL--WHAT WITH BOTH OF US VYING FOR FIRST IN OUR CLASS AND ALL--
--AND I KNOW THAT ENDED VERY BADLY--
YOU MEAN BECAUSE I WON.
YES, WELL, CASEY--LET'S BE FAIR NOW--

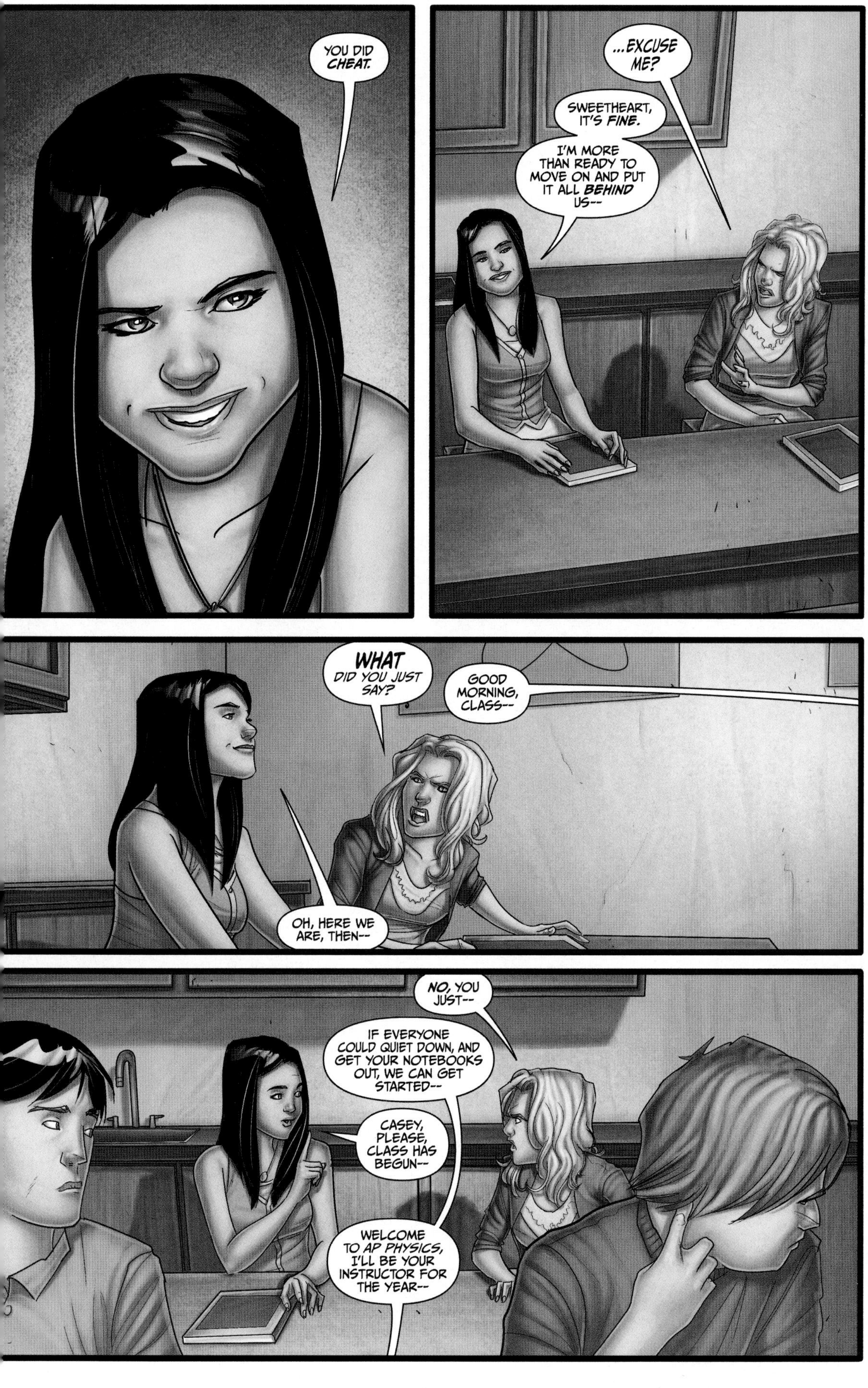

YOU DID *CHEAT.*
...EXCUSE ME?
SWEETHEART, IT'S *FINE.*
I'M MORE THAN READY TO MOVE ON AND PUT IT ALL *BEHIND* US--
WHAT *DID YOU JUST SAY?*
GOOD MORNING, CLASS--
OH, HERE WE ARE, THEN--
NO, YOU JUST--
IF EVERYONE COULD QUIET DOWN, AND GET YOUR NOTEBOOKS OUT, WE CAN GET STARTED--
CASEY, PLEASE, CLASS HAS BEGUN--
WELCOME TO *AP PHYSICS,* I'LL BE YOUR INSTRUCTOR FOR THE YEAR--

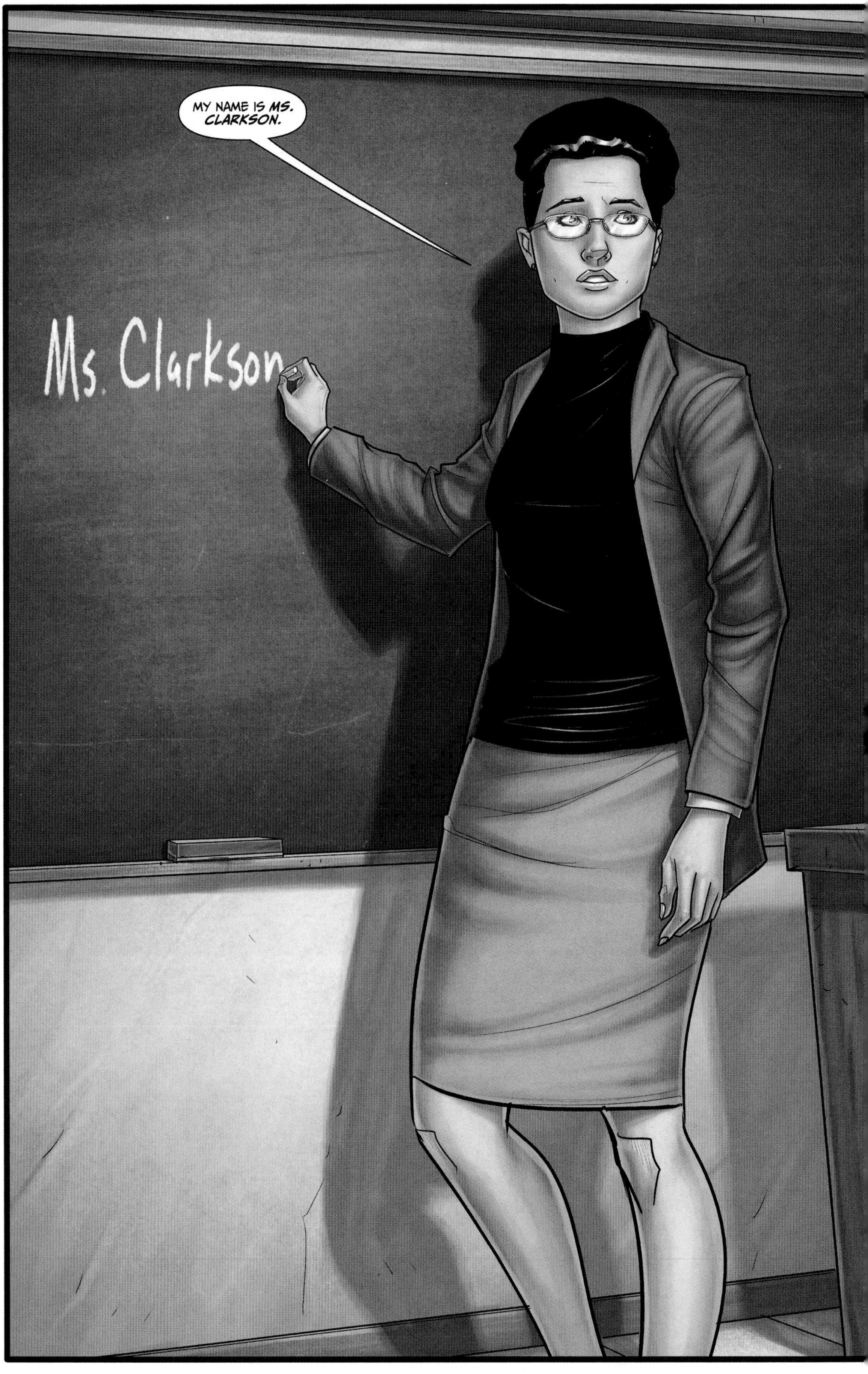
MY NAME IS MS. CLARKSON.
Ms. Clarkson

twentyseven

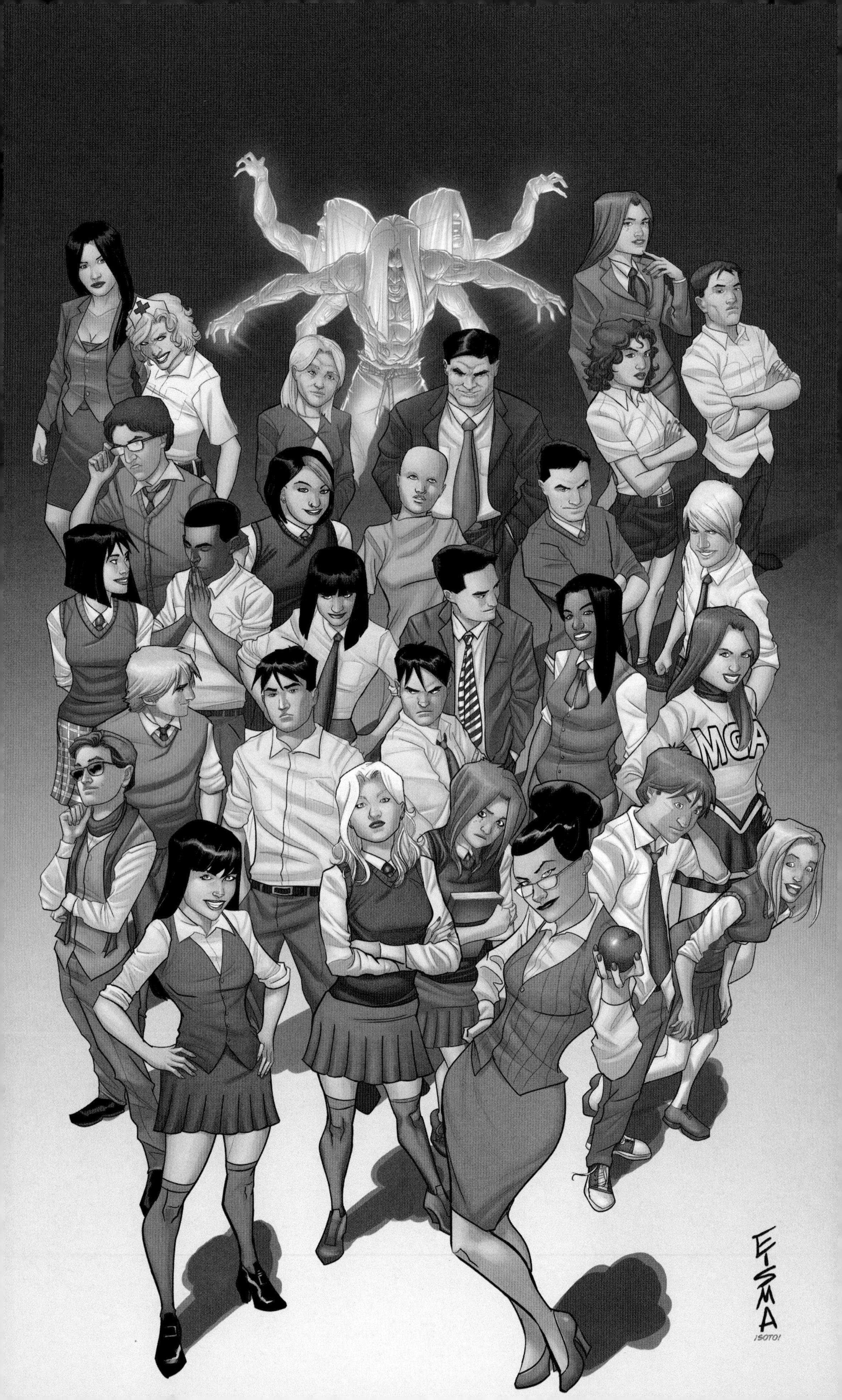
MCA
EISMA
!SOTO!

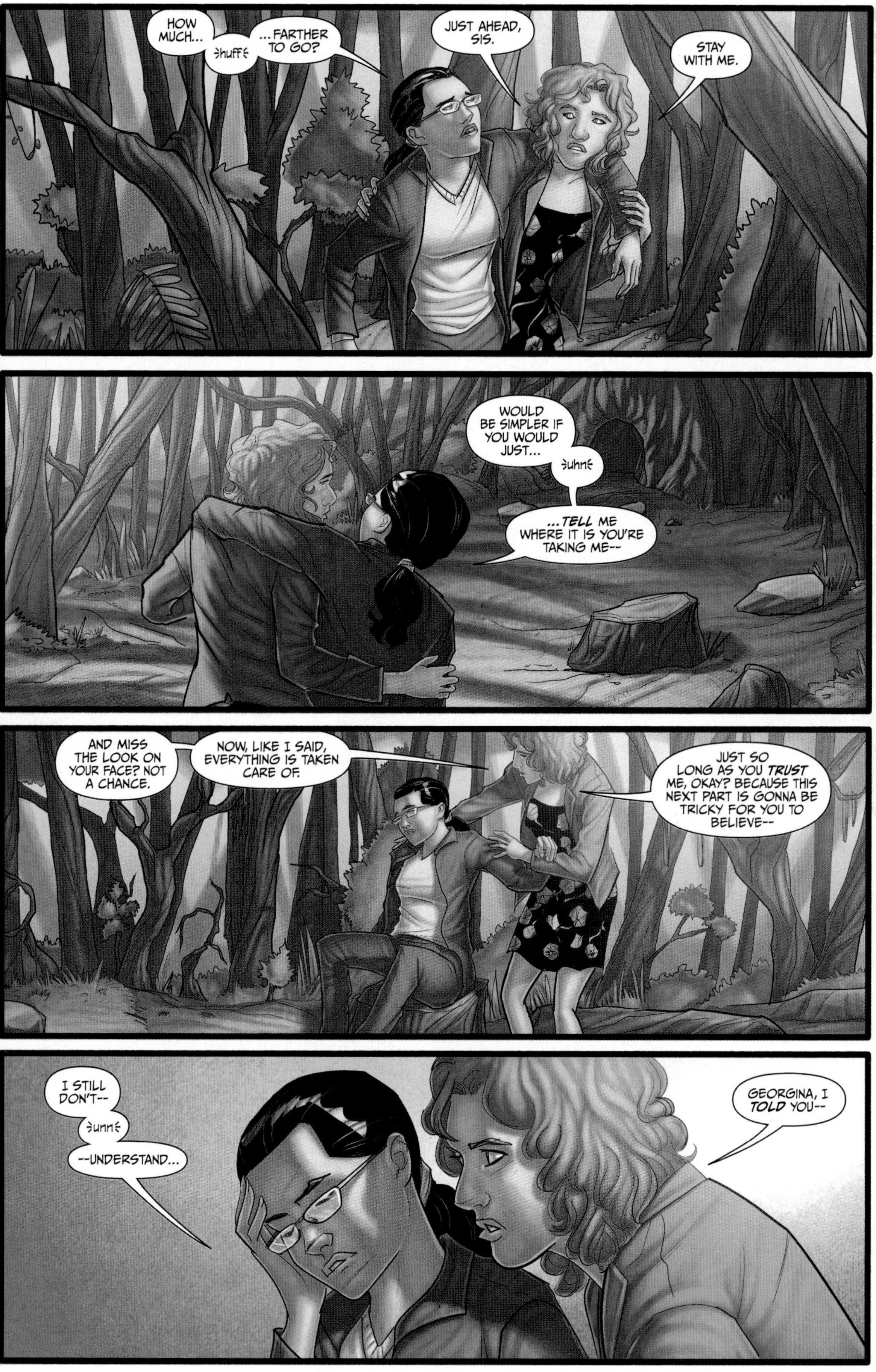
HOW MUCH...
huff
...FARTHER TO GO?
JUST AHEAD, SIS.
STAY WITH ME.
WOULD BE SIMPLER IF YOU WOULD JUST...
uhn
...TELL ME WHERE IT IS YOU'RE TAKING ME--
AND MISS THE LOOK ON YOUR FACE? NOT A CHANCE.
NOW, LIKE I SAID, EVERYTHING IS TAKEN CARE OF.
JUST SO LONG AS YOU TRUST ME, OKAY? BECAUSE THIS NEXT PART IS GONNA BE TRICKY FOR YOU TO BELIEVE--
I STILL DON'T--
unn
--UNDERSTAND...
GEORGINA, I TOLD YOU--

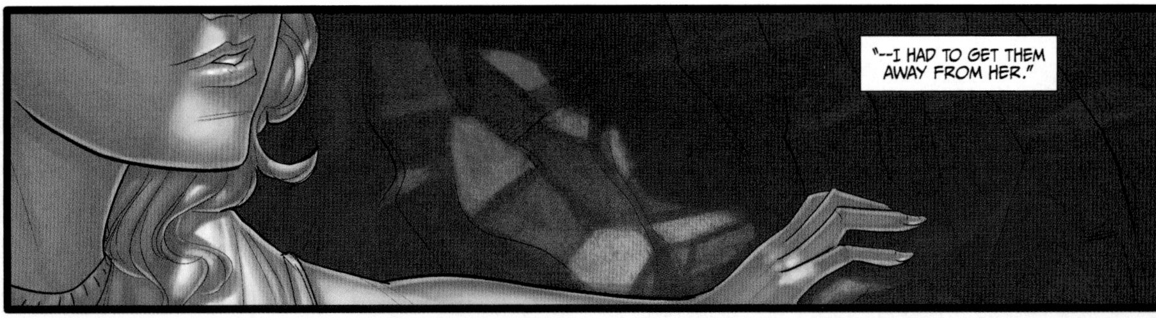
"--I HAD TO GET THEM AWAY FROM HER."

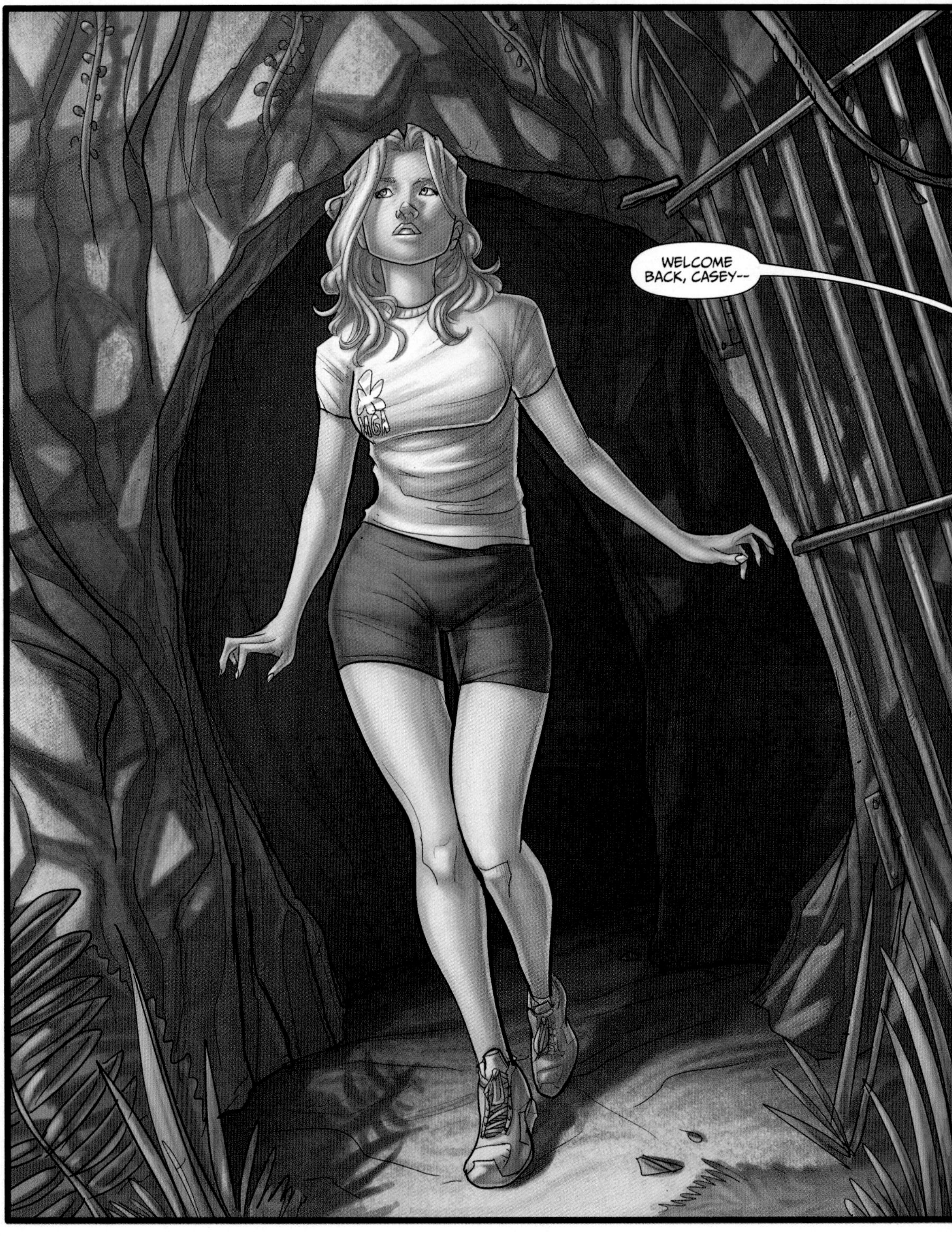
WELCOME BACK, CASEY--

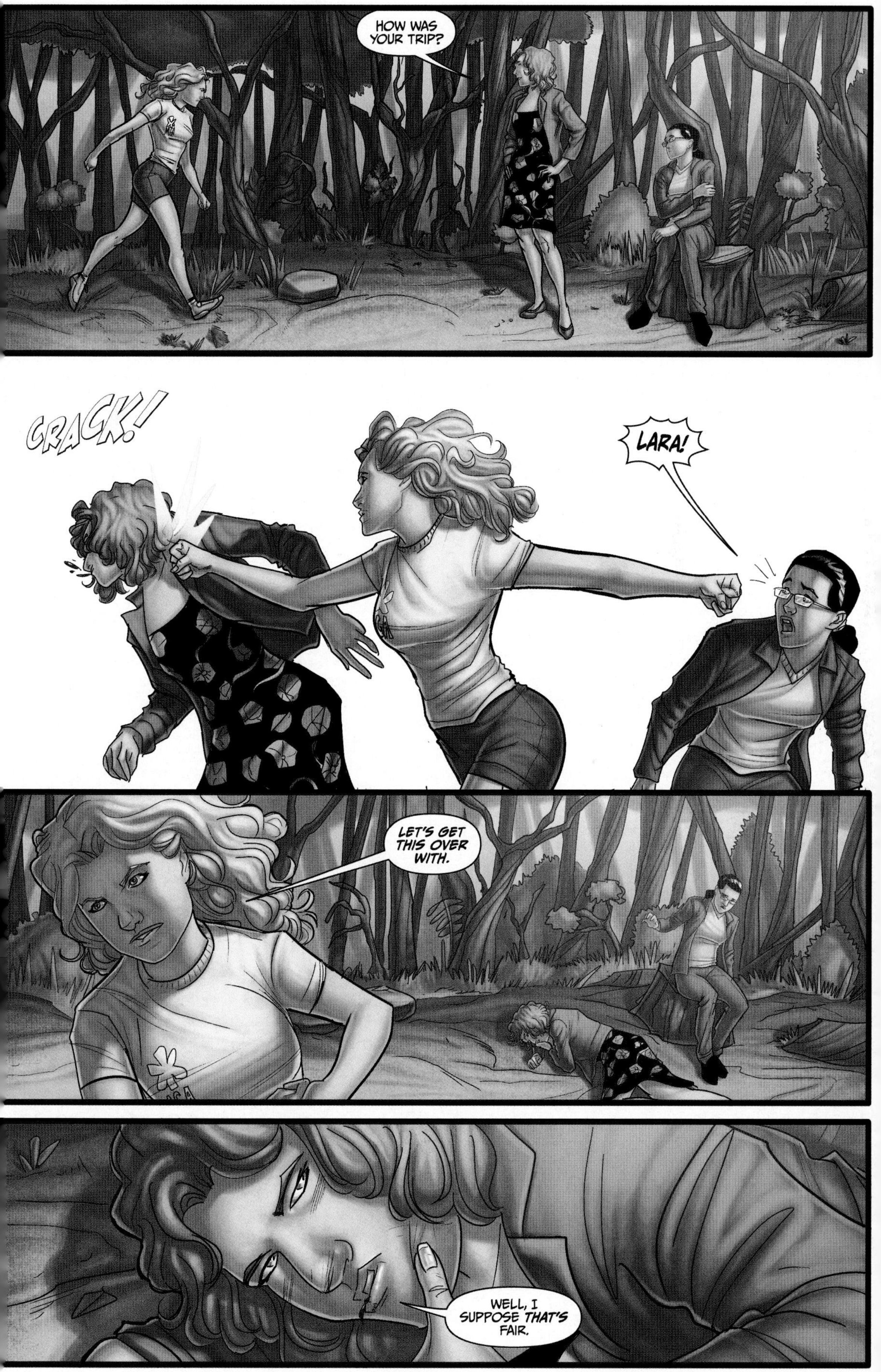

HOW WAS YOUR TRIP?
CRACK!
LARA!
LET'S GET THIS OVER WITH.
WELL, I SUPPOSE *THAT'S* FAIR.

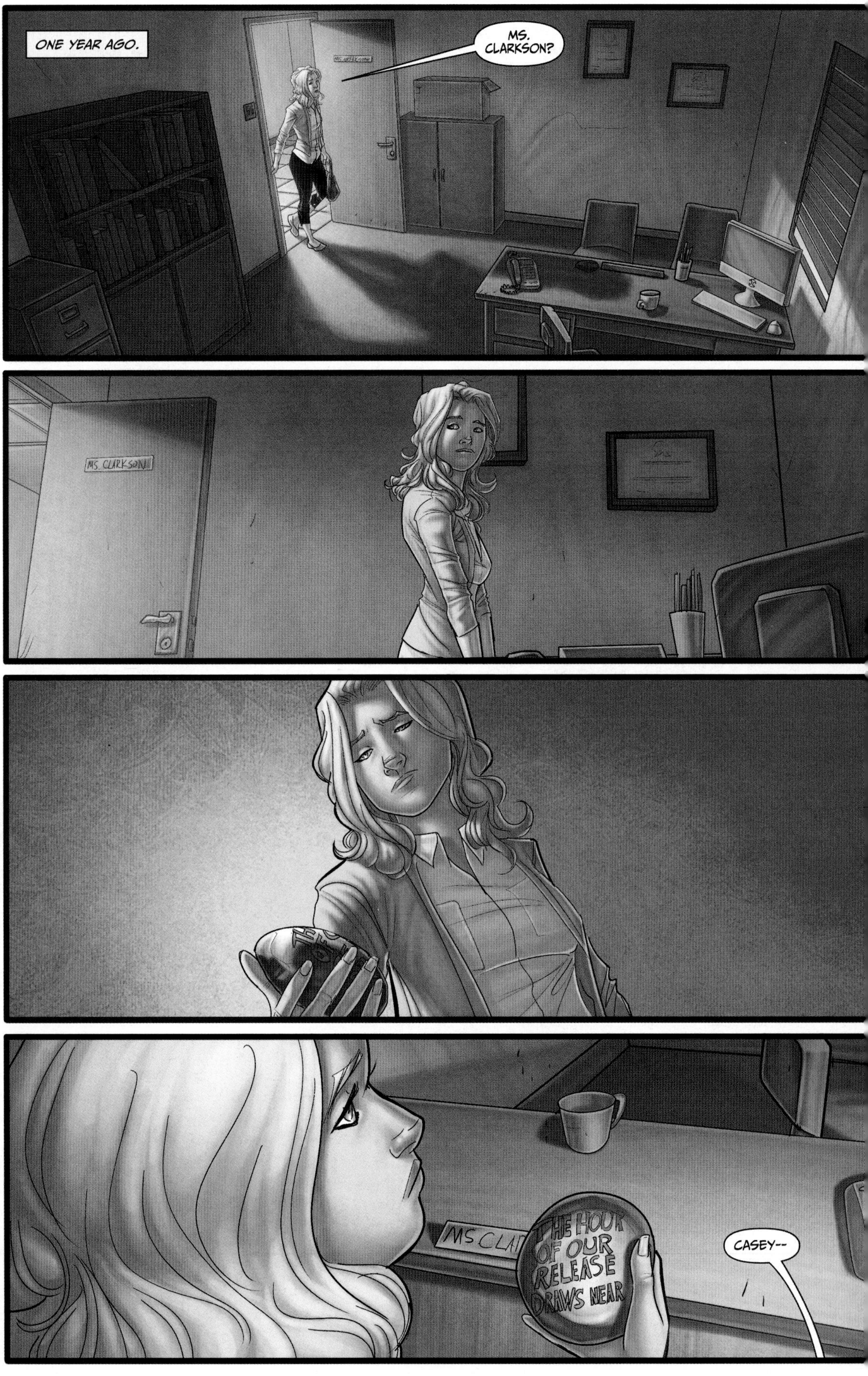
ONE YEAR AGO.
MS. CLARKSON?
MS. CLARKSON
THE HOUR OF OUR RELEASE DRAWS NEAR
CASEY--

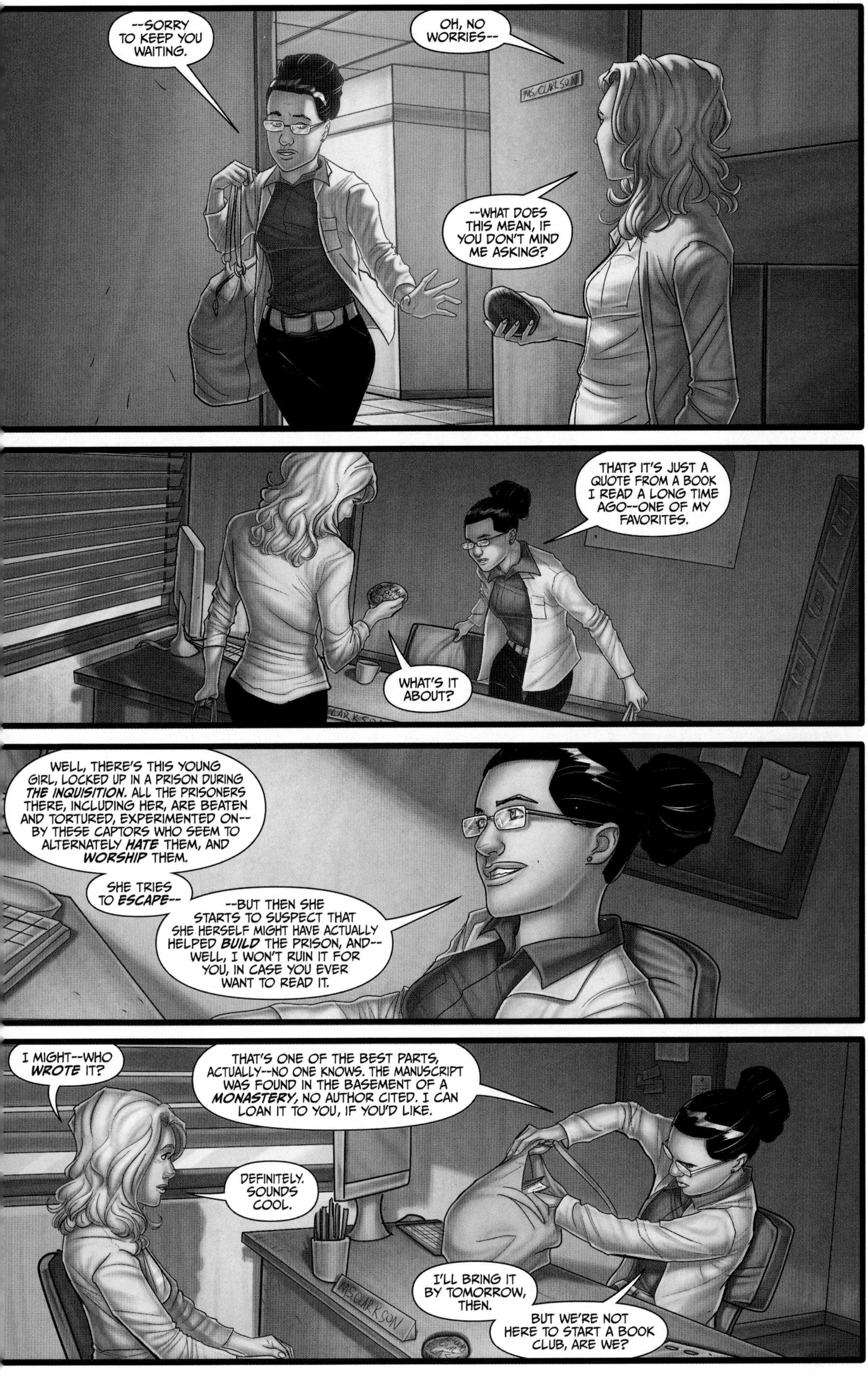

--SORRY TO KEEP YOU WAITING.
OH, NO WORRIES--
MS. CLARKSON
--WHAT DOES THIS MEAN, IF YOU DON'T MIND ME ASKING?
THAT? IT'S JUST A QUOTE FROM A BOOK I READ A LONG TIME AGO--ONE OF MY FAVORITES.
WHAT'S IT ABOUT?
WELL, THERE'S THIS YOUNG GIRL, LOCKED UP IN A PRISON DURING *THE INQUISITION*. ALL THE PRISONERS THERE, INCLUDING HER, ARE BEATEN AND TORTURED, EXPERIMENTED ON--BY THESE CAPTORS WHO SEEM TO ALTERNATELY *HATE* THEM, AND *WORSHIP* THEM.
SHE TRIES TO *ESCAPE*--
--BUT THEN SHE STARTS TO SUSPECT THAT SHE HERSELF MIGHT HAVE ACTUALLY HELPED *BUILD* THE PRISON, AND--WELL, I WON'T RUIN IT FOR YOU, IN CASE YOU EVER WANT TO READ IT.
I MIGHT--WHO *WROTE* IT?
THAT'S ONE OF THE BEST PARTS, ACTUALLY--NO ONE KNOWS. THE MANUSCRIPT WAS FOUND IN THE BASEMENT OF A *MONASTERY*, NO AUTHOR CITED. I CAN LOAN IT TO YOU, IF YOU'D LIKE.
DEFINITELY. SOUNDS COOL.
MS. CLARKSON
I'LL BRING IT BY TOMORROW, THEN.
BUT WE'RE NOT HERE TO START A BOOK CLUB, ARE WE?

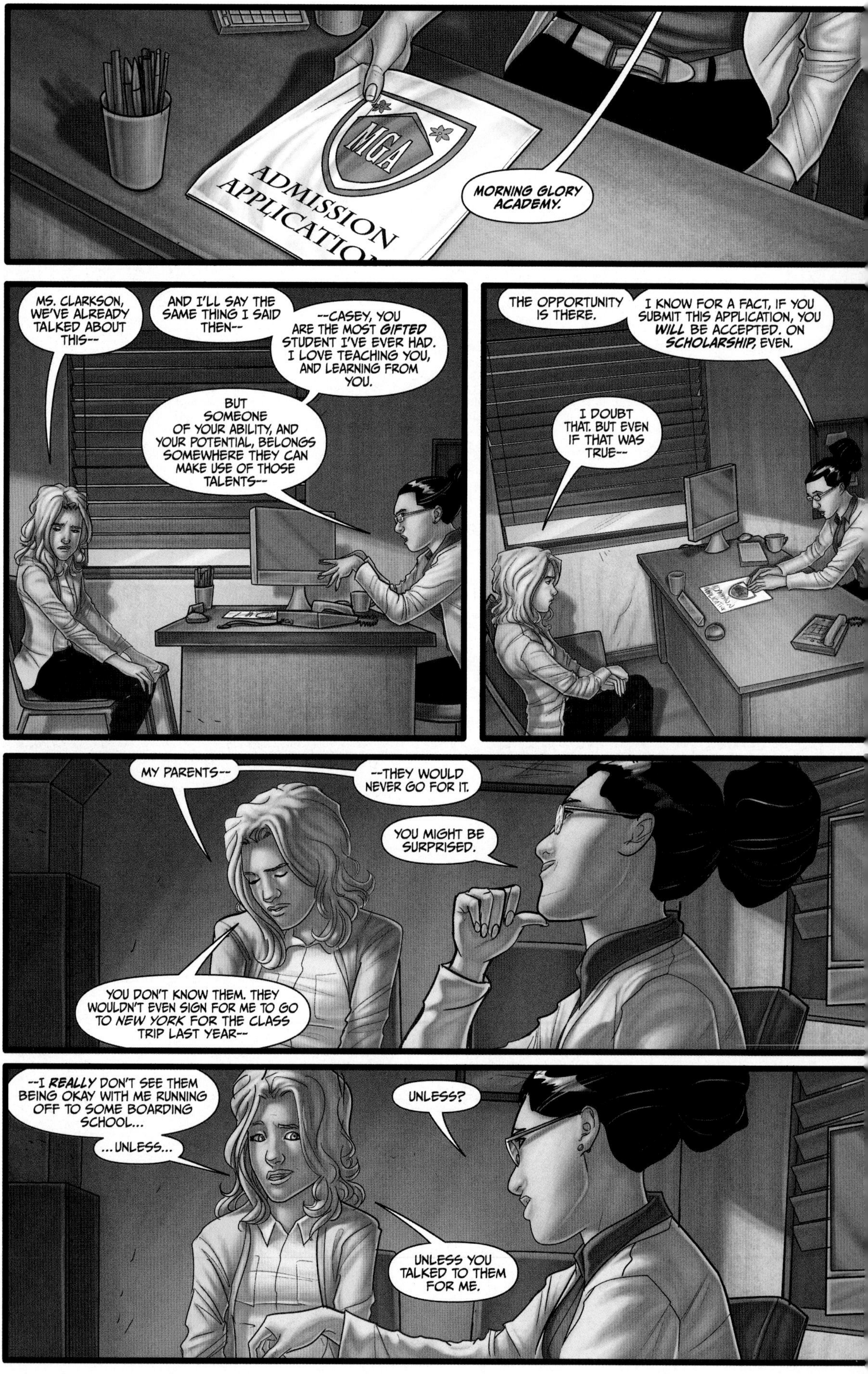
MGA
ADMISSION
APPLICATIO
MORNING GLORY ACADEMY.
MS. CLARKSON, WE'VE ALREADY TALKED ABOUT THIS--
AND I'LL SAY THE SAME THING I SAID THEN--
--CASEY, YOU ARE THE MOST GIFTED STUDENT I'VE EVER HAD. I LOVE TEACHING YOU, AND LEARNING FROM YOU.
BUT SOMEONE OF YOUR ABILITY, AND YOUR POTENTIAL, BELONGS SOMEWHERE THEY CAN MAKE USE OF THOSE TALENTS--
THE OPPORTUNITY IS THERE.
I KNOW FOR A FACT, IF YOU SUBMIT THIS APPLICATION, YOU WILL BE ACCEPTED. ON SCHOLARSHIP, EVEN.
I DOUBT THAT. BUT EVEN IF THAT WAS TRUE--
MY PARENTS--
--THEY WOULD NEVER GO FOR IT.
YOU MIGHT BE SURPRISED.
YOU DON'T KNOW THEM. THEY WOULDN'T EVEN SIGN FOR ME TO GO TO NEW YORK FOR THE CLASS TRIP LAST YEAR--
--I REALLY DON'T SEE THEM BEING OKAY WITH ME RUNNING OFF TO SOME BOARDING SCHOOL...
...UNLESS...
UNLESS?
UNLESS YOU TALKED TO THEM FOR ME.

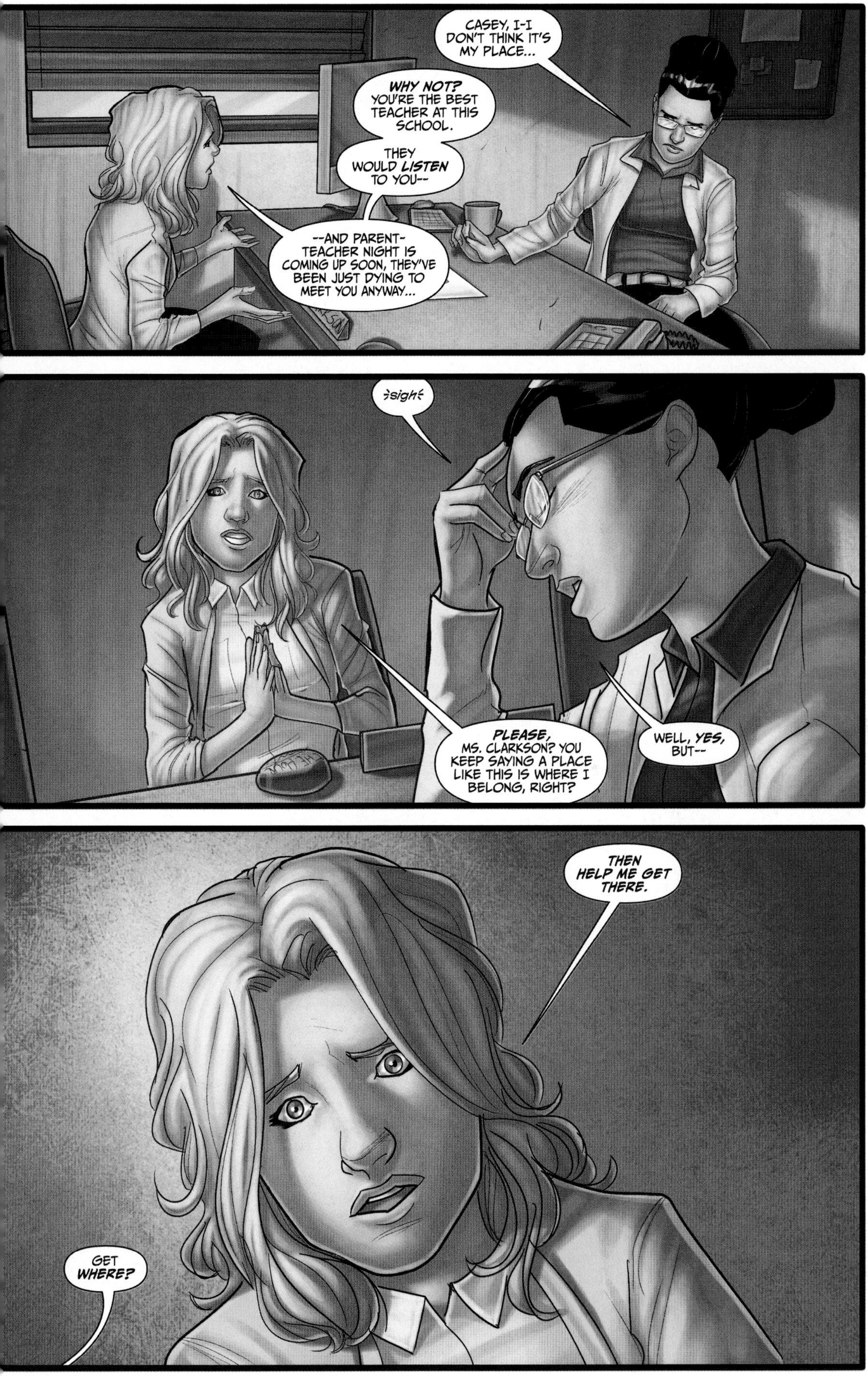
CASEY, I-I DON'T THINK IT'S MY PLACE...
WHY NOT? YOU'RE THE BEST TEACHER AT THIS SCHOOL.
THEY WOULD LISTEN TO YOU--
--AND PARENT-TEACHER NIGHT IS COMING UP SOON, THEY'VE BEEN JUST DYING TO MEET YOU ANYWAY...
sigh
PLEASE, MS. CLARKSON? YOU KEEP SAYING A PLACE LIKE THIS IS WHERE I BELONG, RIGHT?
WELL, YES, BUT--
THEN HELP ME GET THERE.
GET WHERE?

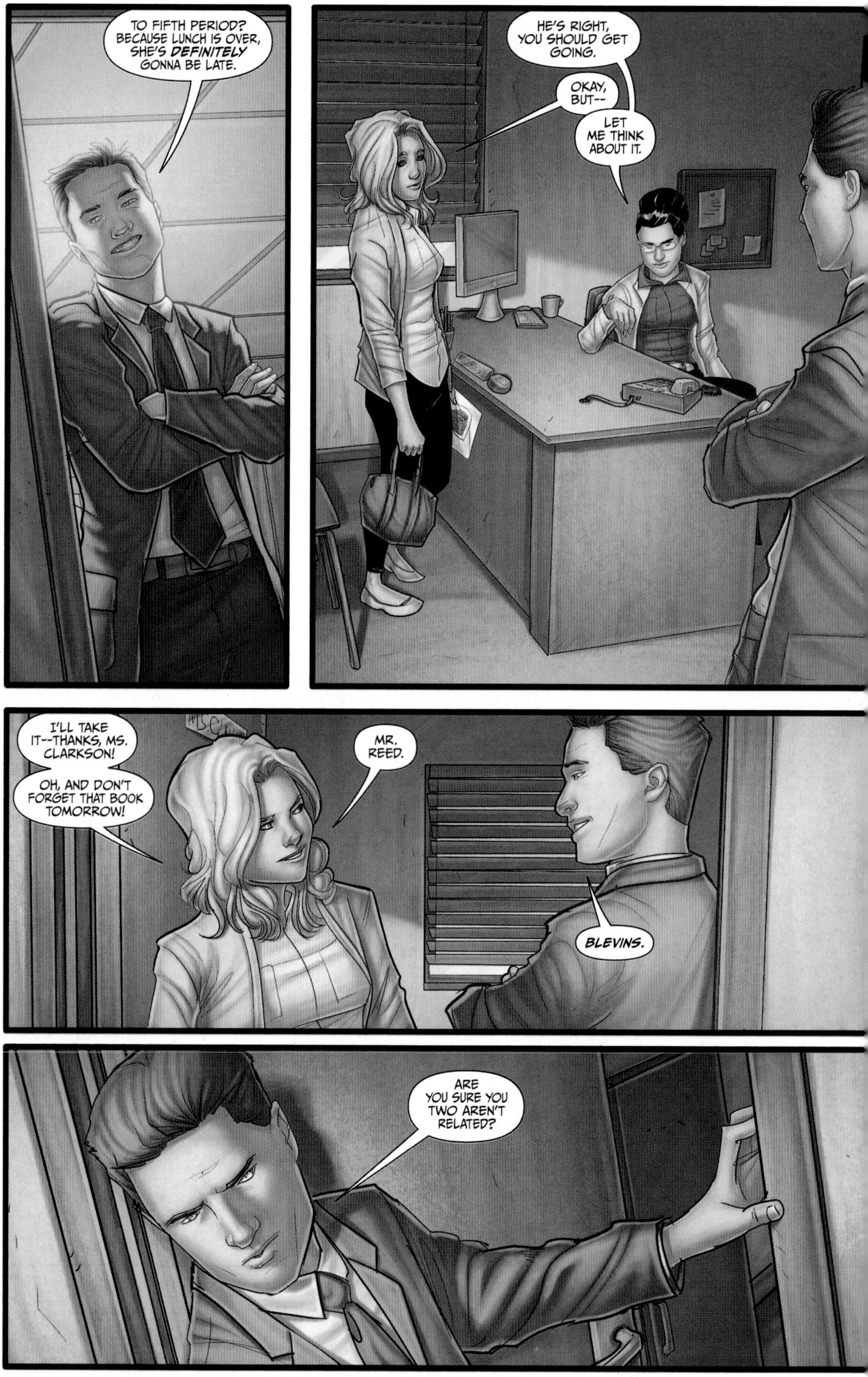
TO FIFTH PERIOD? BECAUSE LUNCH IS OVER, SHE'S *DEFINITELY* GONNA BE LATE.
HE'S RIGHT, YOU SHOULD GET GOING.
OKAY, BUT--
LET ME THINK ABOUT IT.
I'LL TAKE IT--THANKS, MS. CLARKSON!
OH, AND DON'T FORGET THAT BOOK TOMORROW!
MR. REED.
BLEVINS.
ARE YOU SURE YOU TWO AREN'T RELATED?

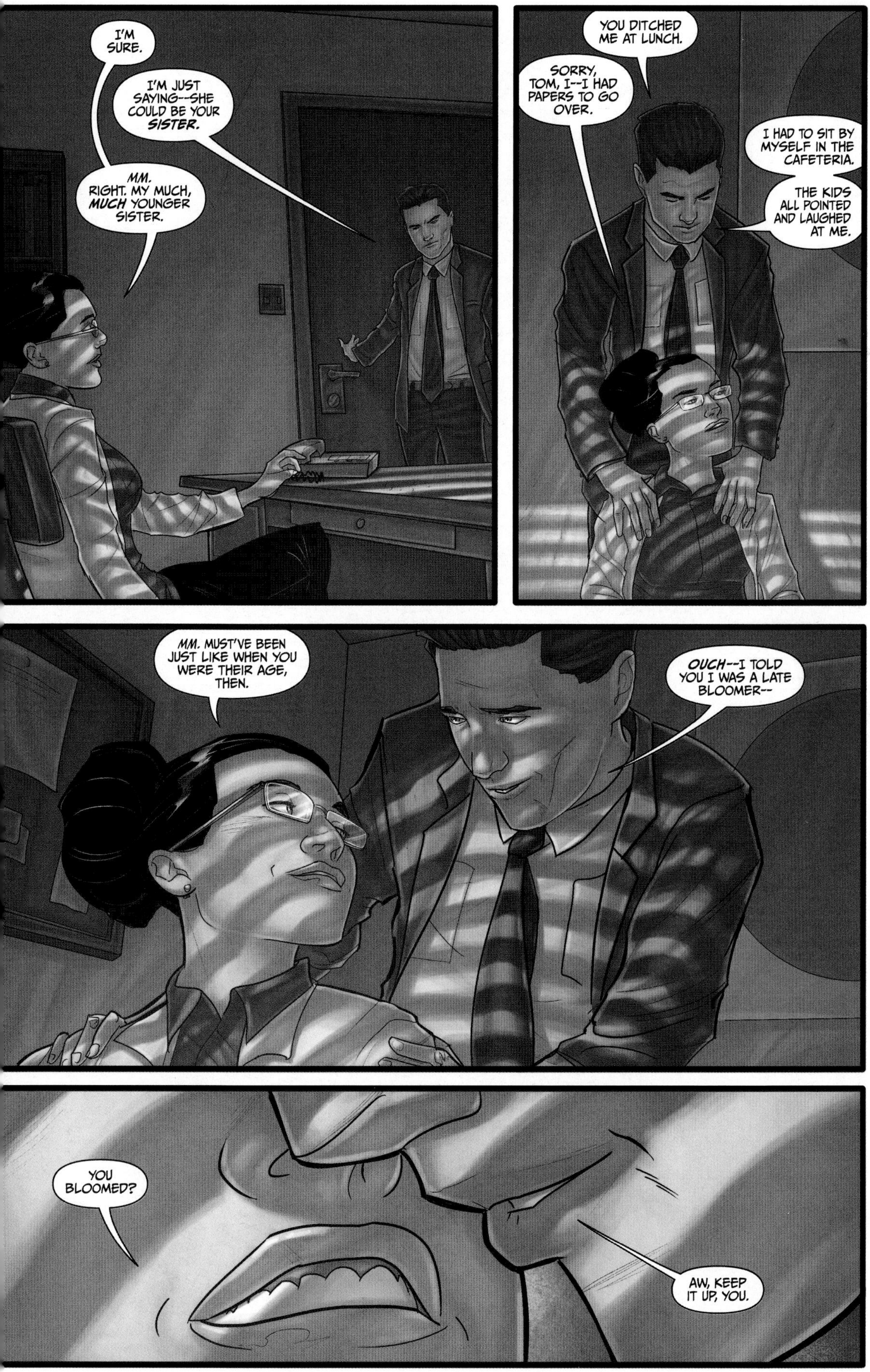
I'M SURE.
I'M JUST SAYING--SHE COULD BE YOUR SISTER.
MM. RIGHT. MY MUCH, MUCH YOUNGER SISTER.
YOU DITCHED ME AT LUNCH.
SORRY, TOM, I--I HAD PAPERS TO GO OVER.
I HAD TO SIT BY MYSELF IN THE CAFETERIA.
THE KIDS ALL POINTED AND LAUGHED AT ME.
MM. MUST'VE BEEN JUST LIKE WHEN YOU WERE THEIR AGE, THEN.
OUCH--I TOLD YOU I WAS A LATE BLOOMER--
YOU BLOOMED?
AW, KEEP IT UP, YOU.

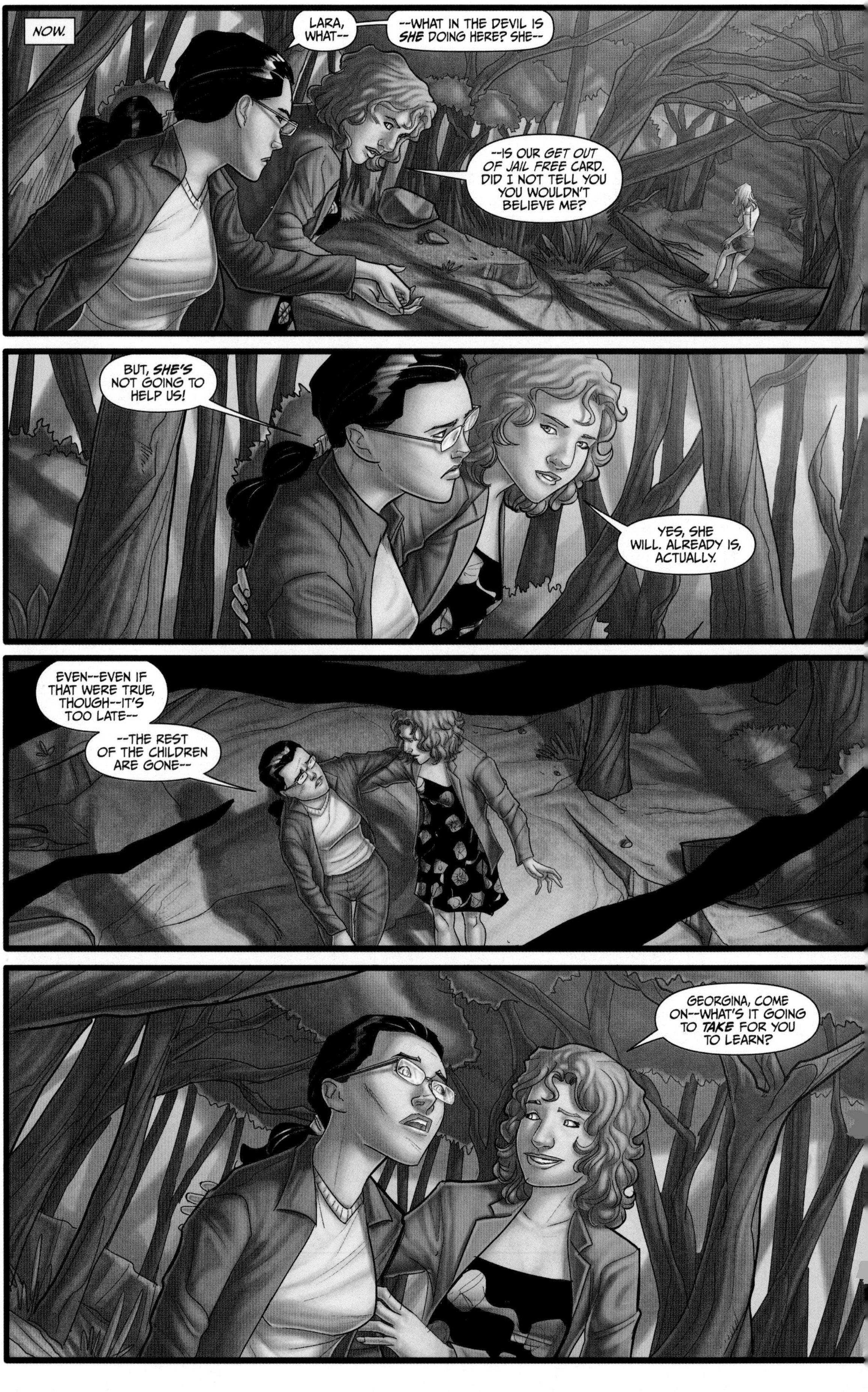

NOW.
LARA, WHAT--
--WHAT IN THE DEVIL IS SHE DOING HERE? SHE--
--IS OUR GET OUT OF JAIL FREE CARD. DID I NOT TELL YOU YOU WOULDN'T BELIEVE ME?
BUT, SHE'S NOT GOING TO HELP US!
YES, SHE WILL. ALREADY IS, ACTUALLY.
EVEN--EVEN IF THAT WERE TRUE, THOUGH--IT'S TOO LATE--
--THE REST OF THE CHILDREN ARE GONE--
GEORGINA, COME ON--WHAT'S IT GOING TO TAKE FOR YOU TO LEARN?

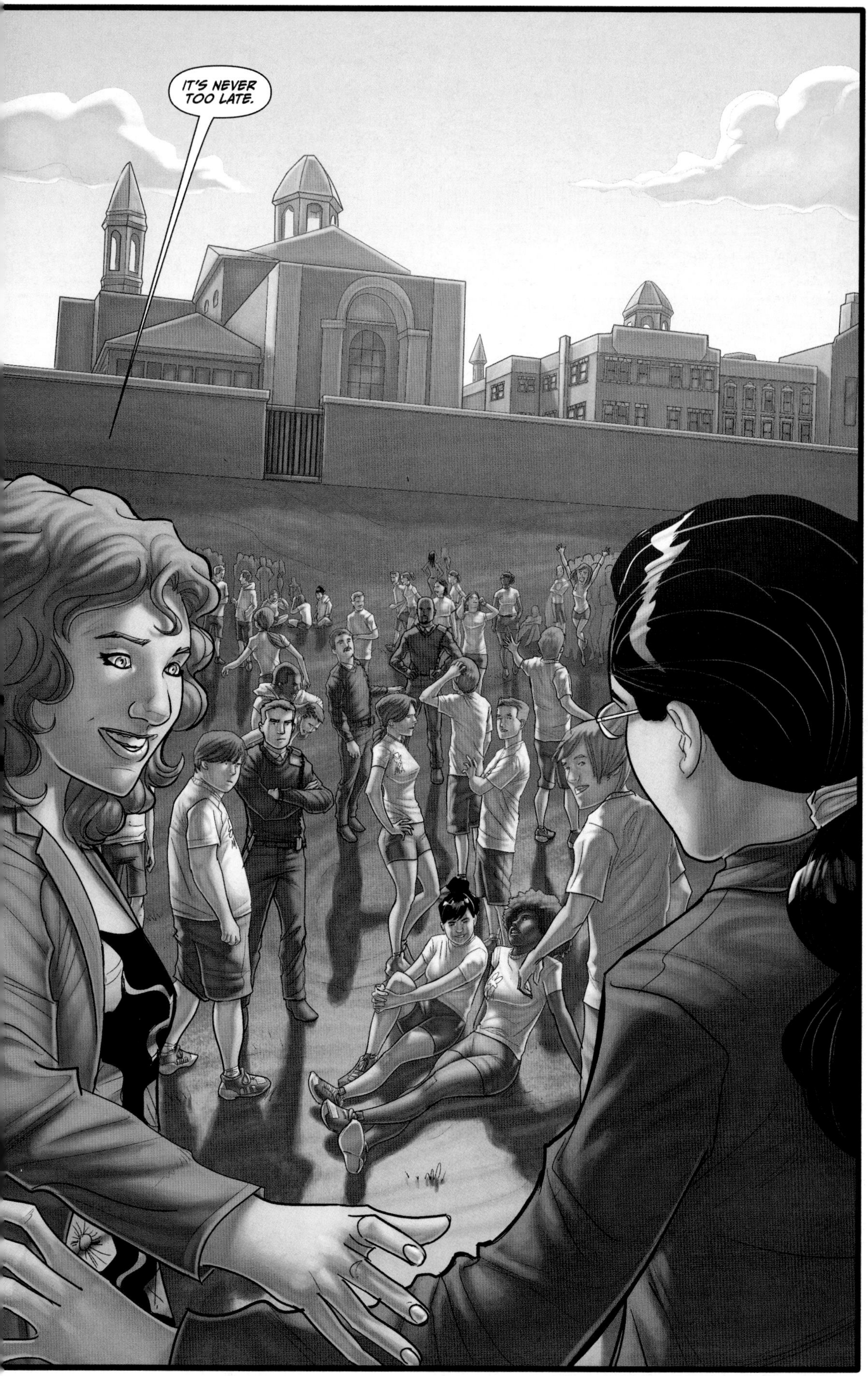
IT'S NEVER TOO LATE.

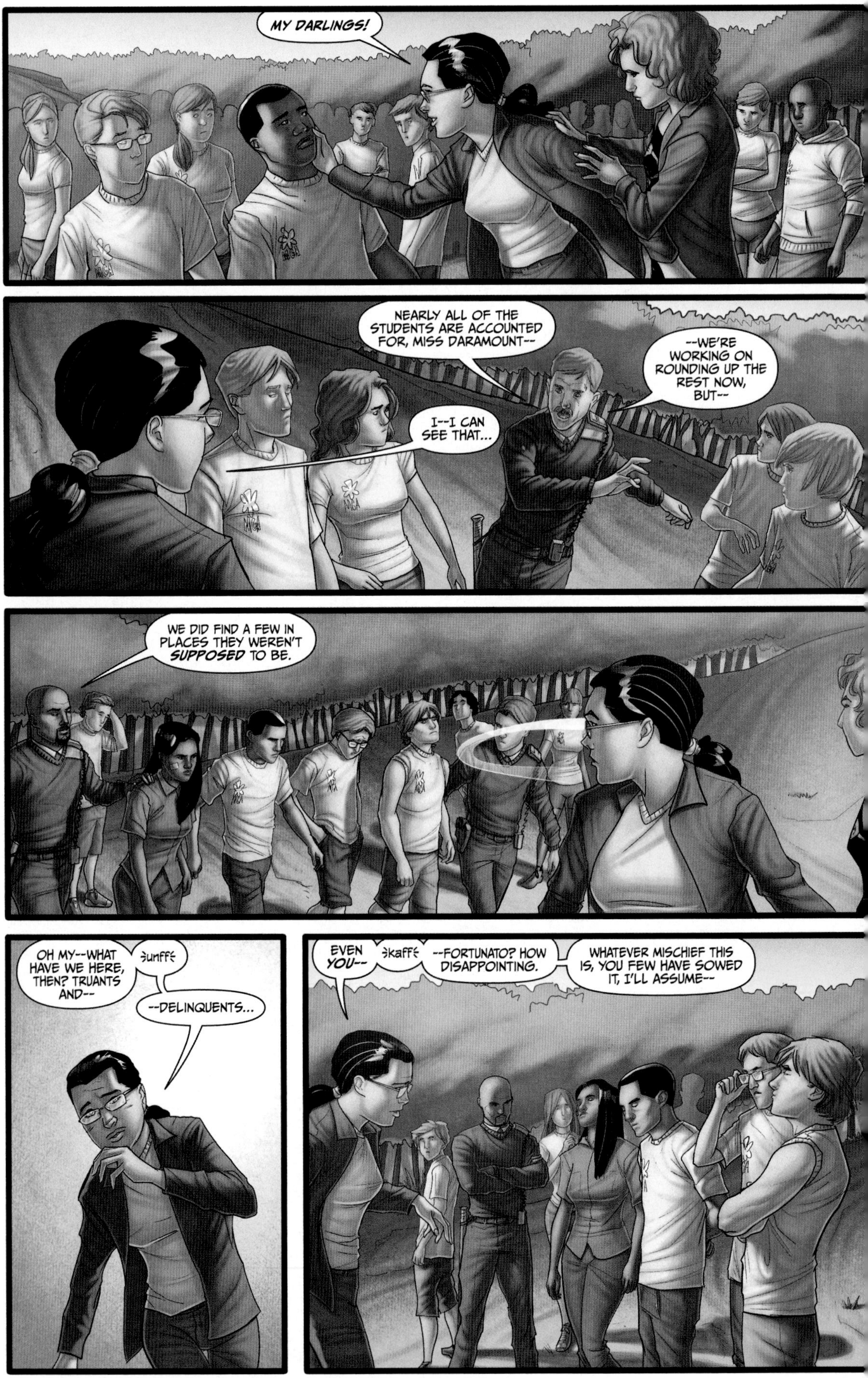
MY DARLINGS!
NEARLY ALL OF THE STUDENTS ARE ACCOUNTED FOR, MISS DARAMOUNT--
--WE'RE WORKING ON ROUNDING UP THE REST NOW, BUT--
I--I CAN SEE THAT...
WE DID FIND A FEW IN PLACES THEY WEREN'T SUPPOSED TO BE.
OH MY--WHAT HAVE WE HERE, THEN? TRUANTS AND--
unff
--DELINQUENTS...
EVEN YOU--
kaff
--FORTUNATO? HOW DISAPPOINTING.
WHATEVER MISCHIEF THIS IS, YOU FEW HAVE SOWED IT, I'LL ASSUME--

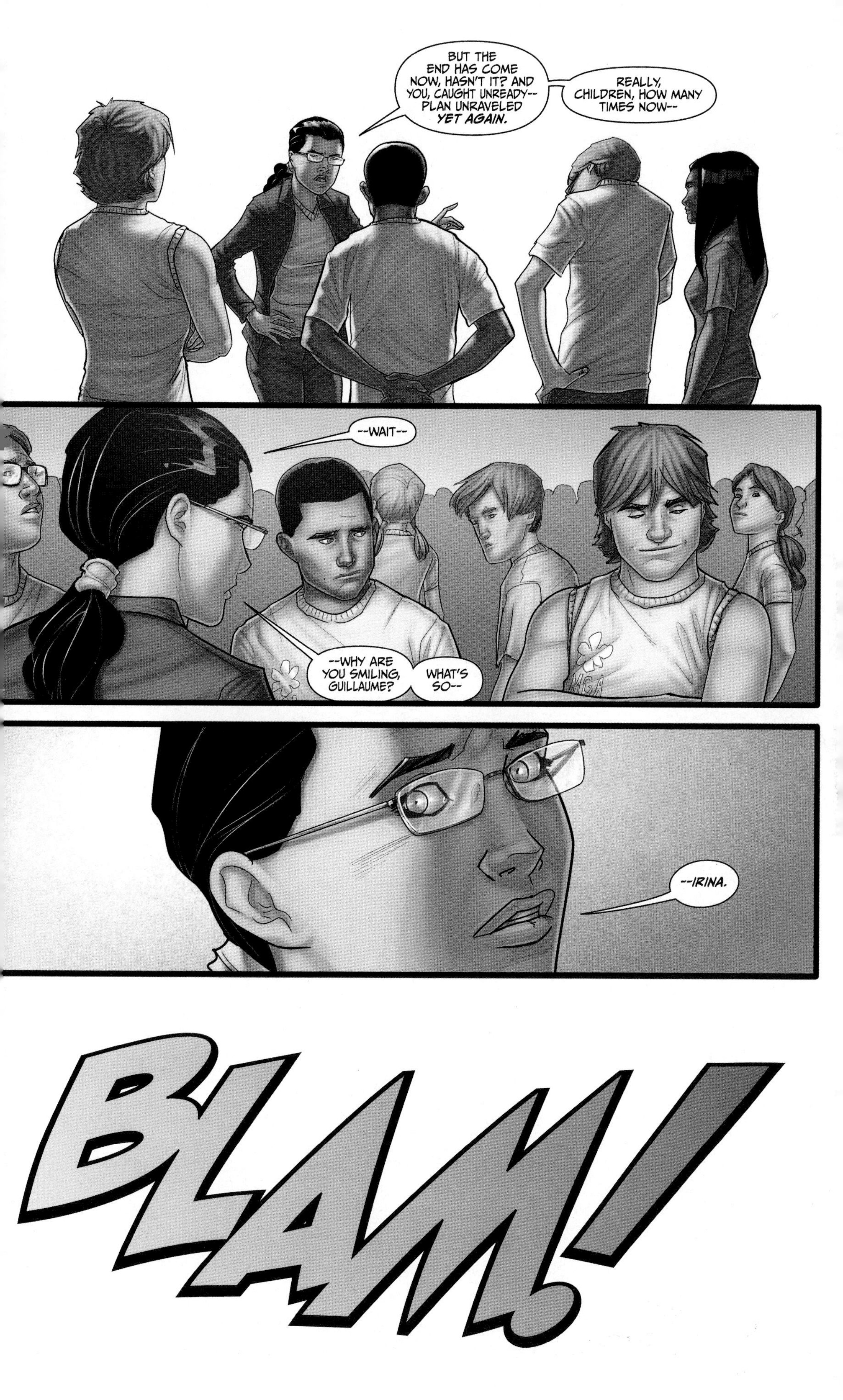
BUT THE END HAS COME NOW, HASN'T IT? AND YOU, CAUGHT UNREADY-- PLAN UNRAVELED *YET AGAIN.*
REALLY, CHILDREN, HOW MANY TIMES NOW--
--WAIT--
--WHY ARE YOU SMILING, GUILLAUME?
WHAT'S SO--
--IRINA.
BLAM!

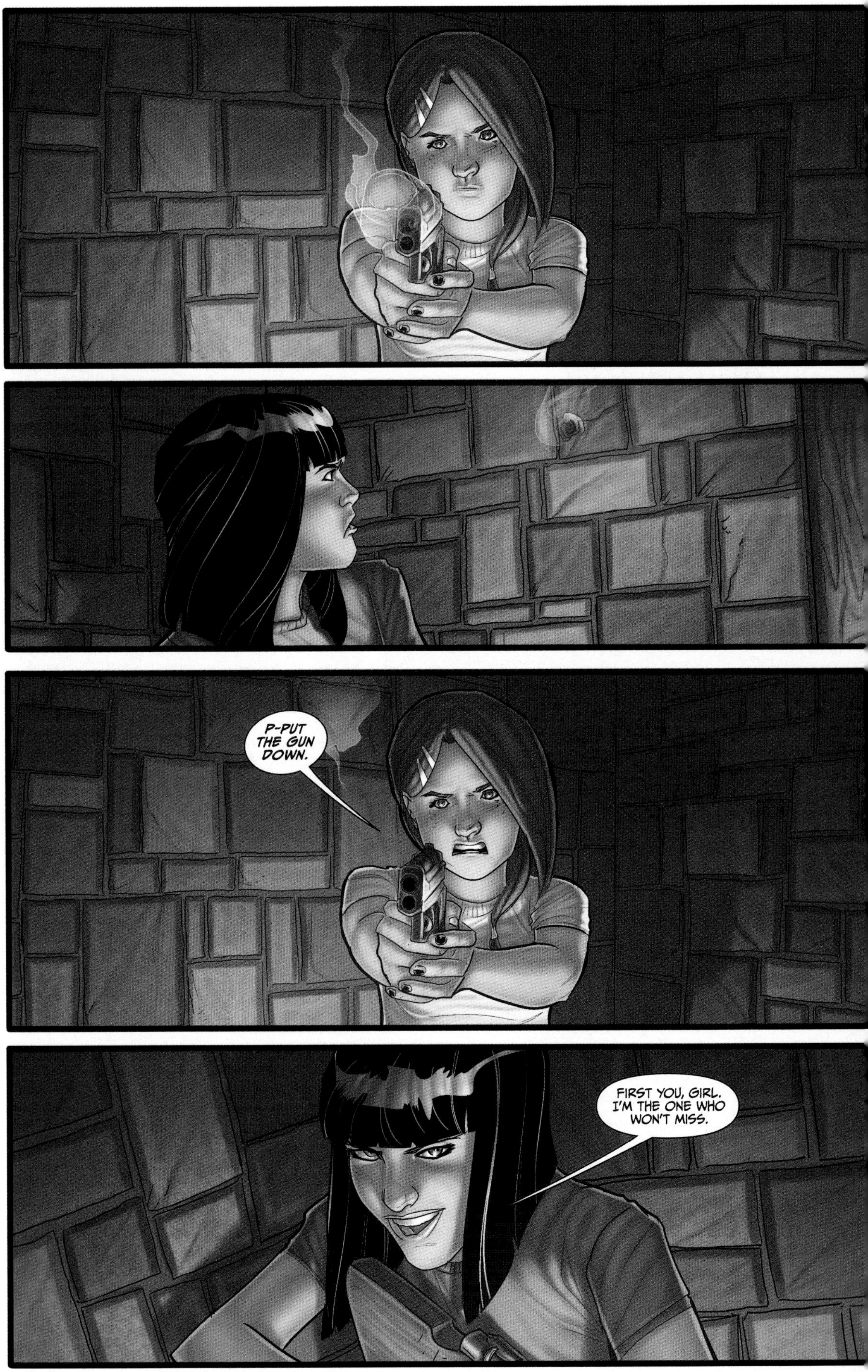
P-PUT THE GUN DOWN.
FIRST YOU, GIRL. I'M THE ONE WHO WON'T MISS.

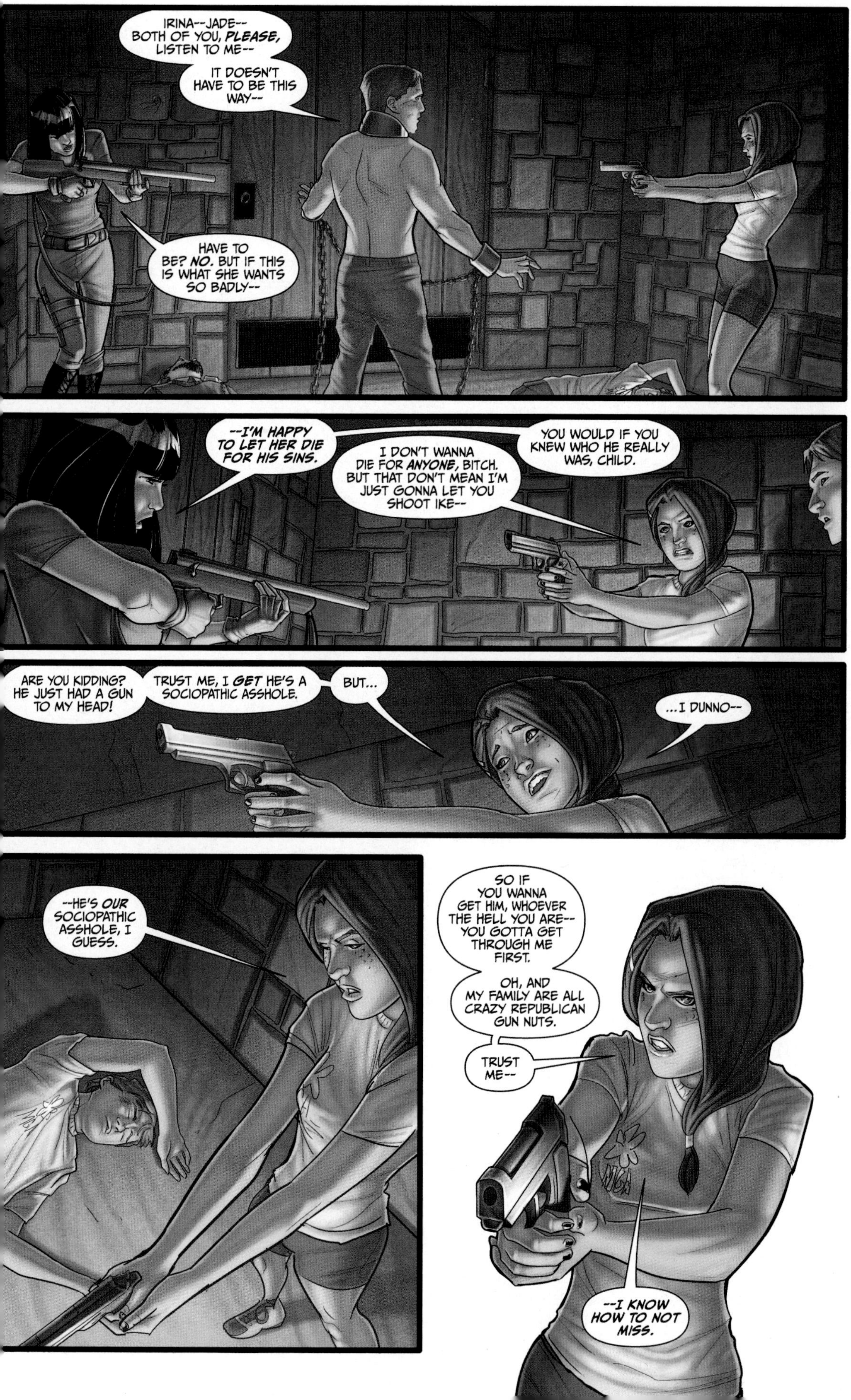
IRINA--JADE--
BOTH OF YOU, PLEASE, LISTEN TO ME--
IT DOESN'T HAVE TO BE THIS WAY--
HAVE TO BE? NO. BUT IF THIS IS WHAT SHE WANTS SO BADLY--
--I'M HAPPY TO LET HER DIE FOR HIS SINS.
YOU WOULD IF YOU KNEW WHO HE REALLY WAS, CHILD.
I DON'T WANNA DIE FOR ANYONE, BITCH. BUT THAT DON'T MEAN I'M JUST GONNA LET YOU SHOOT IKE--
ARE YOU KIDDING? HE JUST HAD A GUN TO MY HEAD!
TRUST ME, I GET HE'S A SOCIOPATHIC ASSHOLE.
BUT...
...I DUNNO--
--HE'S OUR SOCIOPATHIC ASSHOLE, I GUESS.
SO IF YOU WANNA GET HIM, WHOEVER THE HELL YOU ARE-- YOU GOTTA GET THROUGH ME FIRST.
OH, AND MY FAMILY ARE ALL CRAZY REPUBLICAN GUN NUTS.
TRUST ME--
--I KNOW HOW TO NOT MISS.

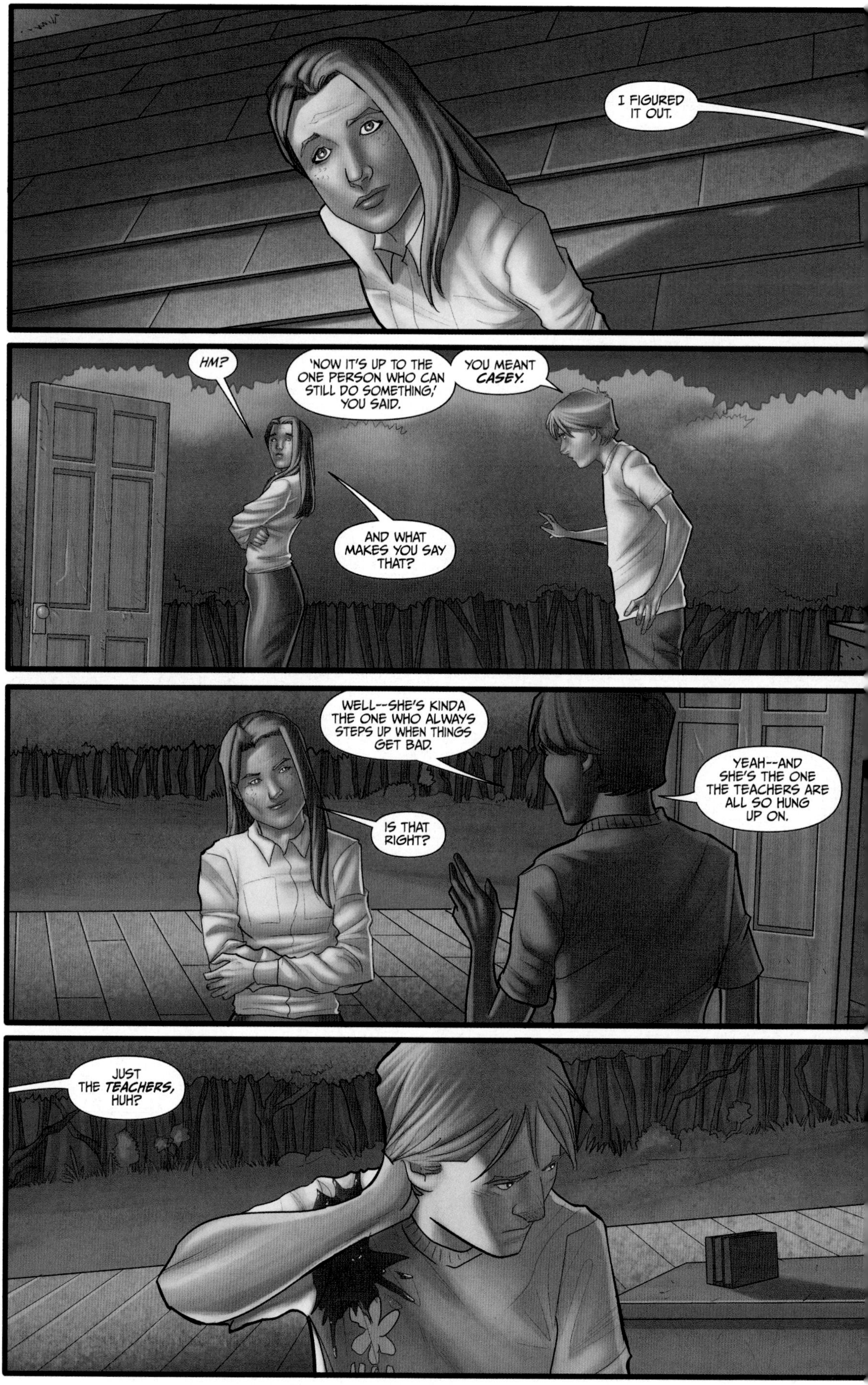
I FIGURED IT OUT.
HM?
'NOW IT'S UP TO THE ONE PERSON WHO CAN STILL DO SOMETHING,' YOU SAID.
YOU MEANT *CASEY.*
AND WHAT MAKES YOU SAY THAT?
WELL--SHE'S KINDA THE ONE WHO ALWAYS STEPS UP WHEN THINGS GET BAD.
IS THAT RIGHT?
YEAH--AND SHE'S THE ONE THE TEACHERS ARE ALL SO HUNG UP ON.
JUST THE *TEACHERS,* HUH?

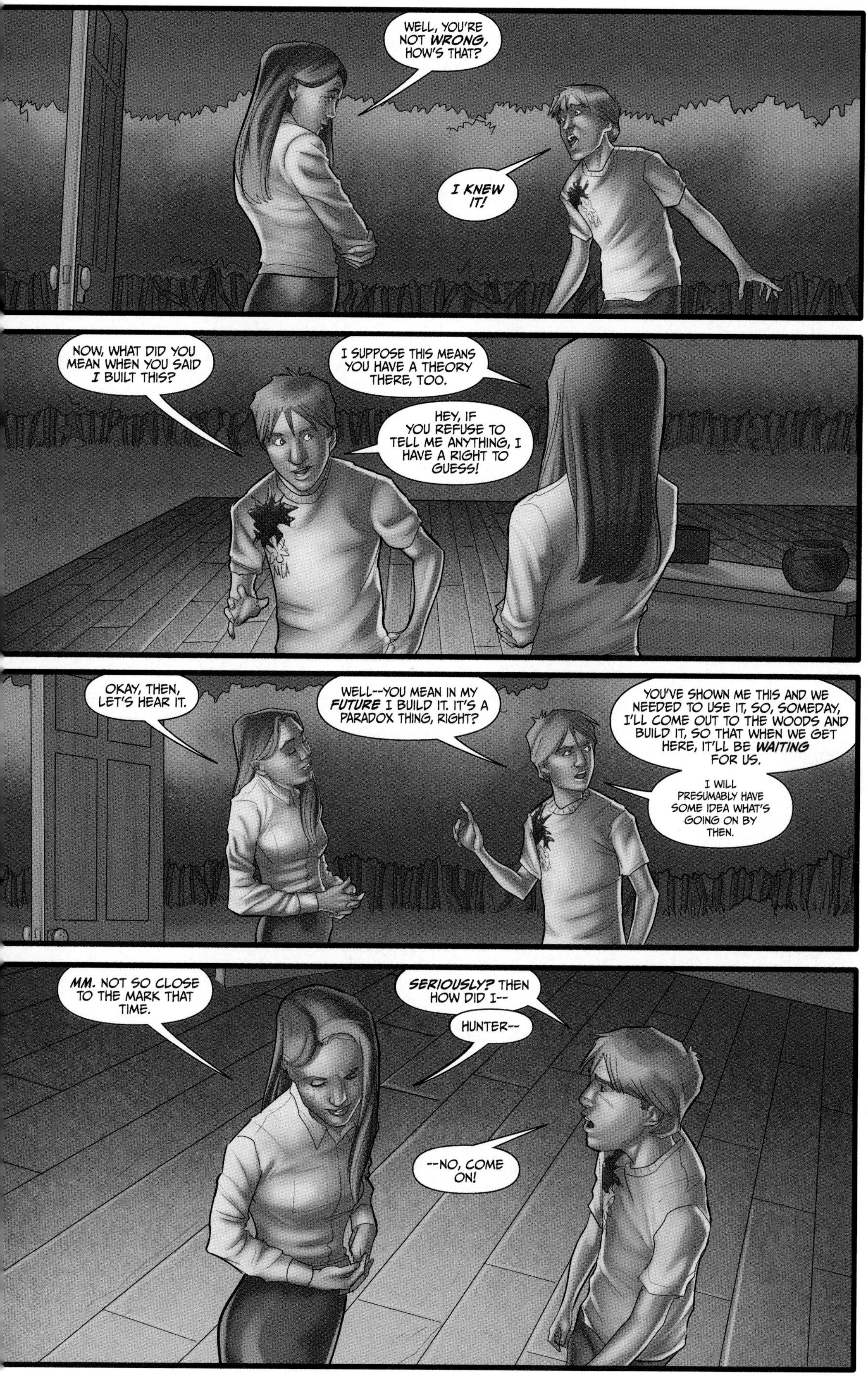
WELL, YOU'RE NOT WRONG, HOW'S THAT?
I KNEW IT!
NOW, WHAT DID YOU MEAN WHEN YOU SAID I BUILT THIS?
I SUPPOSE THIS MEANS YOU HAVE A THEORY THERE, TOO.
HEY, IF YOU REFUSE TO TELL ME ANYTHING, I HAVE A RIGHT TO GUESS!
OKAY, THEN, LET'S HEAR IT.
WELL--YOU MEAN IN MY FUTURE I BUILD IT. IT'S A PARADOX THING, RIGHT?
YOU'VE SHOWN ME THIS AND WE NEEDED TO USE IT, SO, SOMEDAY, I'LL COME OUT TO THE WOODS AND BUILD IT, SO THAT WHEN WE GET HERE, IT'LL BE WAITING FOR US.
I WILL PRESUMABLY HAVE SOME IDEA WHAT'S GOING ON BY THEN.
MM. NOT SO CLOSE TO THE MARK THAT TIME.
SERIOUSLY? THEN HOW DID I--
HUNTER--
--NO, COME ON!

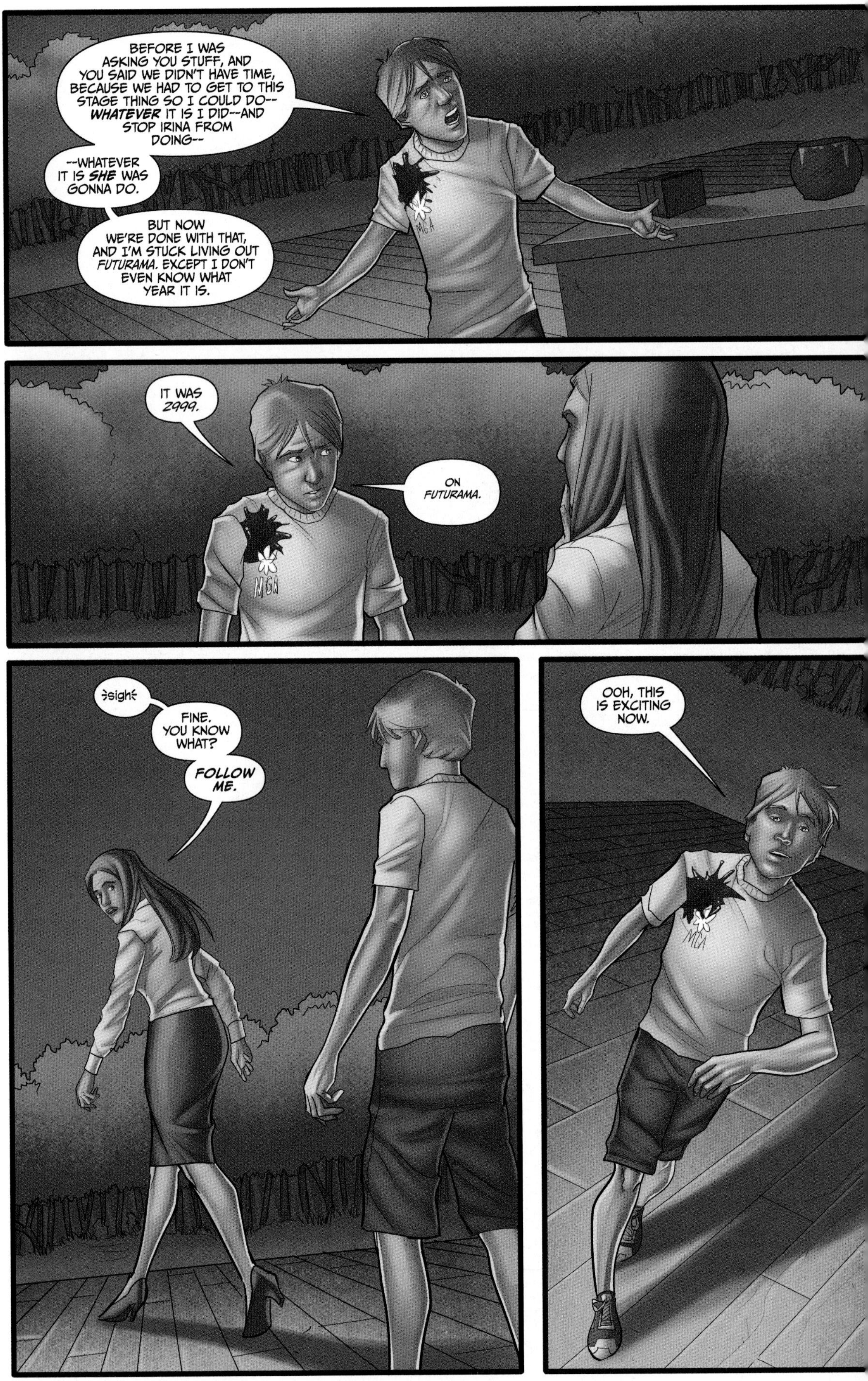

BEFORE I WAS ASKING YOU STUFF, AND YOU SAID WE DIDN'T HAVE TIME, BECAUSE WE HAD TO GET TO THIS STAGE THING SO I COULD DO-- WHATEVER IT IS I DID--AND STOP IRINA FROM DOING--
--WHATEVER IT IS SHE WAS GONNA DO.
BUT NOW WE'RE DONE WITH THAT, AND I'M STUCK LIVING OUT FUTURAMA. EXCEPT I DON'T EVEN KNOW WHAT YEAR IT IS.
MGA
IT WAS 2999.
ON FUTURAMA.
MGA
sigh
FINE. YOU KNOW WHAT?
FOLLOW ME.
OOH, THIS IS EXCITING NOW.
MGA

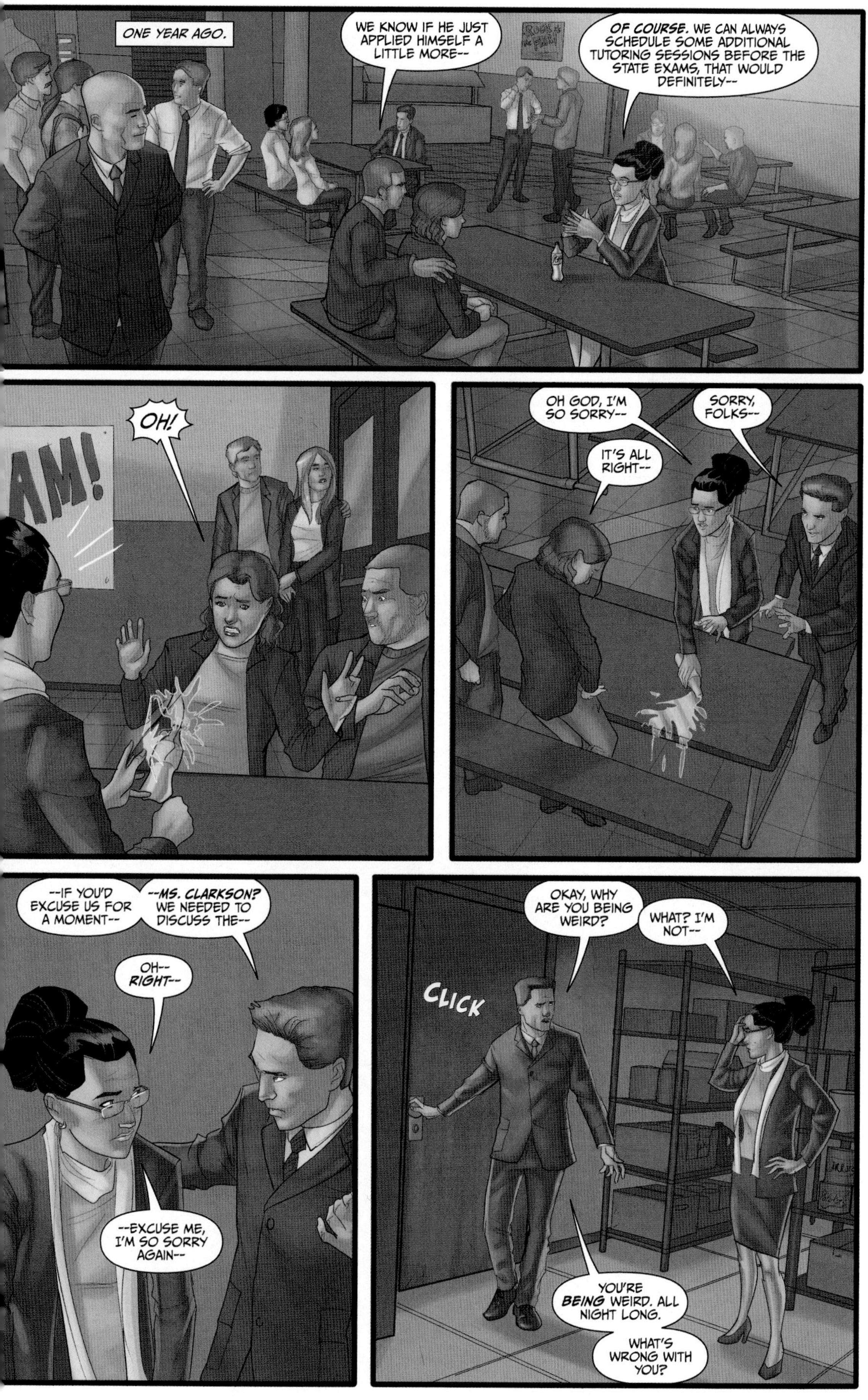
ONE YEAR AGO.
WE KNOW IF HE JUST APPLIED HIMSELF A LITTLE MORE--
OF COURSE. WE CAN ALWAYS SCHEDULE SOME ADDITIONAL TUTORING SESSIONS BEFORE THE STATE EXAMS, THAT WOULD DEFINITELY--
AM!
OH!
OH GOD, I'M SO SORRY--
SORRY, FOLKS--
IT'S ALL RIGHT--
--IF YOU'D EXCUSE US FOR A MOMENT--
--*MS. CLARKSON?* WE NEEDED TO DISCUSS THE--
OH-- *RIGHT*--
--EXCUSE ME, I'M SO SORRY AGAIN--
OKAY, WHY ARE YOU BEING WEIRD?
WHAT? I'M NOT--
CLICK
YOU'RE *BEING* WEIRD. ALL NIGHT LONG.
WHAT'S WRONG WITH YOU?

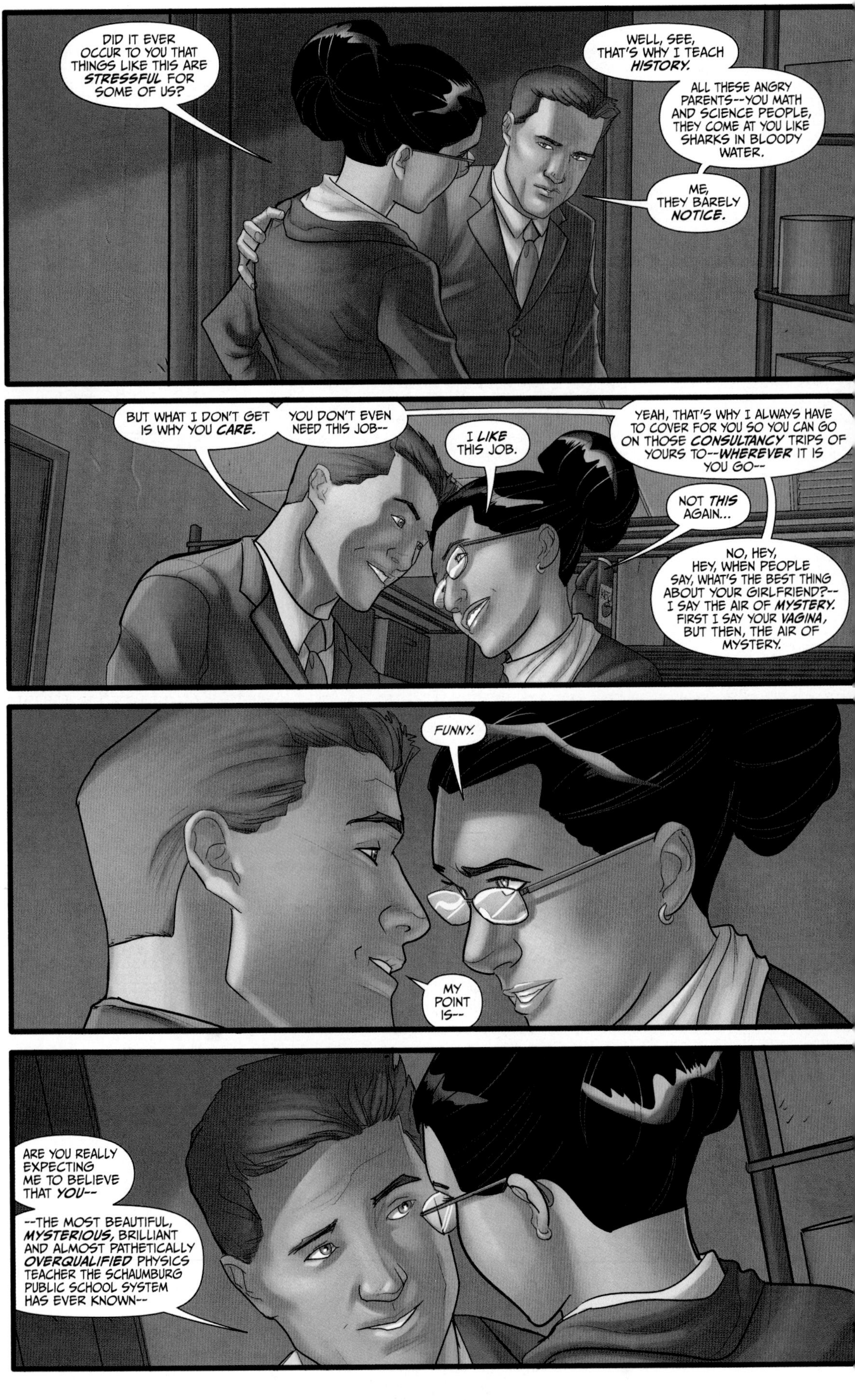
DID IT EVER OCCUR TO YOU THAT THINGS LIKE THIS ARE STRESSFUL FOR SOME OF US?
WELL, SEE, THAT'S WHY I TEACH HISTORY.
ALL THESE ANGRY PARENTS--YOU MATH AND SCIENCE PEOPLE, THEY COME AT YOU LIKE SHARKS IN BLOODY WATER.
ME, THEY BARELY NOTICE.
BUT WHAT I DON'T GET IS WHY YOU CARE.
YOU DON'T EVEN NEED THIS JOB--
I LIKE THIS JOB.
YEAH, THAT'S WHY I ALWAYS HAVE TO COVER FOR YOU SO YOU CAN GO ON THOSE CONSULTANCY TRIPS OF YOURS TO--WHEREVER IT IS YOU GO--
NOT THIS AGAIN...
NO, HEY, HEY, WHEN PEOPLE SAY, WHAT'S THE BEST THING ABOUT YOUR GIRLFRIEND?--I SAY THE AIR OF MYSTERY. FIRST I SAY YOUR VAGINA, BUT THEN, THE AIR OF MYSTERY.
FUNNY.
MY POINT IS--
ARE YOU REALLY EXPECTING ME TO BELIEVE THAT YOU--
--THE MOST BEAUTIFUL, MYSTERIOUS, BRILLIANT AND ALMOST PATHETICALLY OVERQUALIFIED PHYSICS TEACHER THE SCHAUMBURG PUBLIC SCHOOL SYSTEM HAS EVER KNOWN--

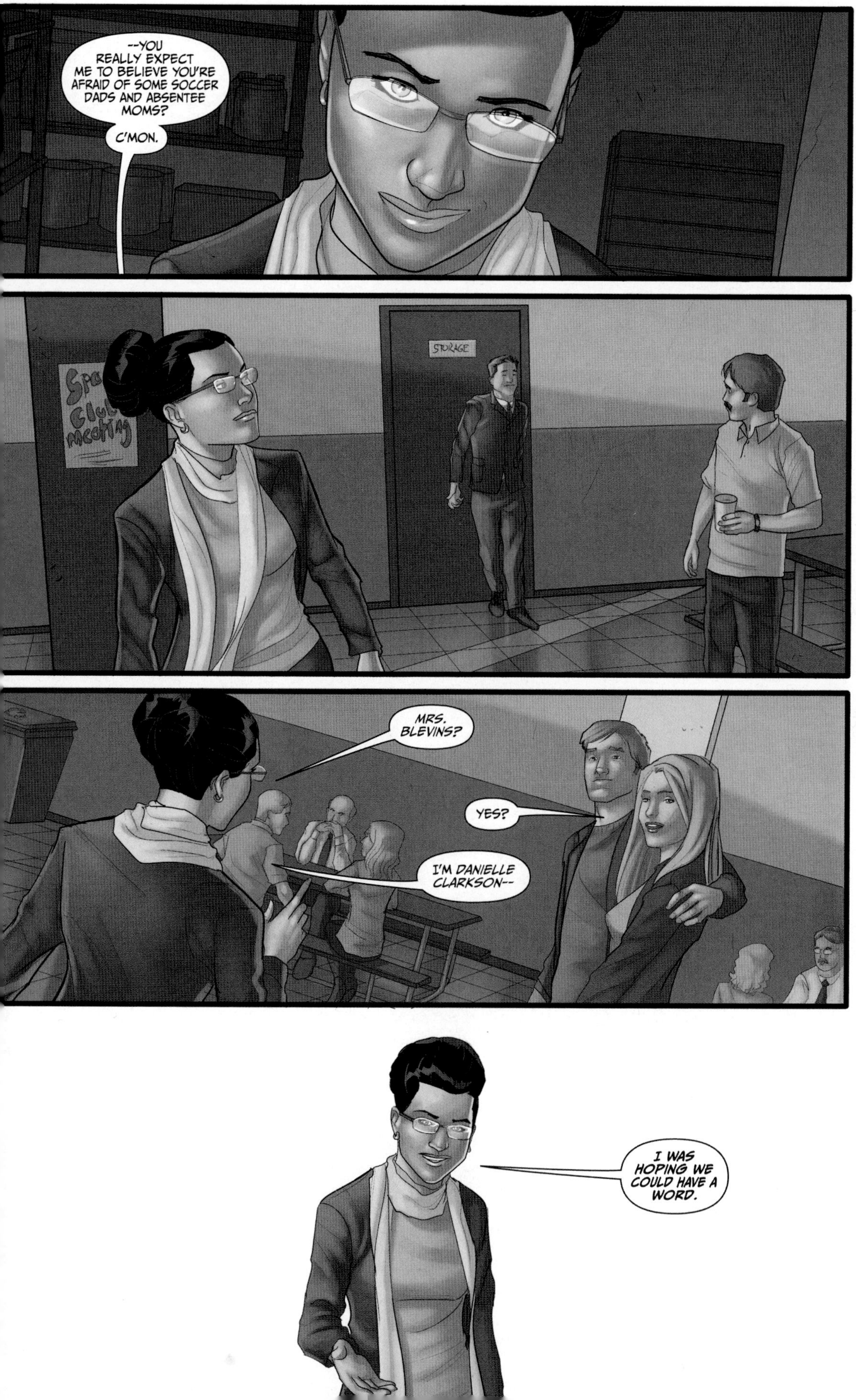
--YOU REALLY EXPECT ME TO BELIEVE YOU'RE AFRAID OF SOME SOCCER DADS AND ABSENTEE MOMS?
C'MON.
STORAGE
MRS. BLEVINS?
YES?
I'M DANIELLE CLARKSON--
I WAS HOPING WE COULD HAVE A WORD.

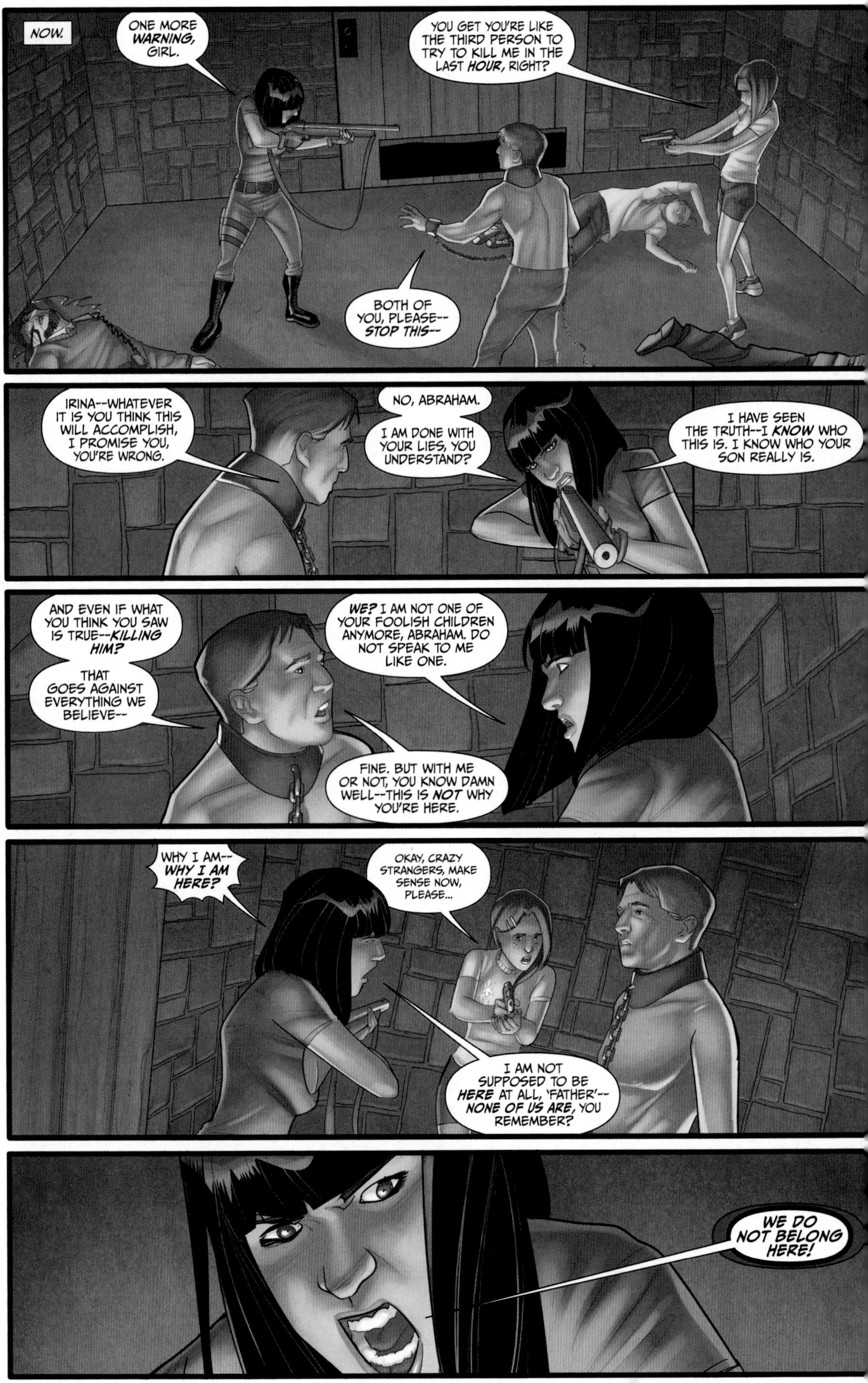
NOW.
ONE MORE WARNING, GIRL.
YOU GET YOU'RE LIKE THE THIRD PERSON TO TRY TO KILL ME IN THE LAST HOUR, RIGHT?
BOTH OF YOU, PLEASE-- STOP THIS--
IRINA--WHATEVER IT IS YOU THINK THIS WILL ACCOMPLISH, I PROMISE YOU, YOU'RE WRONG.
NO, ABRAHAM.
I AM DONE WITH YOUR LIES, YOU UNDERSTAND?
I HAVE SEEN THE TRUTH--I KNOW WHO THIS IS. I KNOW WHO YOUR SON REALLY IS.
AND EVEN IF WHAT YOU THINK YOU SAW IS TRUE--KILLING HIM?
THAT GOES AGAINST EVERYTHING WE BELIEVE--
WE? I AM NOT ONE OF YOUR FOOLISH CHILDREN ANYMORE, ABRAHAM. DO NOT SPEAK TO ME LIKE ONE.
FINE. BUT WITH ME OR NOT, YOU KNOW DAMN WELL--THIS IS NOT WHY YOU'RE HERE.
WHY I AM-- WHY I AM HERE?
OKAY, CRAZY STRANGERS, MAKE SENSE NOW, PLEASE...
I AM NOT SUPPOSED TO BE HERE AT ALL, 'FATHER'-- NONE OF US ARE, YOU REMEMBER?
WE DO NOT BELONG HERE!

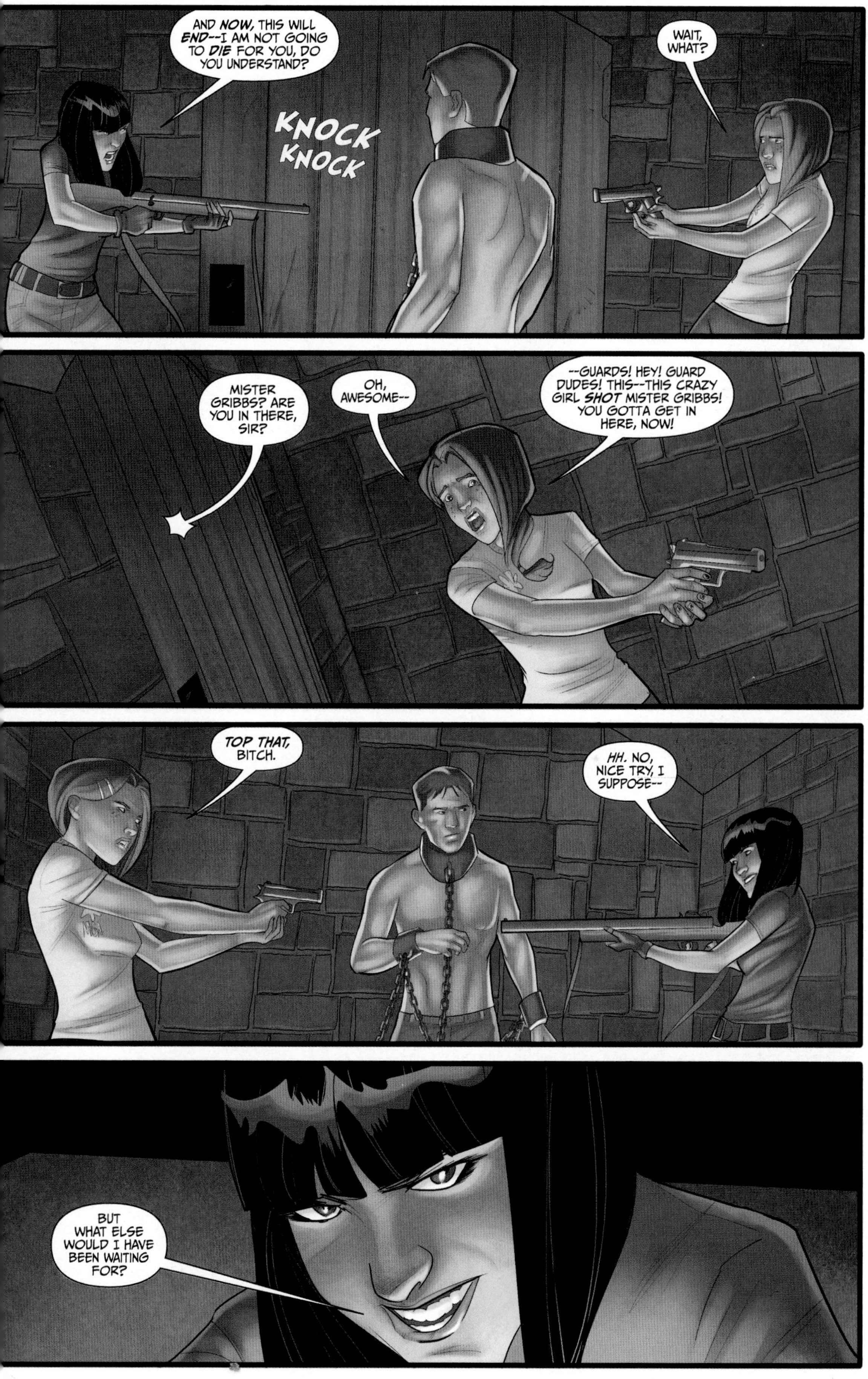
AND *NOW*, THIS WILL *END*--I AM NOT GOING TO *DIE* FOR YOU, DO YOU UNDERSTAND?
KNOCK KNOCK
WAIT, WHAT?
MISTER GRIBBS? ARE YOU IN THERE, SIR?
OH, AWESOME--
--GUARDS! HEY! GUARD DUDES! THIS--THIS CRAZY GIRL *SHOT* MISTER GRIBBS! YOU GOTTA GET IN HERE, NOW!
TOP THAT, BITCH.
HH. NO, NICE TRY, I SUPPOSE--
BUT WHAT ELSE WOULD I HAVE BEEN WAITING FOR?

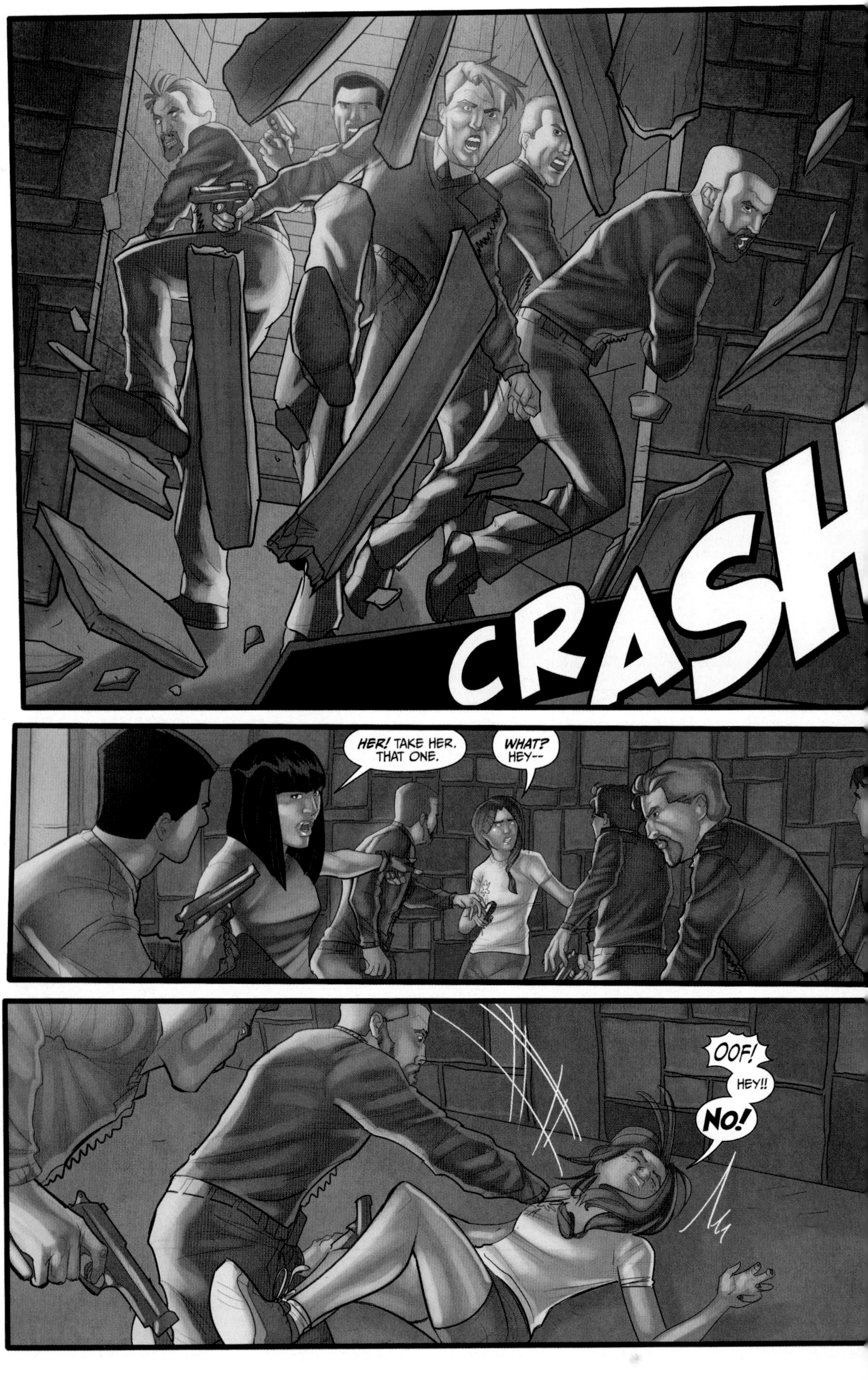
CRASH
HER! TAKE HER. THAT ONE.
WHAT? HEY--
OOF!
HEY!!
NO!

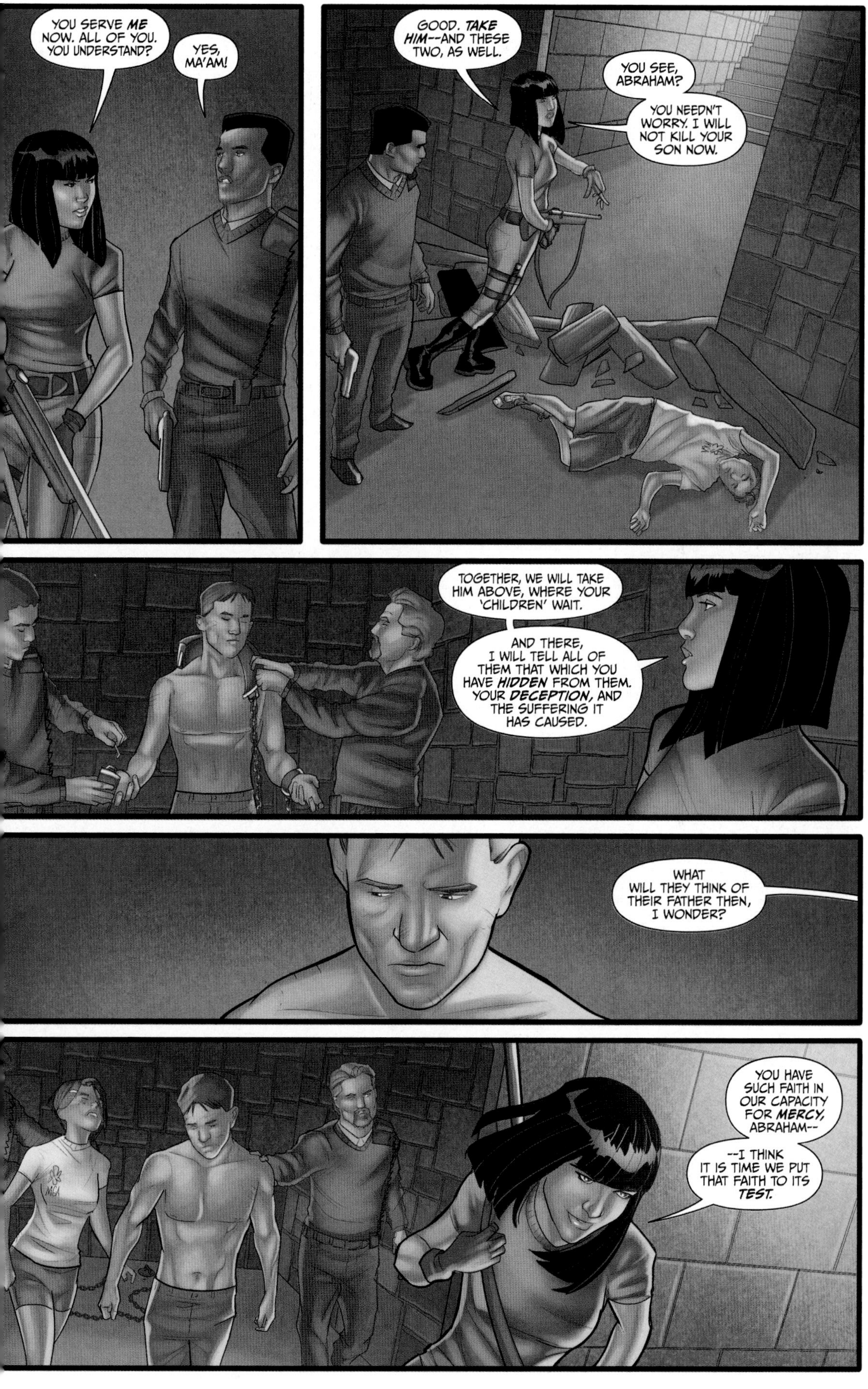
YOU SERVE *ME* NOW. ALL OF YOU. YOU UNDERSTAND?
YES, MA'AM!
GOOD. *TAKE HIM*--AND THESE TWO, AS WELL.
YOU SEE, ABRAHAM?
YOU NEEDN'T WORRY. I WILL NOT KILL YOUR SON NOW.
TOGETHER, WE WILL TAKE HIM ABOVE, WHERE YOUR 'CHILDREN' WAIT.
AND THERE, I WILL TELL ALL OF THEM THAT WHICH YOU HAVE *HIDDEN* FROM THEM. YOUR *DECEPTION,* AND THE SUFFERING IT HAS CAUSED.
WHAT WILL THEY THINK OF THEIR FATHER THEN, I WONDER?
YOU HAVE SUCH FAITH IN OUR CAPACITY FOR *MERCY,* ABRAHAM--
--I THINK IT IS TIME WE PUT THAT FAITH TO ITS *TEST.*

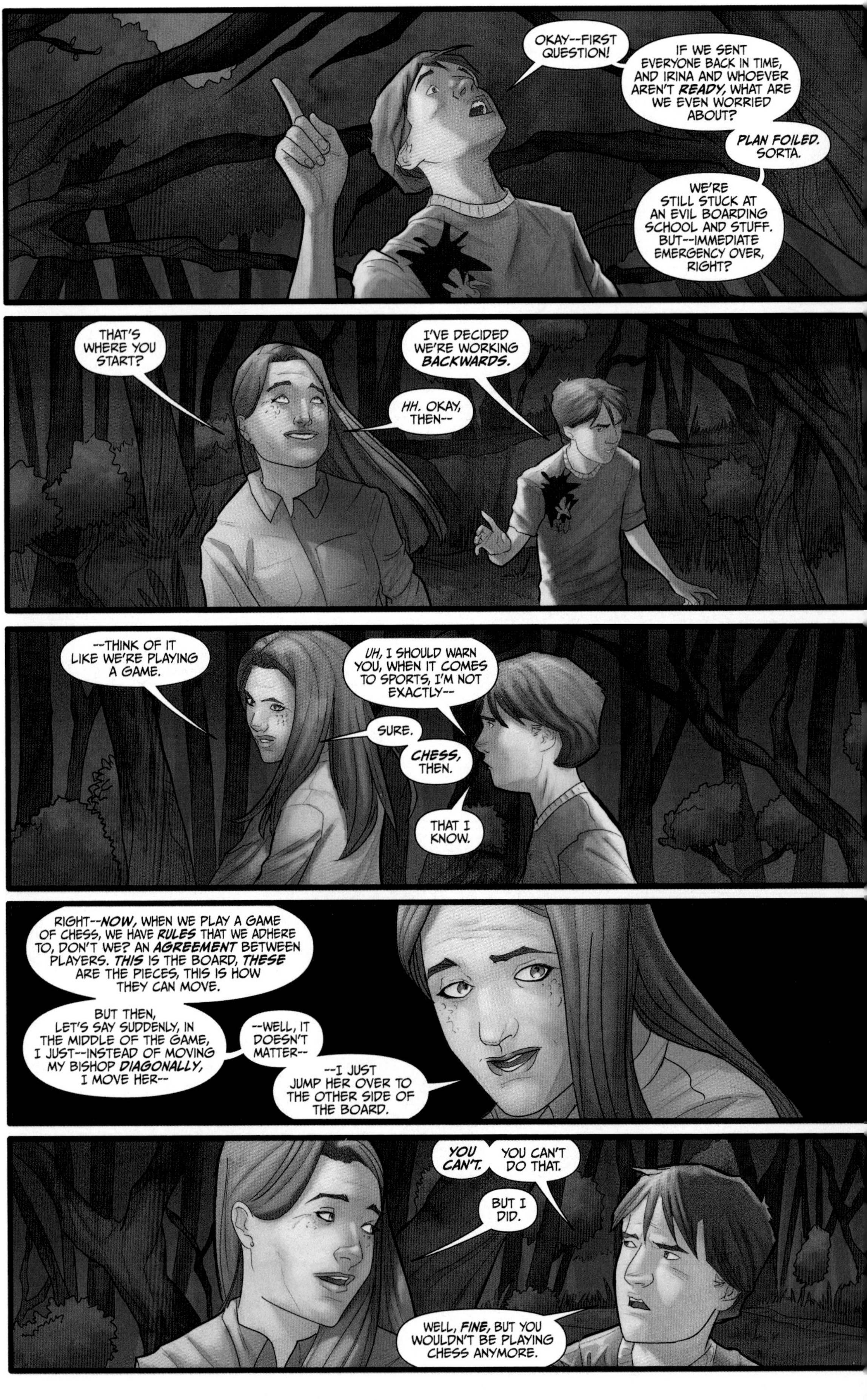
OKAY--FIRST QUESTION!
IF WE SENT EVERYONE BACK IN TIME, AND IRINA AND WHOEVER AREN'T READY, WHAT ARE WE EVEN WORRIED ABOUT?
PLAN FOILED. SORTA.
WE'RE STILL STUCK AT AN EVIL BOARDING SCHOOL AND STUFF. BUT--IMMEDIATE EMERGENCY OVER, RIGHT?
THAT'S WHERE YOU START?
I'VE DECIDED WE'RE WORKING BACKWARDS.
HH. OKAY, THEN--
--THINK OF IT LIKE WE'RE PLAYING A GAME.
UH, I SHOULD WARN YOU, WHEN IT COMES TO SPORTS, I'M NOT EXACTLY--
SURE.
CHESS, THEN.
THAT I KNOW.
RIGHT--NOW, WHEN WE PLAY A GAME OF CHESS, WE HAVE RULES THAT WE ADHERE TO, DON'T WE? AN AGREEMENT BETWEEN PLAYERS. THIS IS THE BOARD, THESE ARE THE PIECES, THIS IS HOW THEY CAN MOVE.
BUT THEN, LET'S SAY SUDDENLY, IN THE MIDDLE OF THE GAME, I JUST--INSTEAD OF MOVING MY BISHOP DIAGONALLY, I MOVE HER--
--WELL, IT DOESN'T MATTER--
--I JUST JUMP HER OVER TO THE OTHER SIDE OF THE BOARD.
YOU CAN'T.
YOU CAN'T DO THAT.
BUT I DID.
WELL, FINE, BUT YOU WOULDN'T BE PLAYING CHESS ANYMORE.

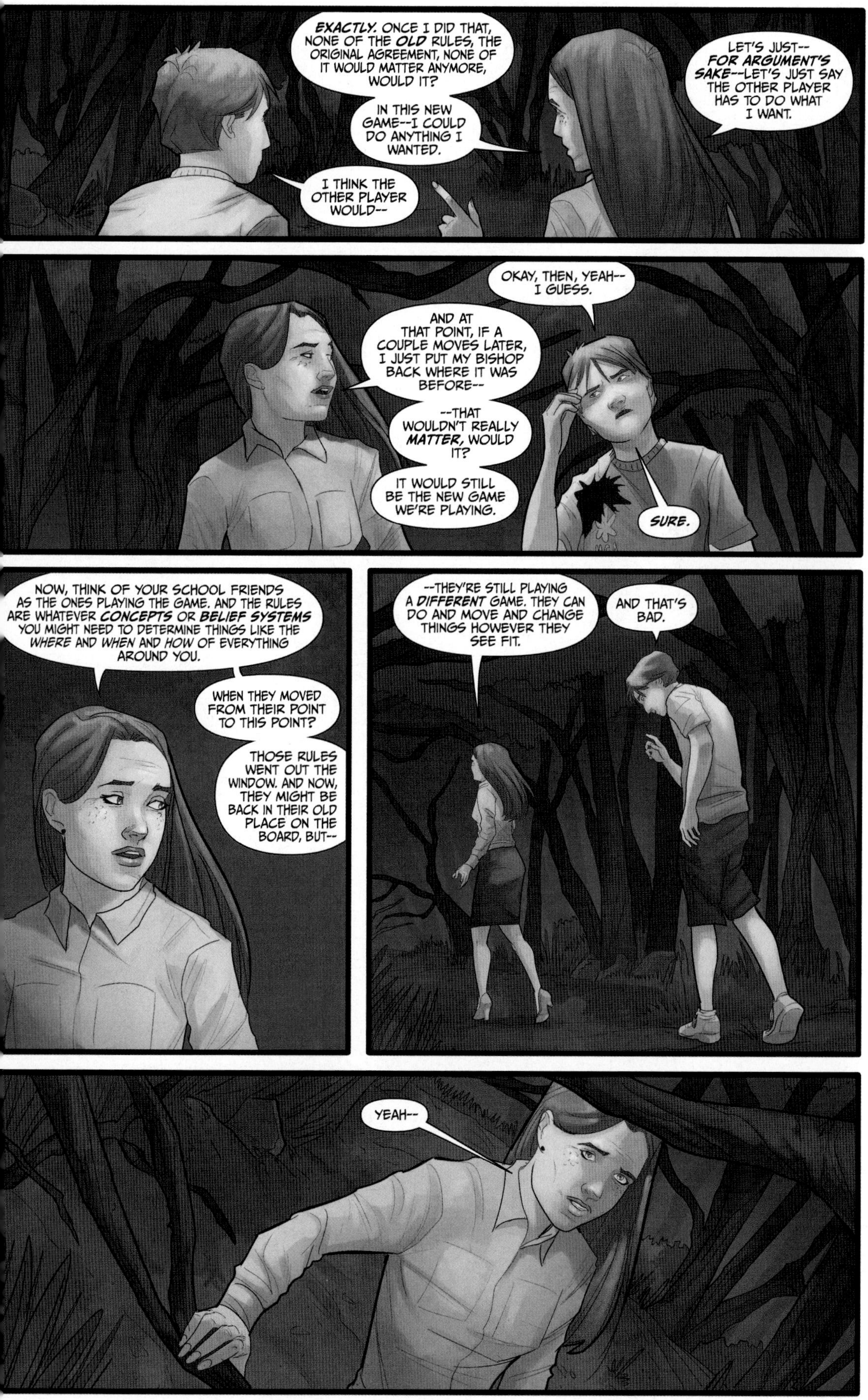
EXACTLY. ONCE I DID THAT, NONE OF THE OLD RULES, THE ORIGINAL AGREEMENT, NONE OF IT WOULD MATTER ANYMORE, WOULD IT?
IN THIS NEW GAME--I COULD DO ANYTHING I WANTED.
I THINK THE OTHER PLAYER WOULD--
LET'S JUST-- FOR ARGUMENT'S SAKE--LET'S JUST SAY THE OTHER PLAYER HAS TO DO WHAT I WANT.
OKAY, THEN, YEAH-- I GUESS.
AND AT THAT POINT, IF A COUPLE MOVES LATER, I JUST PUT MY BISHOP BACK WHERE IT WAS BEFORE--
--THAT WOULDN'T REALLY MATTER, WOULD IT?
IT WOULD STILL BE THE NEW GAME WE'RE PLAYING.
SURE.
NOW, THINK OF YOUR SCHOOL FRIENDS AS THE ONES PLAYING THE GAME. AND THE RULES ARE WHATEVER CONCEPTS OR BELIEF SYSTEMS YOU MIGHT NEED TO DETERMINE THINGS LIKE THE WHERE AND WHEN AND HOW OF EVERYTHING AROUND YOU.
WHEN THEY MOVED FROM THEIR POINT TO THIS POINT?
THOSE RULES WENT OUT THE WINDOW. AND NOW, THEY MIGHT BE BACK IN THEIR OLD PLACE ON THE BOARD, BUT--
--THEY'RE STILL PLAYING A DIFFERENT GAME. THEY CAN DO AND MOVE AND CHANGE THINGS HOWEVER THEY SEE FIT.
AND THAT'S BAD.
YEAH--

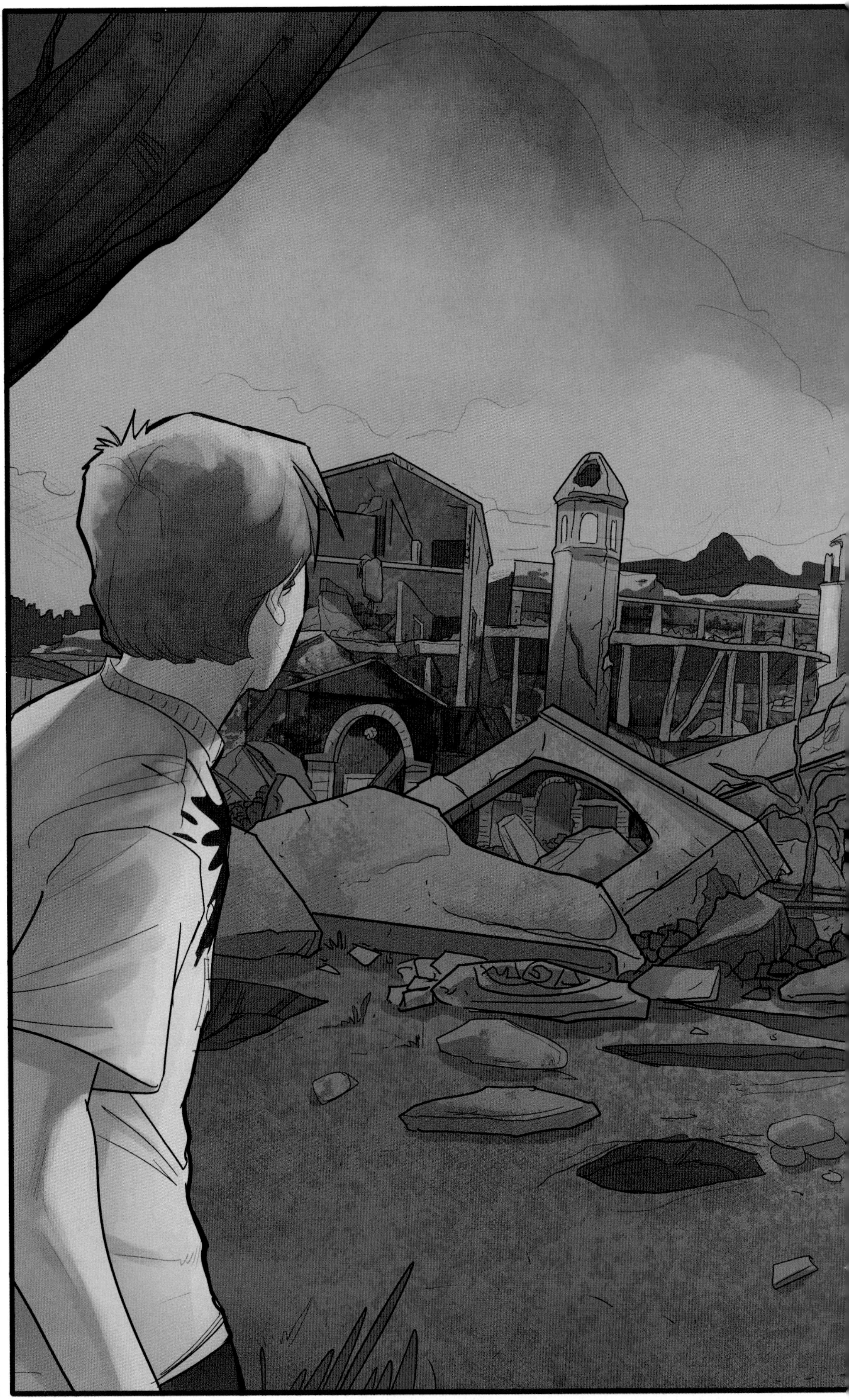

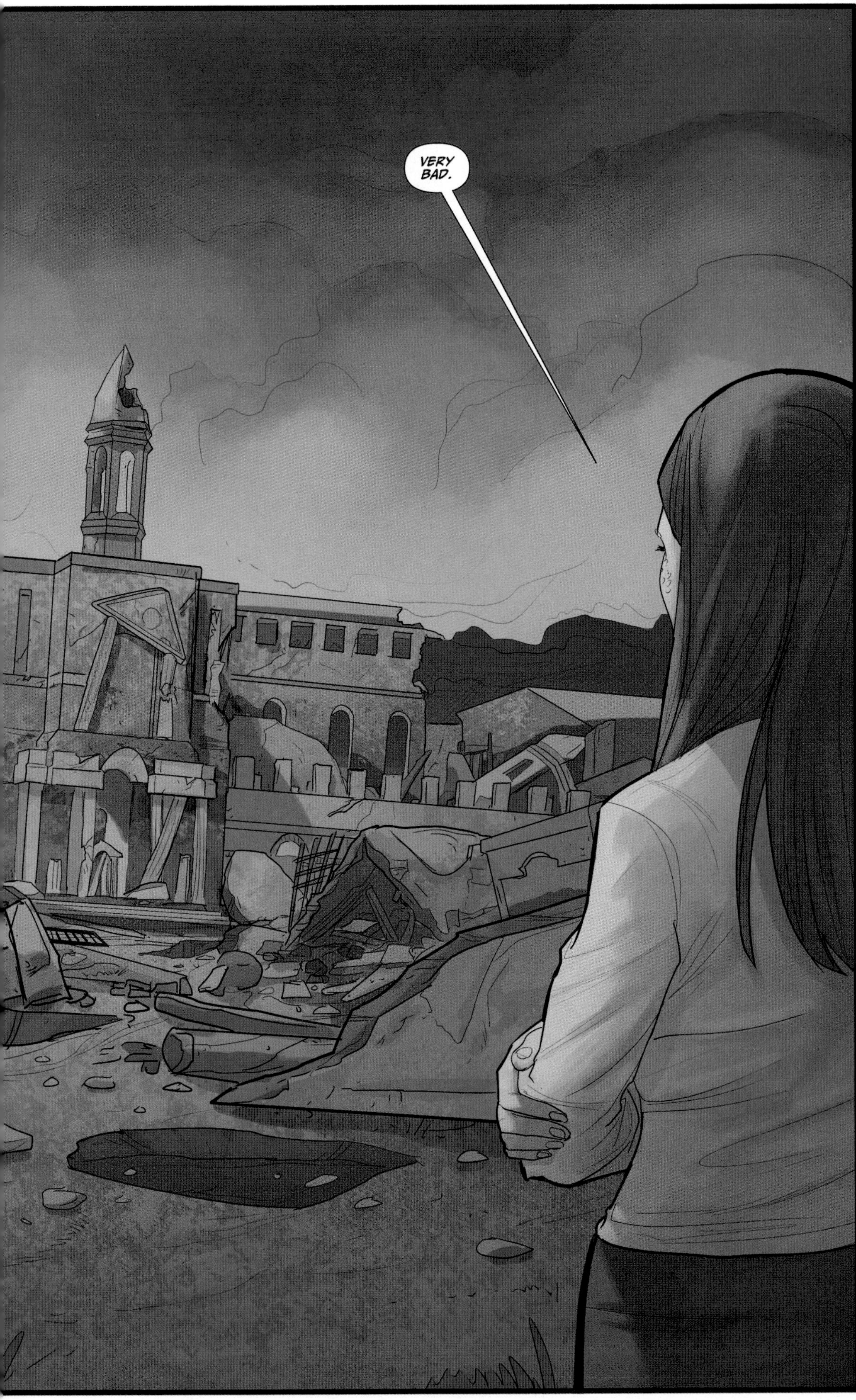
VERY BAD.

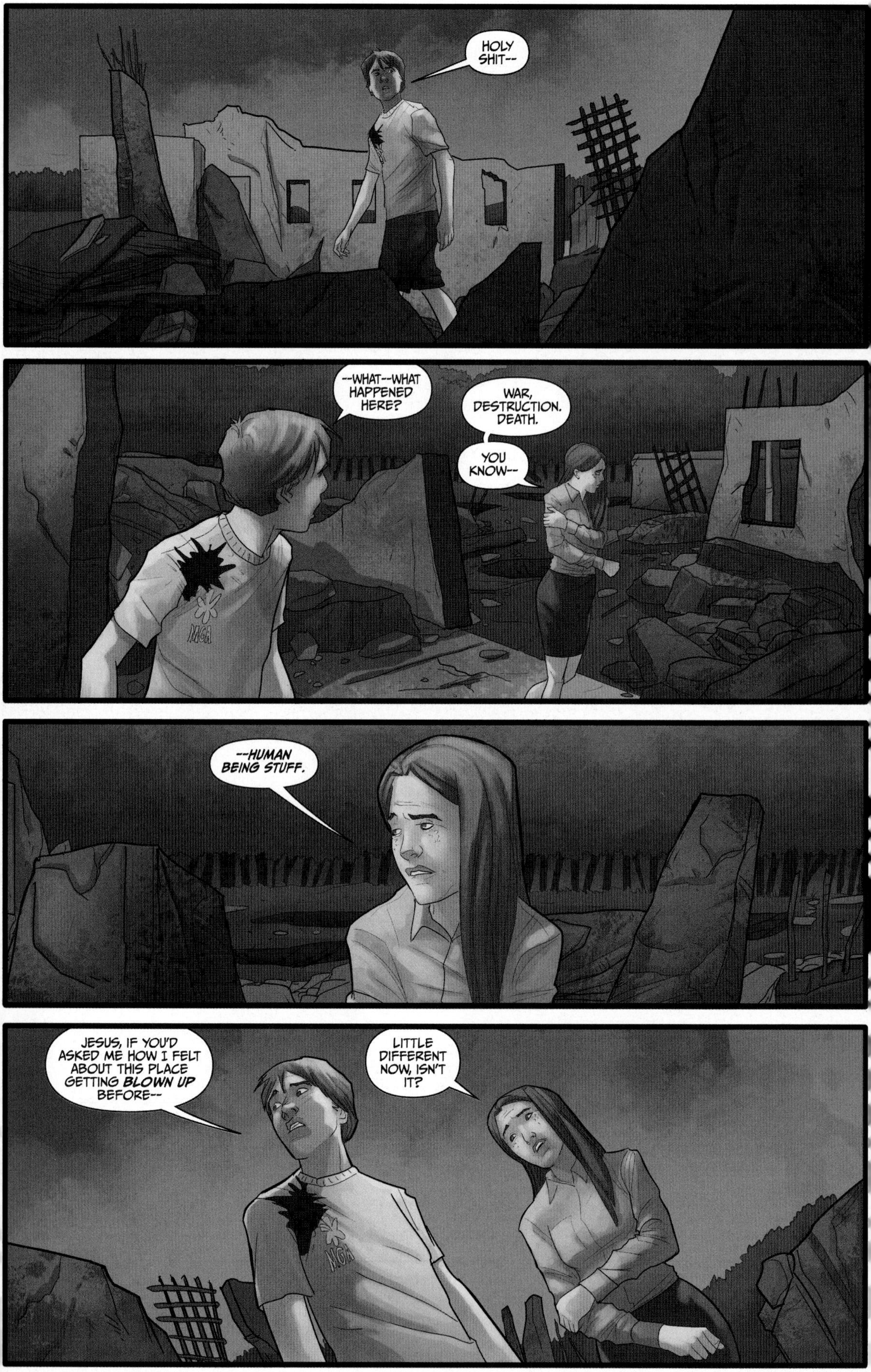
HOLY SHIT--
--WHAT--WHAT HAPPENED HERE?
WAR, DESTRUCTION. DEATH.
YOU KNOW--
--HUMAN BEING STUFF.
JESUS, IF YOU'D ASKED ME HOW I FELT ABOUT THIS PLACE GETTING BLOWN UP BEFORE--
LITTLE DIFFERENT NOW, ISN'T IT?

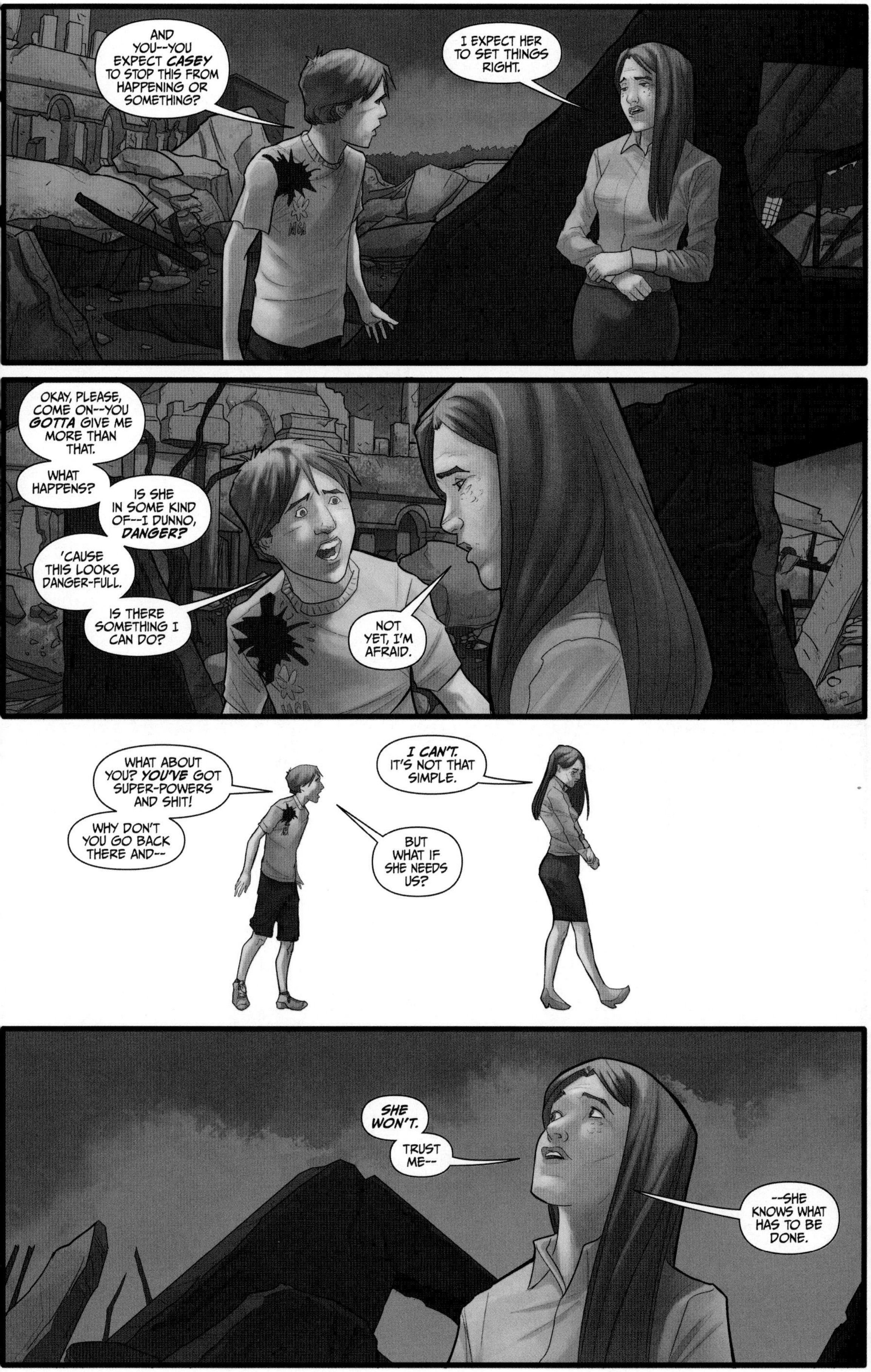
AND YOU--YOU EXPECT CASEY TO STOP THIS FROM HAPPENING OR SOMETHING?
I EXPECT HER TO SET THINGS RIGHT.
OKAY, PLEASE, COME ON--YOU GOTTA GIVE ME MORE THAN THAT.
WHAT HAPPENS?
IS SHE IN SOME KIND OF--I DUNNO, DANGER?
'CAUSE THIS LOOKS DANGER-FULL.
IS THERE SOMETHING I CAN DO?
NOT YET, I'M AFRAID.
WHAT ABOUT YOU? YOU'VE GOT SUPER-POWERS AND SHIT!
WHY DON'T YOU GO BACK THERE AND--
I CAN'T. IT'S NOT THAT SIMPLE.
BUT WHAT IF SHE NEEDS US?
SHE WON'T.
TRUST ME--
--SHE KNOWS WHAT HAS TO BE DONE.

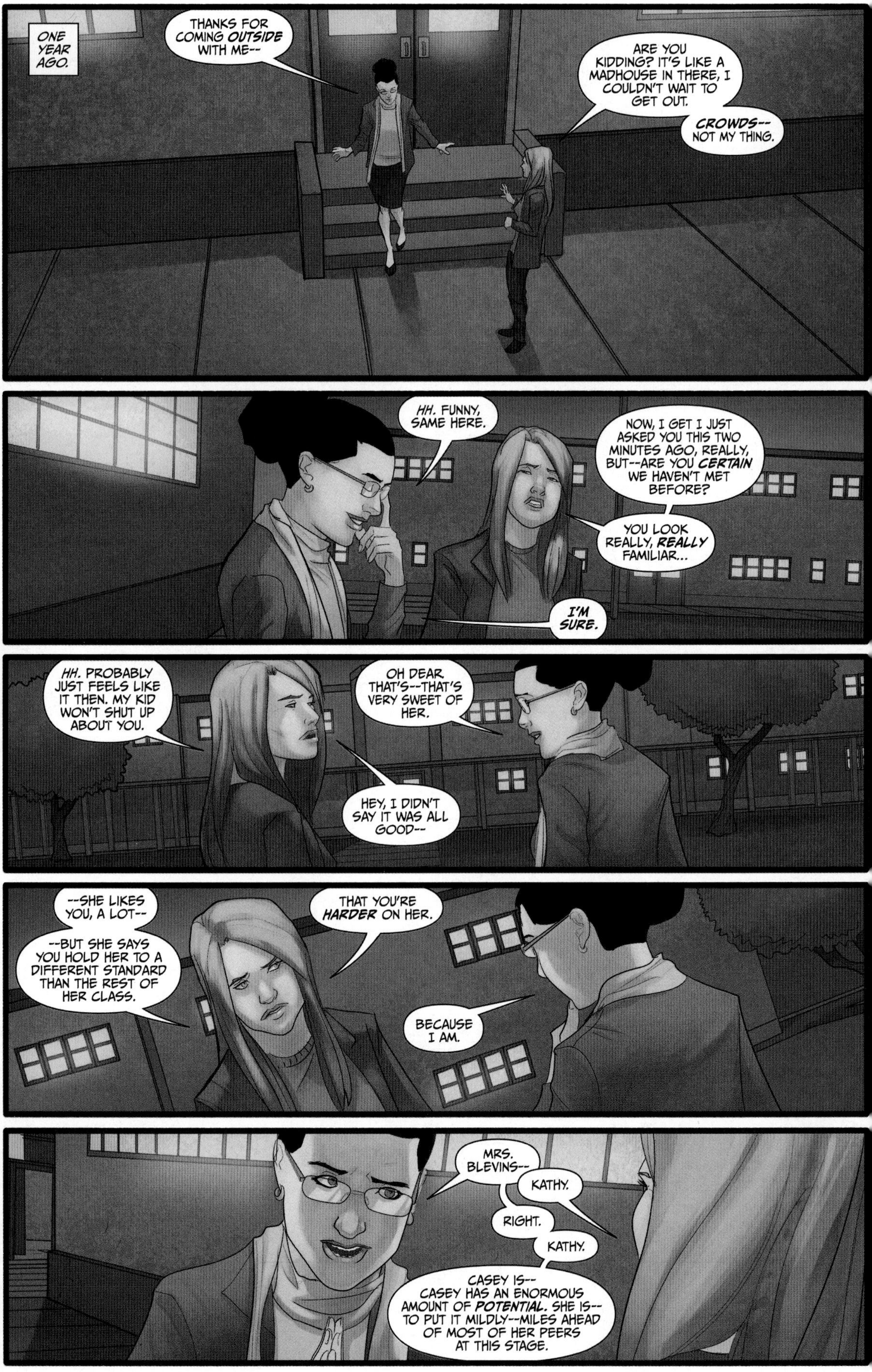
ONE YEAR AGO.
THANKS FOR COMING OUTSIDE WITH ME--
ARE YOU KIDDING? IT'S LIKE A MADHOUSE IN THERE, I COULDN'T WAIT TO GET OUT.
CROWDS-- NOT MY THING.
HH. FUNNY, SAME HERE.
NOW, I GET I JUST ASKED YOU THIS TWO MINUTES AGO, REALLY, BUT--ARE YOU CERTAIN WE HAVEN'T MET BEFORE?
YOU LOOK REALLY, REALLY FAMILIAR...
I'M SURE.
HH. PROBABLY JUST FEELS LIKE IT THEN. MY KID WON'T SHUT UP ABOUT YOU.
OH DEAR. THAT'S--THAT'S VERY SWEET OF HER.
HEY, I DIDN'T SAY IT WAS ALL GOOD--
--SHE LIKES YOU, A LOT--
--BUT SHE SAYS YOU HOLD HER TO A DIFFERENT STANDARD THAN THE REST OF HER CLASS.
THAT YOU'RE HARDER ON HER.
BECAUSE I AM.
MRS. BLEVINS--
KATHY.
RIGHT.
KATHY.
CASEY IS-- CASEY HAS AN ENORMOUS AMOUNT OF POTENTIAL. SHE IS-- TO PUT IT MILDLY--MILES AHEAD OF MOST OF HER PEERS AT THIS STAGE.

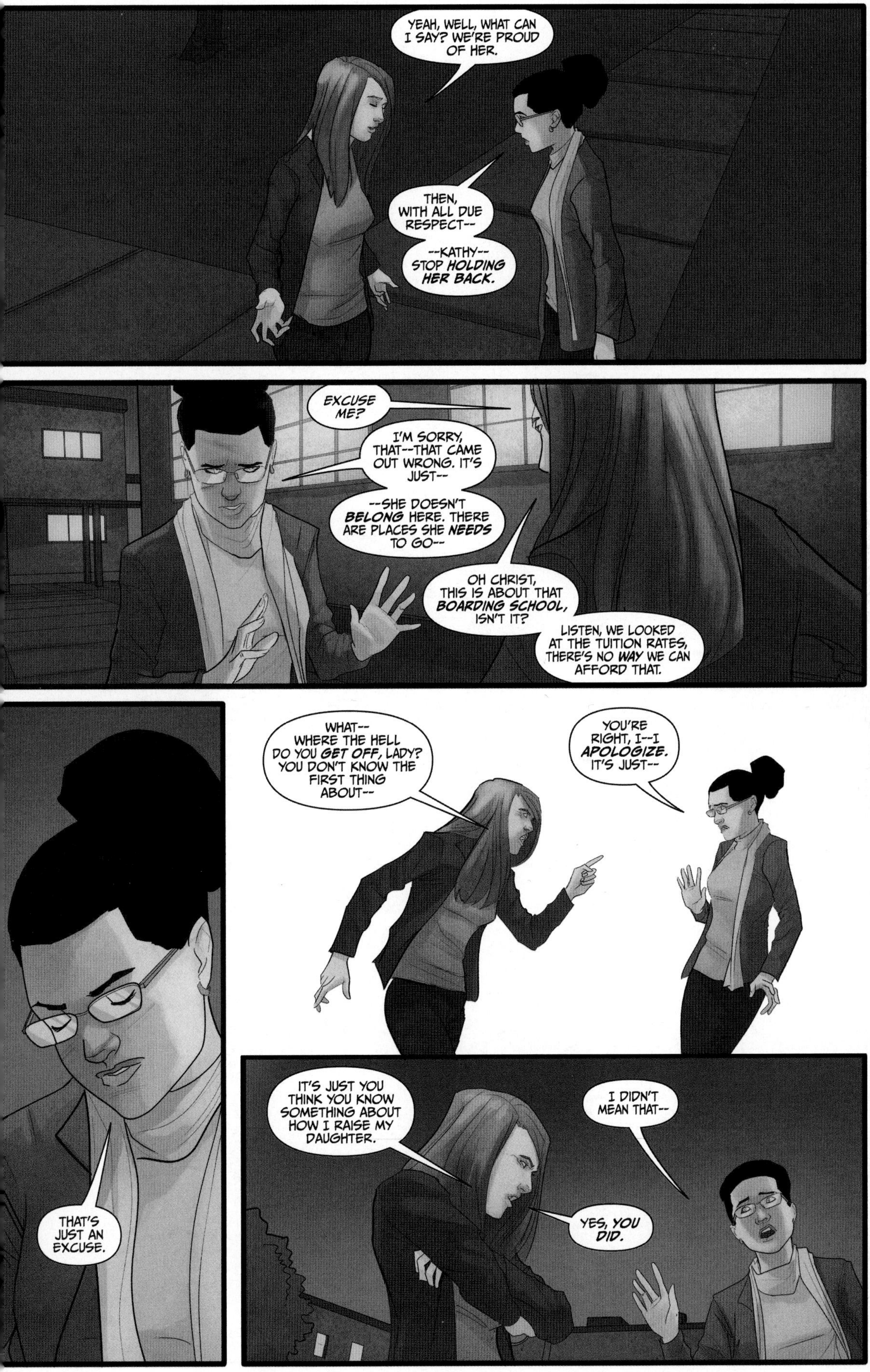
YEAH, WELL, WHAT CAN I SAY? WE'RE PROUD OF HER.
THEN, WITH ALL DUE RESPECT--
--KATHY-- STOP *HOLDING HER BACK.*
EXCUSE ME?
I'M SORRY, THAT--THAT CAME OUT WRONG. IT'S JUST--
--SHE DOESN'T *BELONG* HERE. THERE ARE PLACES SHE *NEEDS* TO GO--
OH CHRIST, THIS IS ABOUT THAT *BOARDING SCHOOL,* ISN'T IT?
LISTEN, WE LOOKED AT THE TUITION RATES, THERE'S NO *WAY* WE CAN AFFORD THAT.
THAT'S JUST AN EXCUSE.
WHAT-- WHERE THE HELL DO YOU *GET OFF,* LADY? YOU DON'T KNOW THE FIRST THING ABOUT--
YOU'RE RIGHT, I--I *APOLOGIZE.* IT'S JUST--
IT'S JUST YOU THINK YOU KNOW SOMETHING ABOUT HOW I RAISE MY DAUGHTER.
I DIDN'T MEAN THAT--
YES, *YOU DID.*

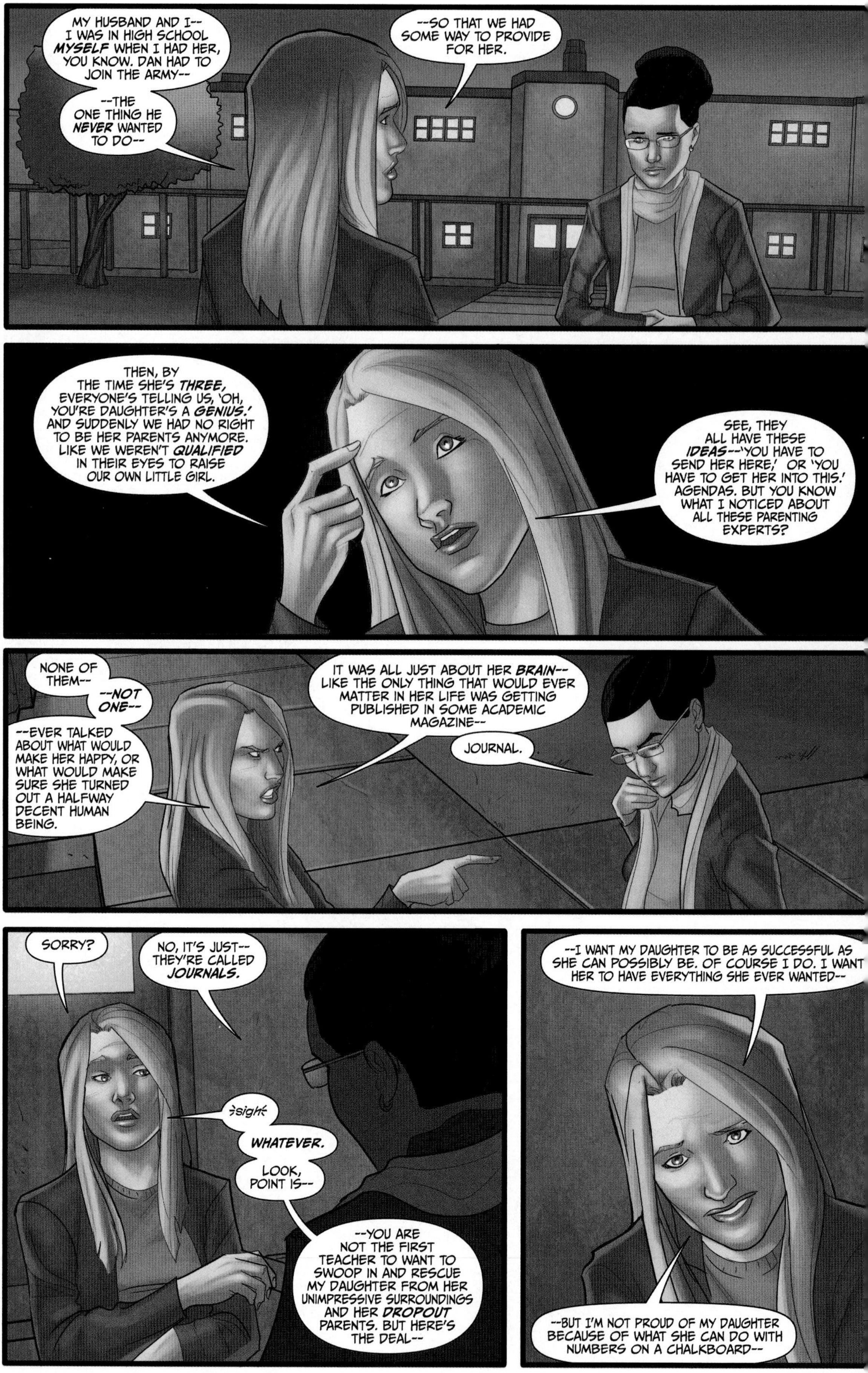
MY HUSBAND AND I-- I WAS IN HIGH SCHOOL MYSELF WHEN I HAD HER, YOU KNOW. DAN HAD TO JOIN THE ARMY--
--THE ONE THING HE NEVER WANTED TO DO--
--SO THAT WE HAD SOME WAY TO PROVIDE FOR HER.
THEN, BY THE TIME SHE'S THREE, EVERYONE'S TELLING US, 'OH, YOU'RE DAUGHTER'S A GENIUS.' AND SUDDENLY WE HAD NO RIGHT TO BE HER PARENTS ANYMORE. LIKE WE WEREN'T QUALIFIED IN THEIR EYES TO RAISE OUR OWN LITTLE GIRL.
SEE, THEY ALL HAVE THESE IDEAS--'YOU HAVE TO SEND HER HERE,' OR 'YOU HAVE TO GET HER INTO THIS.' AGENDAS. BUT YOU KNOW WHAT I NOTICED ABOUT ALL THESE PARENTING EXPERTS?
NONE OF THEM--
--NOT ONE--
--EVER TALKED ABOUT WHAT WOULD MAKE HER HAPPY, OR WHAT WOULD MAKE SURE SHE TURNED OUT A HALFWAY DECENT HUMAN BEING.
IT WAS ALL JUST ABOUT HER BRAIN-- LIKE THE ONLY THING THAT WOULD EVER MATTER IN HER LIFE WAS GETTING PUBLISHED IN SOME ACADEMIC MAGAZINE--
JOURNAL.
SORRY?
NO, IT'S JUST-- THEY'RE CALLED JOURNALS.
sigh
WHATEVER.
LOOK, POINT IS--
--YOU ARE NOT THE FIRST TEACHER TO WANT TO SWOOP IN AND RESCUE MY DAUGHTER FROM HER UNIMPRESSIVE SURROUNDINGS AND HER DROPOUT PARENTS. BUT HERE'S THE DEAL--
--I WANT MY DAUGHTER TO BE AS SUCCESSFUL AS SHE CAN POSSIBLY BE. OF COURSE I DO. I WANT HER TO HAVE EVERYTHING SHE EVER WANTED--
--BUT I'M NOT PROUD OF MY DAUGHTER BECAUSE OF WHAT SHE CAN DO WITH NUMBERS ON A CHALKBOARD--

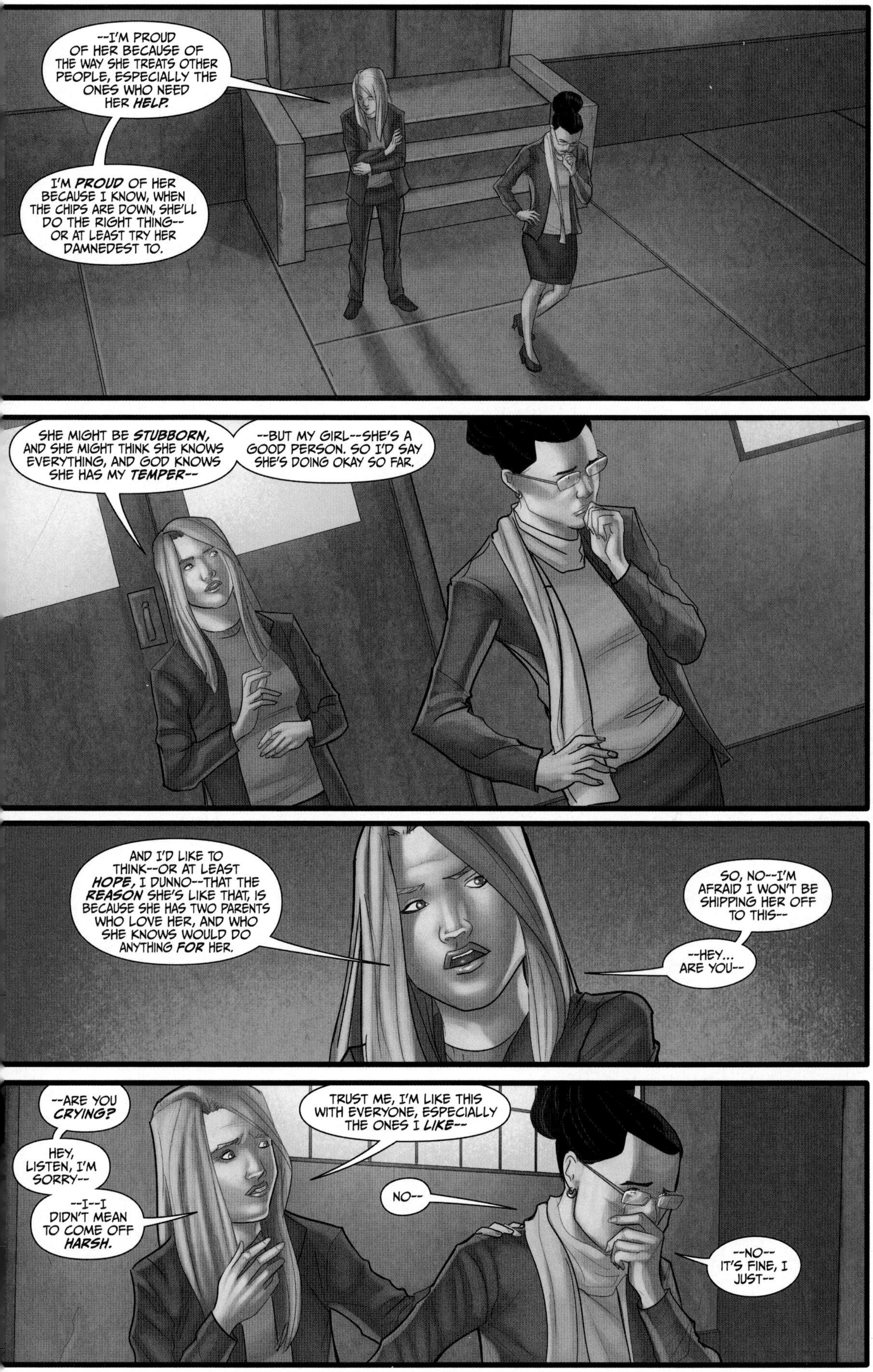
--I'M PROUD OF HER BECAUSE OF THE WAY SHE TREATS OTHER PEOPLE, ESPECIALLY THE ONES WHO NEED HER HELP.
I'M PROUD OF HER BECAUSE I KNOW, WHEN THE CHIPS ARE DOWN, SHE'LL DO THE RIGHT THING-- OR AT LEAST TRY HER DAMNEDEST TO.
SHE MIGHT BE STUBBORN, AND SHE MIGHT THINK SHE KNOWS EVERYTHING, AND GOD KNOWS SHE HAS MY TEMPER--
--BUT MY GIRL--SHE'S A GOOD PERSON. SO I'D SAY SHE'S DOING OKAY SO FAR.
AND I'D LIKE TO THINK--OR AT LEAST HOPE, I DUNNO--THAT THE REASON SHE'S LIKE THAT, IS BECAUSE SHE HAS TWO PARENTS WHO LOVE HER, AND WHO SHE KNOWS WOULD DO ANYTHING FOR HER.
SO, NO--I'M AFRAID I WON'T BE SHIPPING HER OFF TO THIS--
--HEY... ARE YOU--
--ARE YOU CRYING?
HEY, LISTEN, I'M SORRY--
--I--I DIDN'T MEAN TO COME OFF HARSH.
TRUST ME, I'M LIKE THIS WITH EVERYONE, ESPECIALLY THE ONES I LIKE--
NO--
--NO-- IT'S FINE, I JUST--

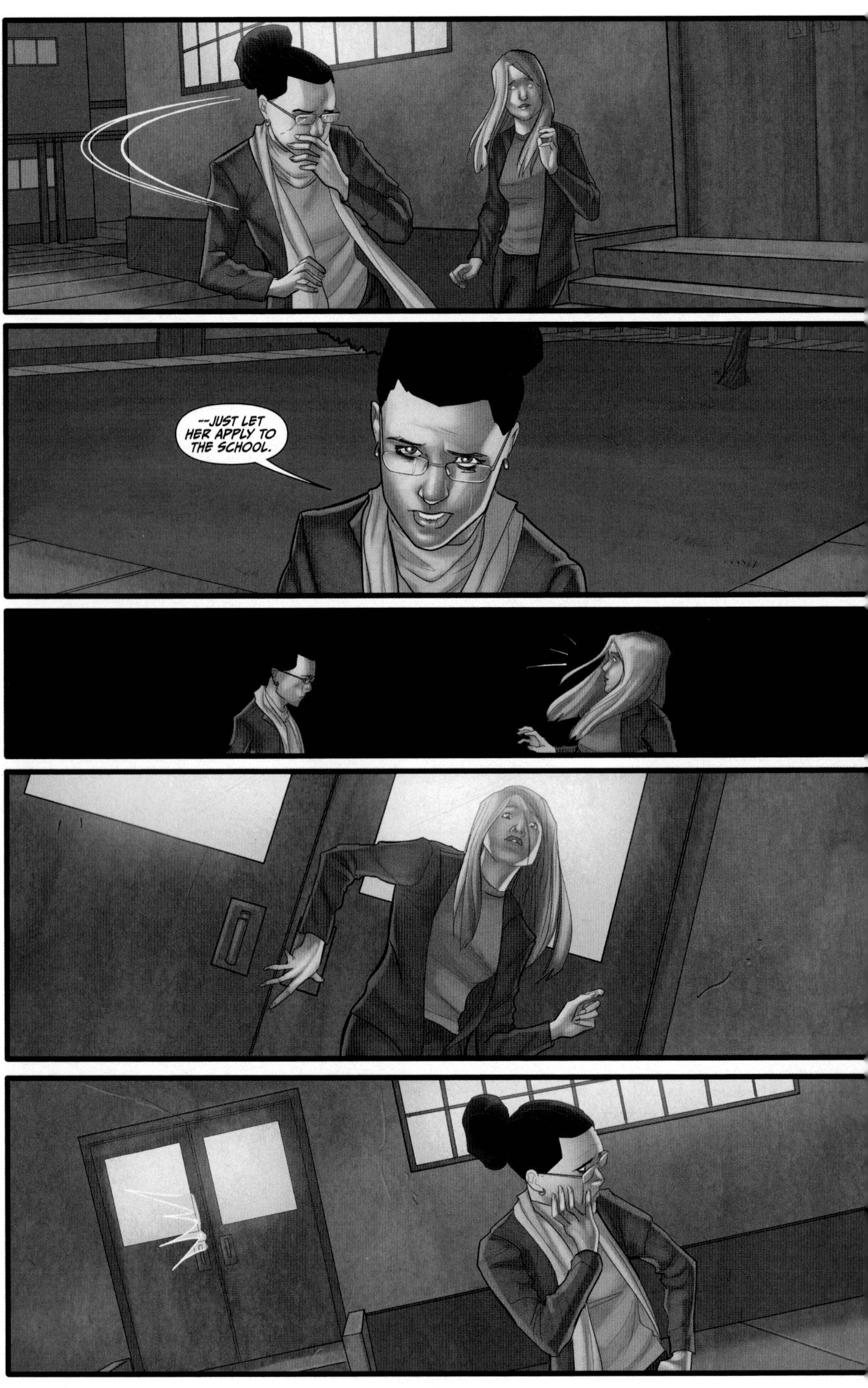
--JUST LET HER APPLY TO THE SCHOOL.

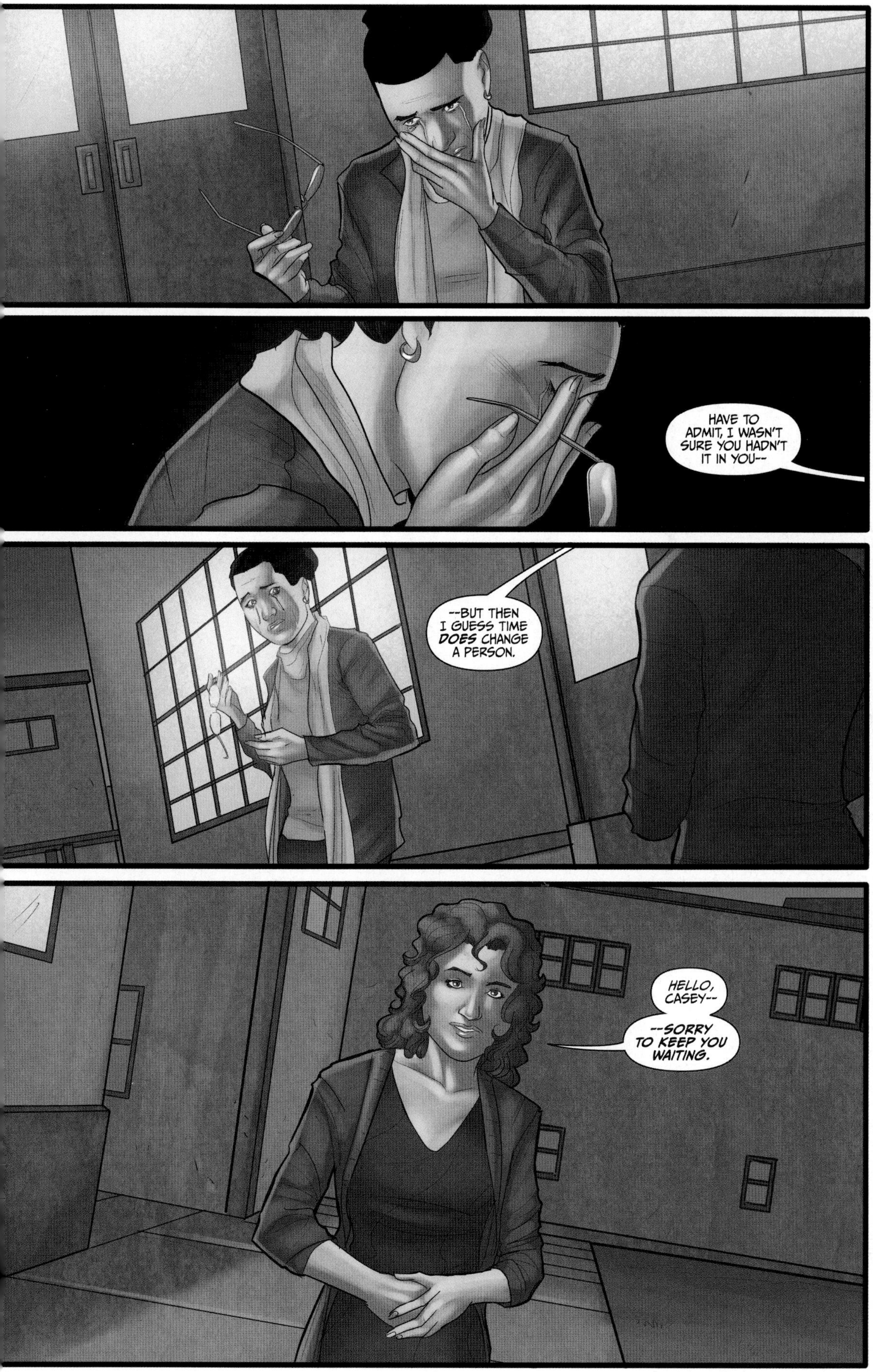
HAVE TO ADMIT, I WASN'T SURE YOU HADN'T IT IN YOU--
--BUT THEN I GUESS TIME DOES CHANGE A PERSON.
HELLO, CASEY--
--SORRY TO KEEP YOU WAITING.

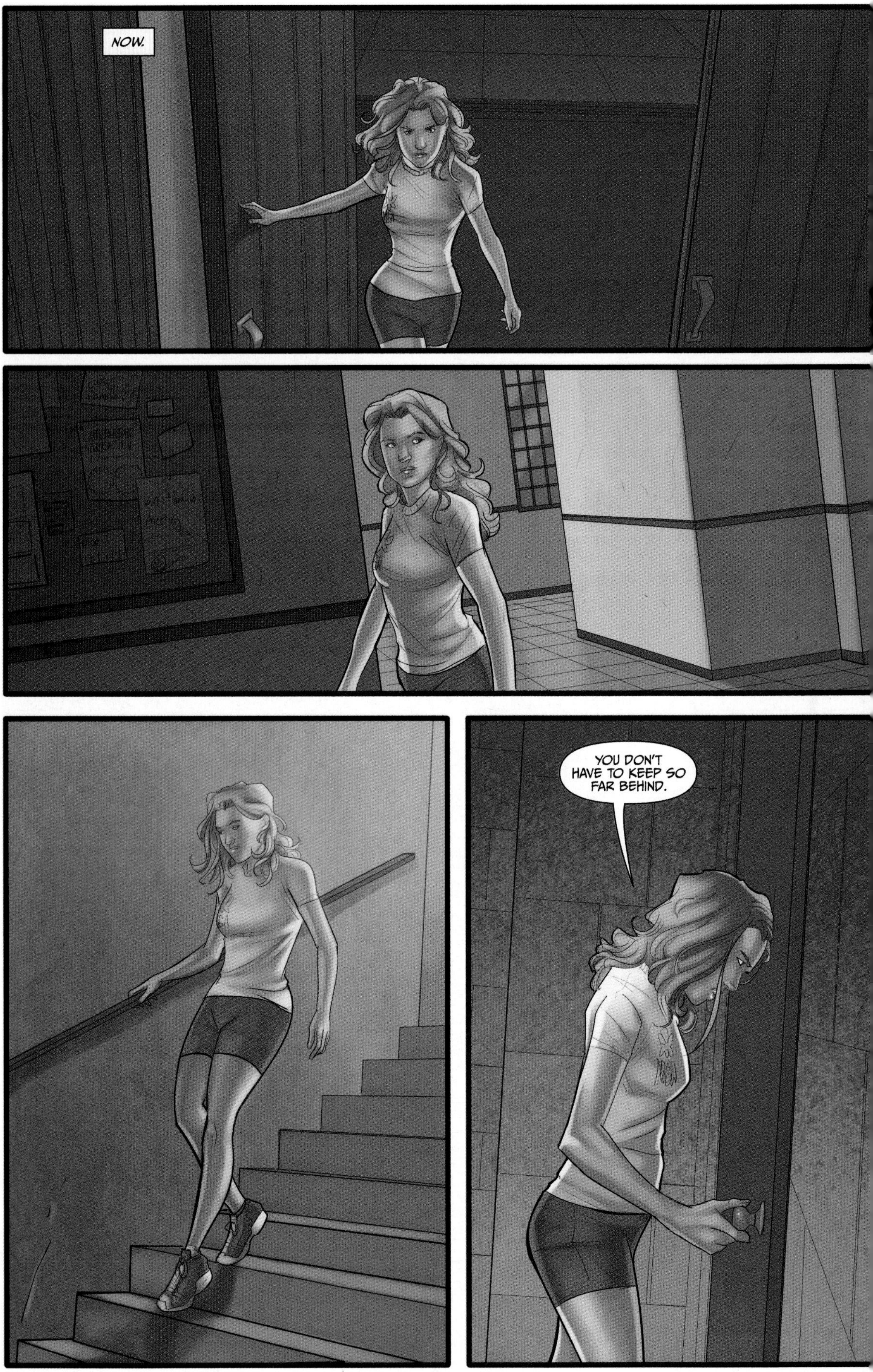
NOW.
YOU DON'T HAVE TO KEEP SO FAR BEHIND.

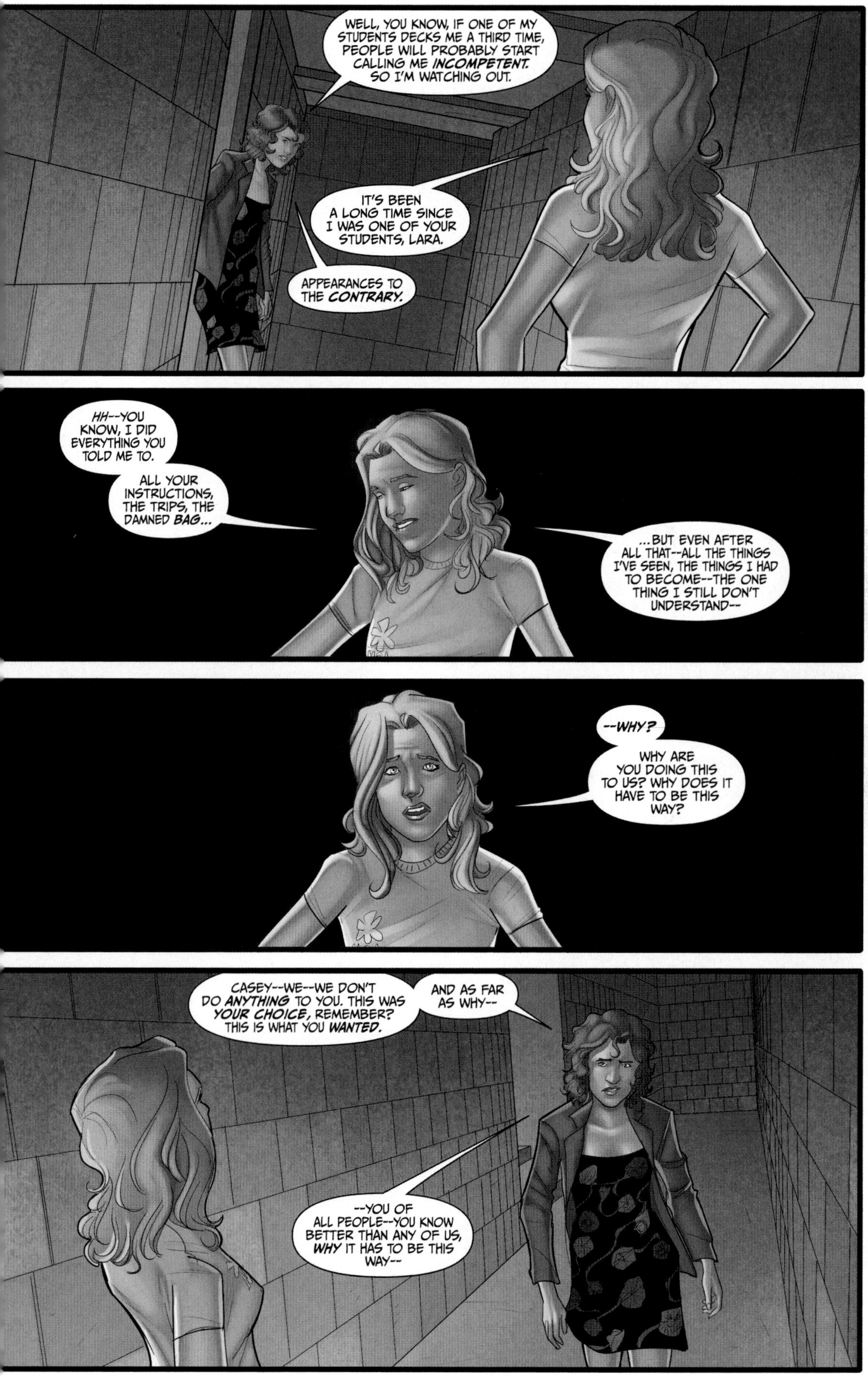
WELL, YOU KNOW, IF ONE OF MY STUDENTS DECKS ME A THIRD TIME, PEOPLE WILL PROBABLY START CALLING ME *INCOMPETENT.* SO I'M WATCHING OUT.
IT'S BEEN A LONG TIME SINCE I WAS ONE OF YOUR STUDENTS, LARA.
APPEARANCES TO THE *CONTRARY.*
HH--YOU KNOW, I DID EVERYTHING YOU TOLD ME TO.
ALL YOUR INSTRUCTIONS, THE TRIPS, THE DAMNED *BAG...*
...BUT EVEN AFTER ALL THAT--ALL THE THINGS I'VE SEEN, THE THINGS I HAD TO BECOME--THE ONE THING I STILL DON'T UNDERSTAND--
--WHY?
WHY ARE YOU DOING THIS TO US? WHY DOES IT HAVE TO BE THIS WAY?
CASEY--WE--WE DON'T DO *ANYTHING* TO YOU. THIS WAS *YOUR CHOICE,* REMEMBER? THIS IS WHAT YOU *WANTED.*
AND AS FAR AS WHY--
--YOU OF ALL PEOPLE--YOU KNOW BETTER THAN ANY OF US, *WHY* IT HAS TO BE THIS WAY--

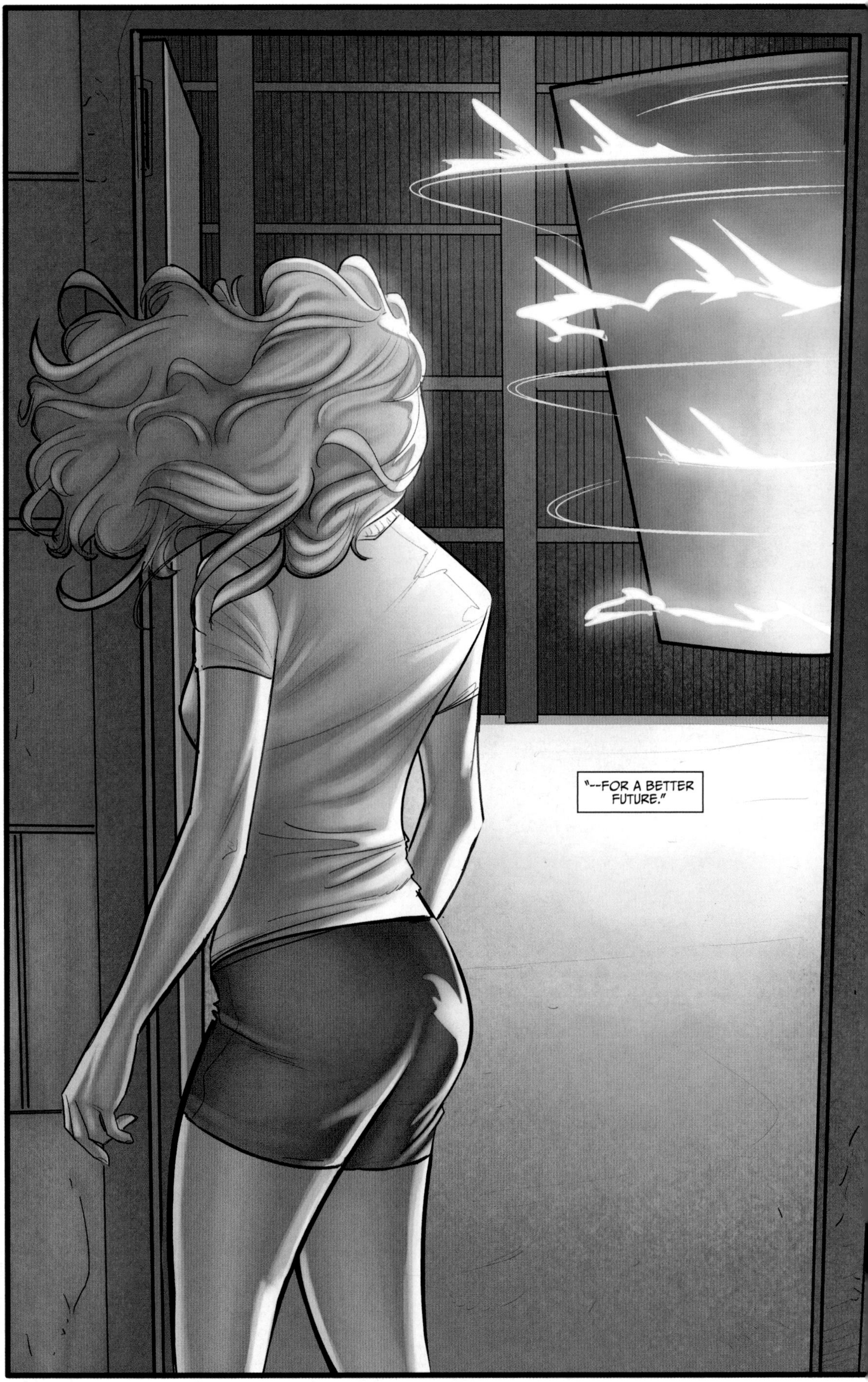
"--FOR A BETTER FUTURE."

twenty**eight**

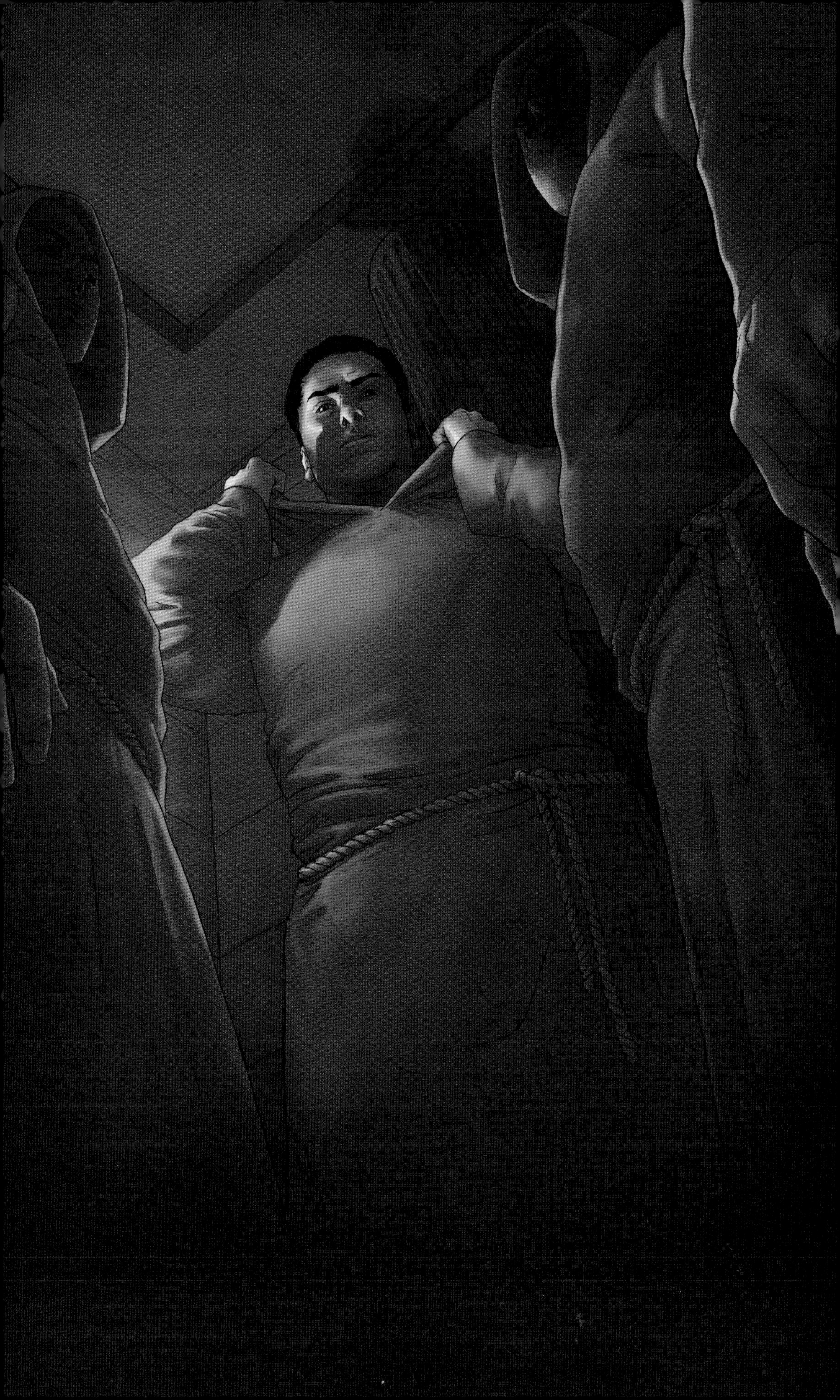

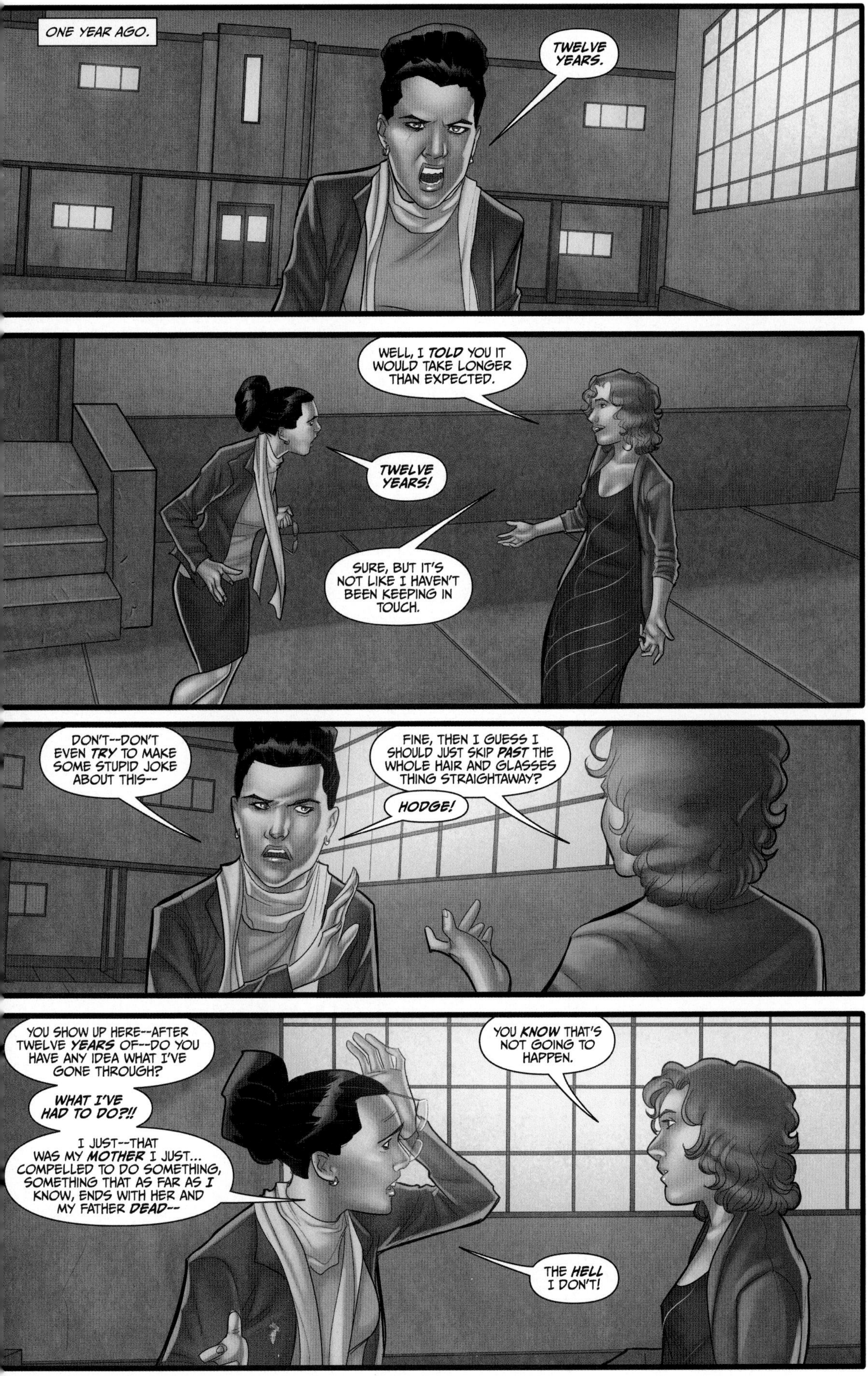
ONE YEAR AGO.
TWELVE YEARS.
WELL, I TOLD YOU IT WOULD TAKE LONGER THAN EXPECTED.
TWELVE YEARS!
SURE, BUT IT'S NOT LIKE I HAVEN'T BEEN KEEPING IN TOUCH.
DON'T--DON'T EVEN TRY TO MAKE SOME STUPID JOKE ABOUT THIS--
FINE, THEN I GUESS I SHOULD JUST SKIP PAST THE WHOLE HAIR AND GLASSES THING STRAIGHTAWAY?
HODGE!
YOU SHOW UP HERE--AFTER TWELVE YEARS OF--DO YOU HAVE ANY IDEA WHAT I'VE GONE THROUGH?
WHAT I'VE HAD TO DO?!!
I JUST--THAT WAS MY MOTHER I JUST... COMPELLED TO DO SOMETHING, SOMETHING THAT AS FAR AS I KNOW, ENDS WITH HER AND MY FATHER DEAD--
YOU KNOW THAT'S NOT GOING TO HAPPEN.
THE HELL I DON'T!

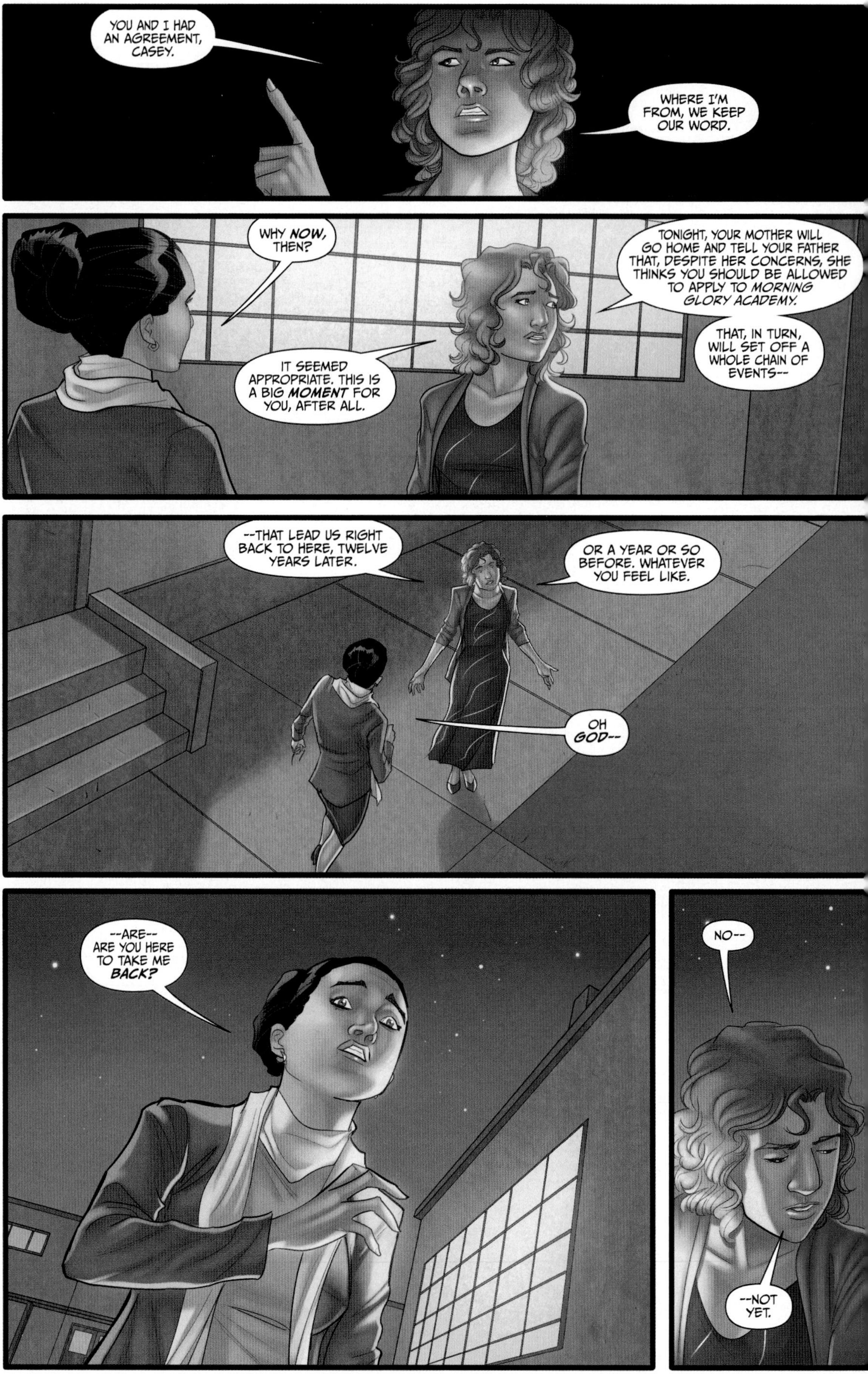

YOU AND I HAD AN AGREEMENT, CASEY.
WHERE I'M FROM, WE KEEP OUR WORD.
WHY NOW, THEN?
IT SEEMED APPROPRIATE. THIS IS A BIG MOMENT FOR YOU, AFTER ALL.
TONIGHT, YOUR MOTHER WILL GO HOME AND TELL YOUR FATHER THAT, DESPITE HER CONCERNS, SHE THINKS YOU SHOULD BE ALLOWED TO APPLY TO MORNING GLORY ACADEMY.
THAT, IN TURN, WILL SET OFF A WHOLE CHAIN OF EVENTS--
--THAT LEAD US RIGHT BACK TO HERE, TWELVE YEARS LATER.
OR A YEAR OR SO BEFORE. WHATEVER YOU FEEL LIKE.
OH GOD--
--ARE-- ARE YOU HERE TO TAKE ME BACK?
NO--
--NOT YET.

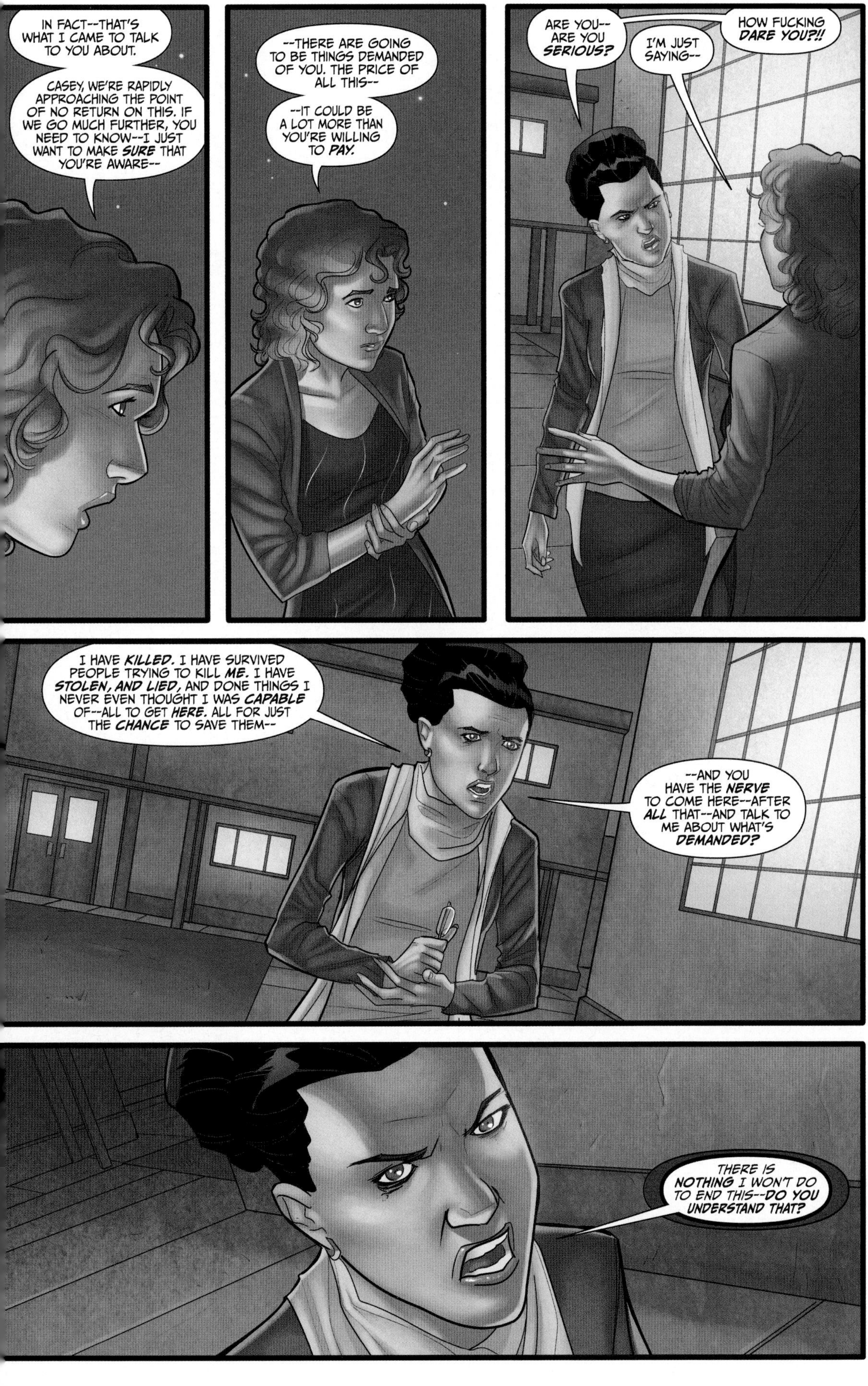
IN FACT--THAT'S WHAT I CAME TO TALK TO YOU ABOUT.
CASEY, WE'RE RAPIDLY APPROACHING THE POINT OF NO RETURN ON THIS. IF WE GO MUCH FURTHER, YOU NEED TO KNOW--I JUST WANT TO MAKE SURE THAT YOU'RE AWARE--
--THERE ARE GOING TO BE THINGS DEMANDED OF YOU. THE PRICE OF ALL THIS--
--IT COULD BE A LOT MORE THAN YOU'RE WILLING TO PAY.
ARE YOU-- ARE YOU SERIOUS?
I'M JUST SAYING--
HOW FUCKING DARE YOU?!!
I HAVE KILLED. I HAVE SURVIVED PEOPLE TRYING TO KILL ME. I HAVE STOLEN, AND LIED, AND DONE THINGS I NEVER EVEN THOUGHT I WAS CAPABLE OF--ALL TO GET HERE. ALL FOR JUST THE CHANCE TO SAVE THEM--
--AND YOU HAVE THE NERVE TO COME HERE--AFTER ALL THAT--AND TALK TO ME ABOUT WHAT'S DEMANDED?
THERE IS NOTHING I WON'T DO TO END THIS--DO YOU UNDERSTAND THAT?

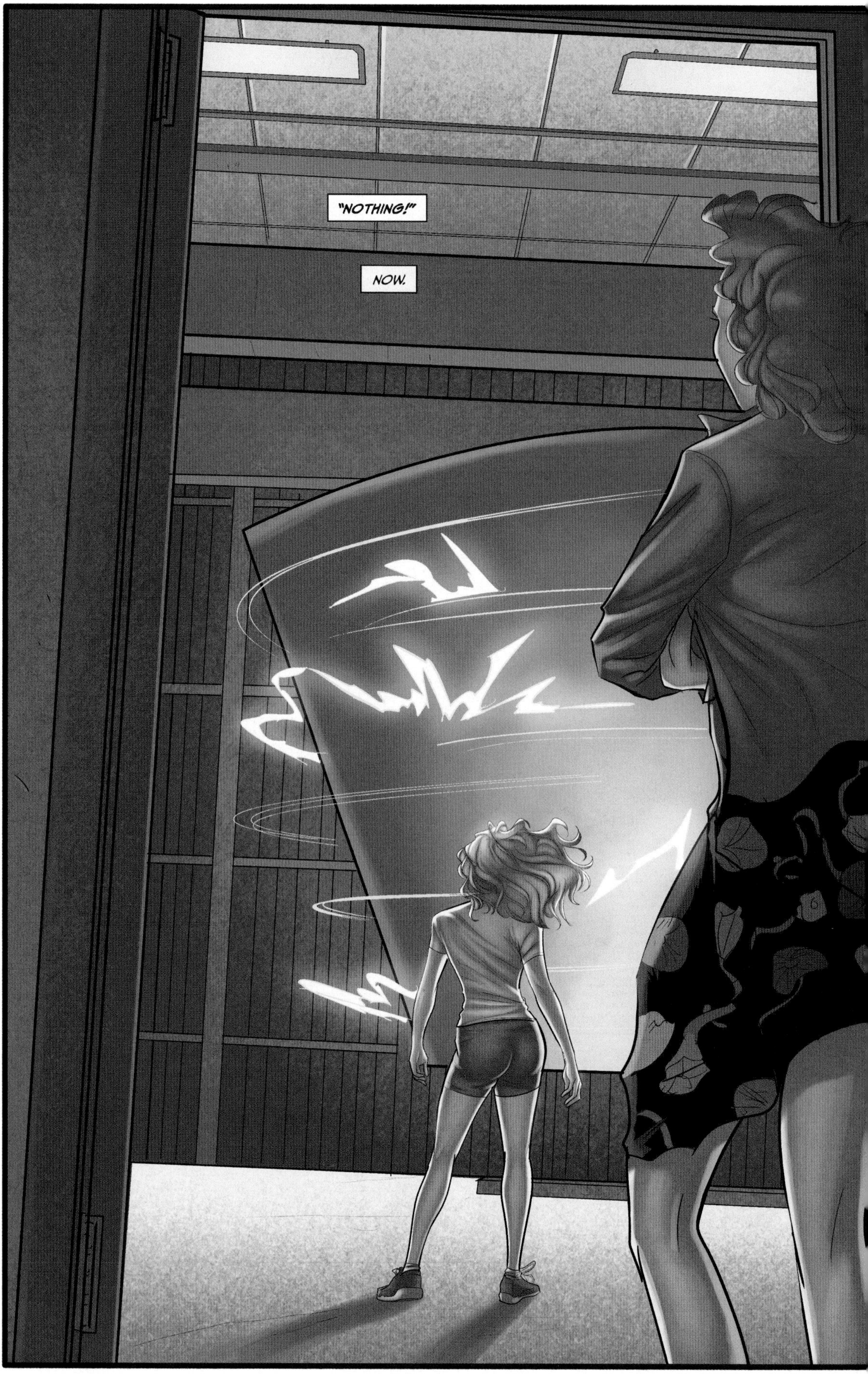
"NOTHING!"
NOW.

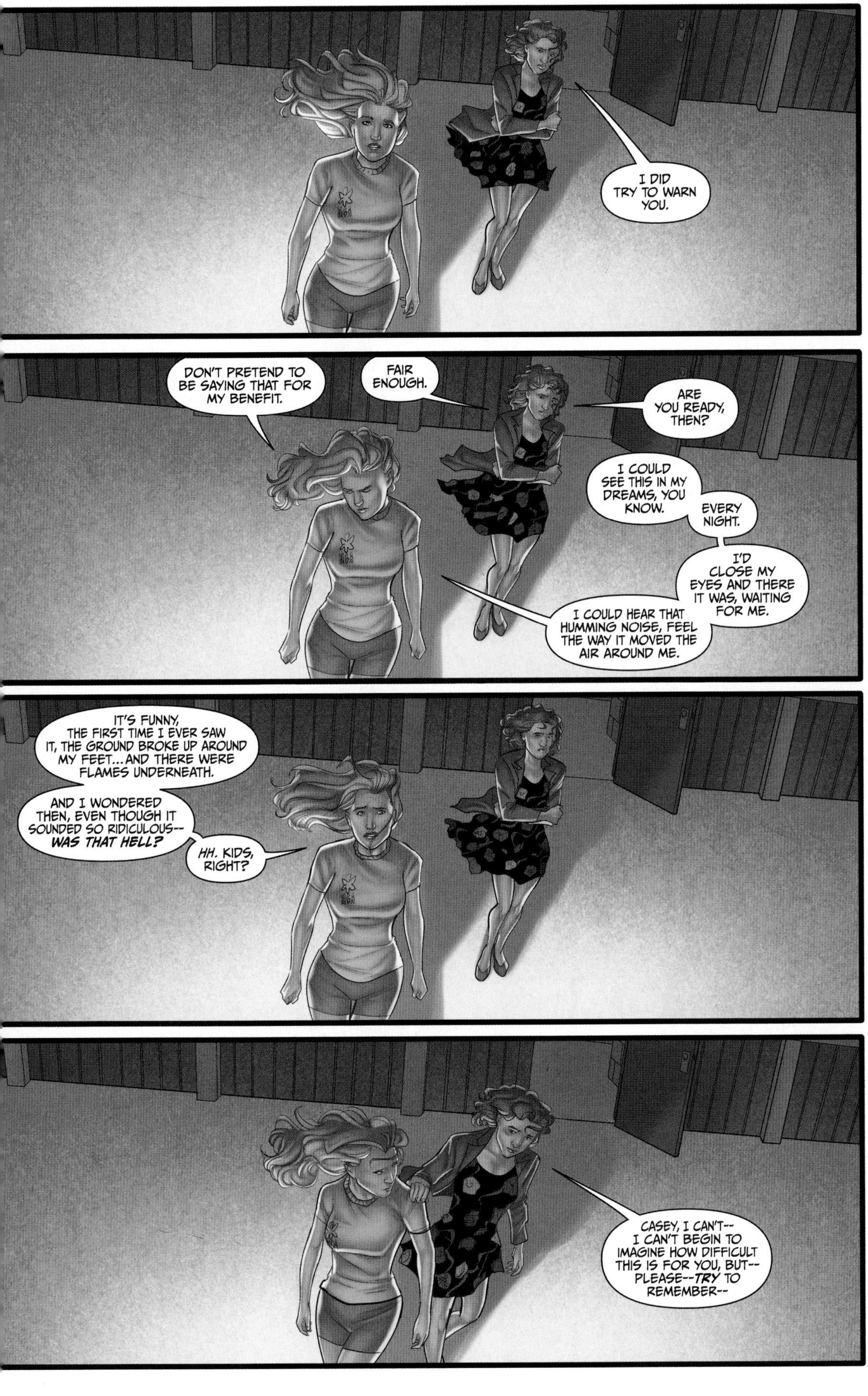
I DID TRY TO WARN YOU.
DON'T PRETEND TO BE SAYING THAT FOR MY BENEFIT.
FAIR ENOUGH.
ARE YOU READY, THEN?
I COULD SEE THIS IN MY DREAMS, YOU KNOW.
EVERY NIGHT.
I'D CLOSE MY EYES AND THERE IT WAS, WAITING FOR ME.
I COULD HEAR THAT HUMMING NOISE, FEEL THE WAY IT MOVED THE AIR AROUND ME.
IT'S FUNNY, THE FIRST TIME I EVER SAW IT, THE GROUND BROKE UP AROUND MY FEET...AND THERE WERE FLAMES UNDERNEATH.
AND I WONDERED THEN, EVEN THOUGH IT SOUNDED SO RIDICULOUS-- ***WAS THAT HELL?***
HH. KIDS, RIGHT?
CASEY, I CAN'T-- I CAN'T BEGIN TO IMAGINE HOW DIFFICULT THIS IS FOR YOU, BUT-- PLEASE--***TRY*** TO REMEMBER--

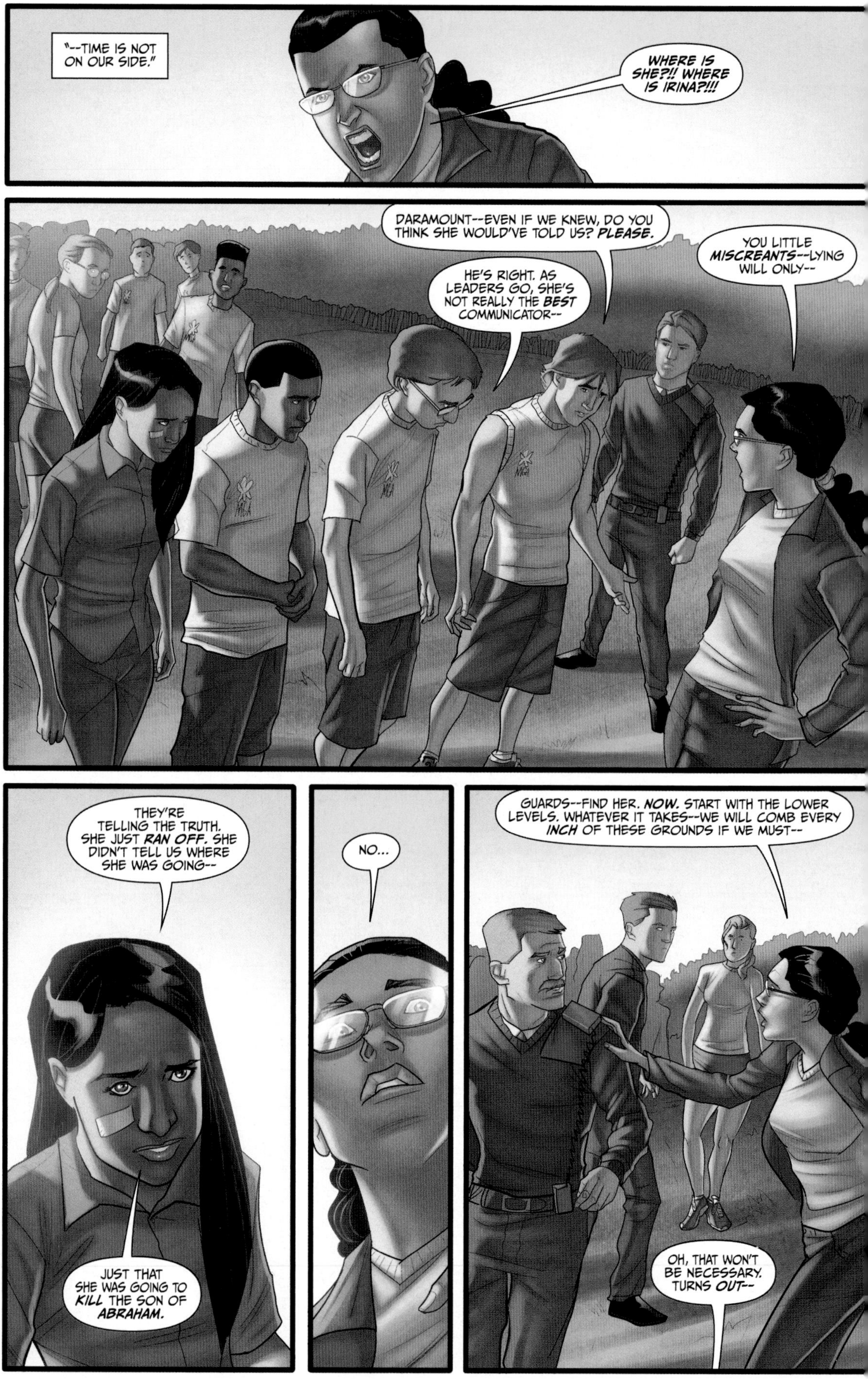

"--TIME IS NOT ON OUR SIDE."
WHERE IS SHE?!! WHERE IS IRINA?!!!
DARAMOUNT--EVEN IF WE KNEW, DO YOU THINK SHE WOULD'VE TOLD US? PLEASE.
HE'S RIGHT. AS LEADERS GO, SHE'S NOT REALLY THE BEST COMMUNICATOR--
YOU LITTLE MISCREANTS--LYING WILL ONLY--
THEY'RE TELLING THE TRUTH. SHE JUST RAN OFF. SHE DIDN'T TELL US WHERE SHE WAS GOING--
JUST THAT SHE WAS GOING TO KILL THE SON OF ABRAHAM.
NO...
GUARDS--FIND HER. NOW. START WITH THE LOWER LEVELS. WHATEVER IT TAKES--WE WILL COMB EVERY INCH OF THESE GROUNDS IF WE MUST--
OH, THAT WON'T BE NECESSARY. TURNS OUT--

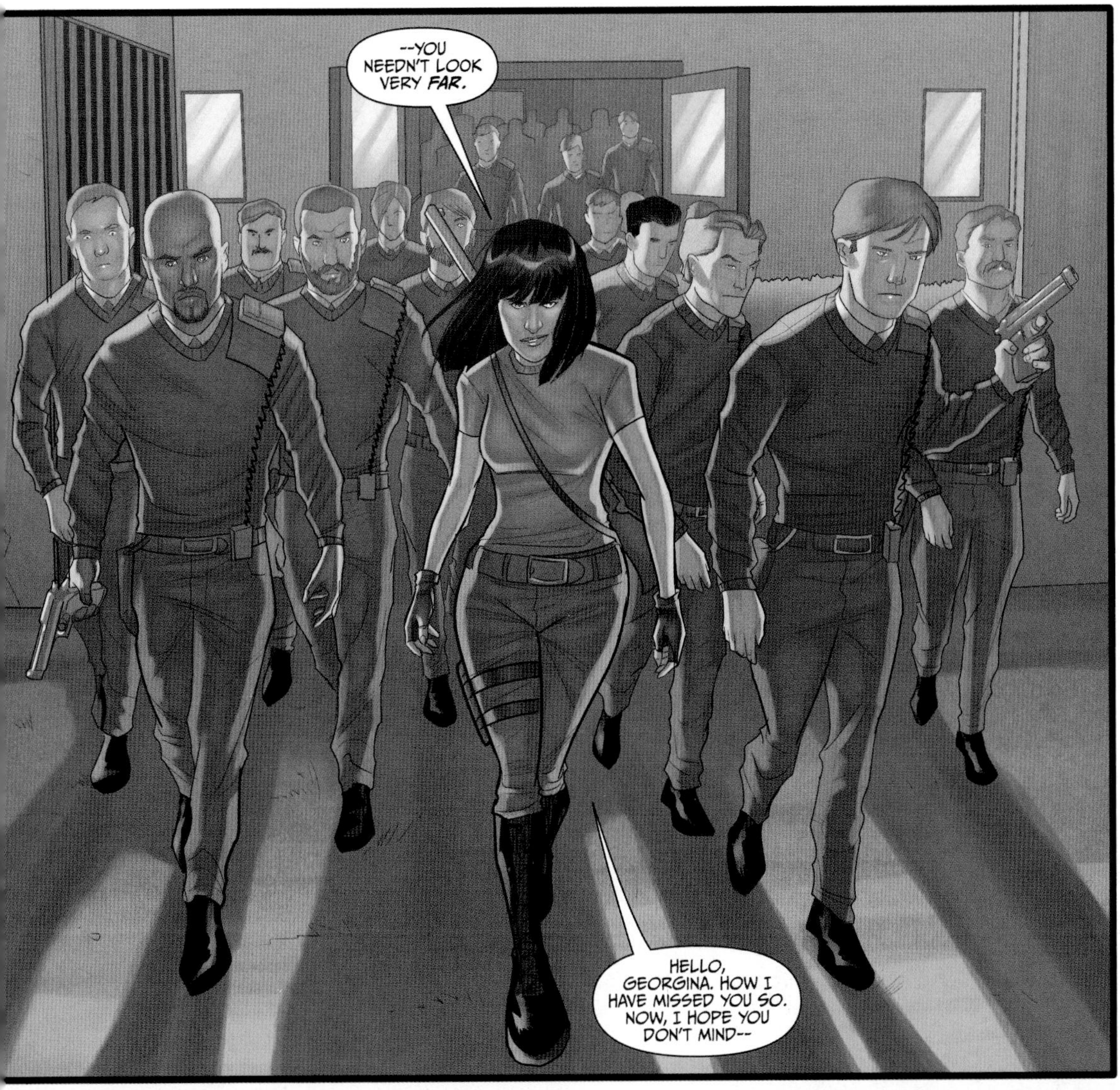
--YOU NEEDN'T LOOK VERY *FAR.*
HELLO, GEORGINA. HOW I HAVE MISSED YOU SO. NOW, I HOPE YOU DON'T MIND--
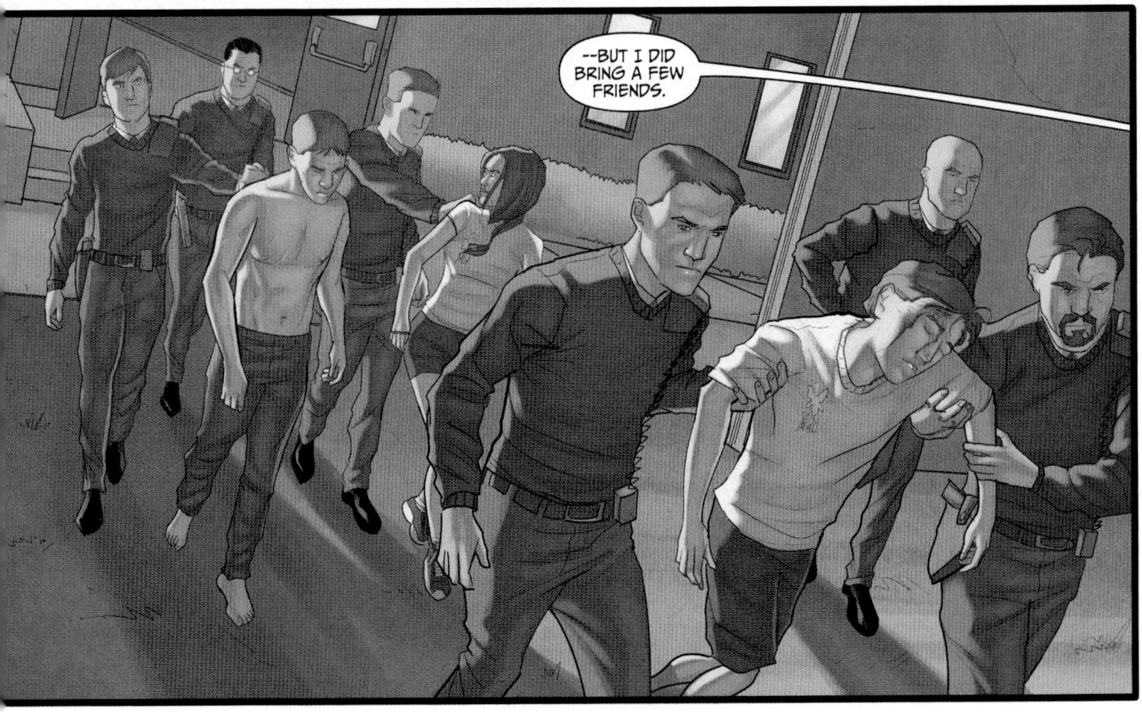
--BUT I DID BRING A FEW FRIENDS.

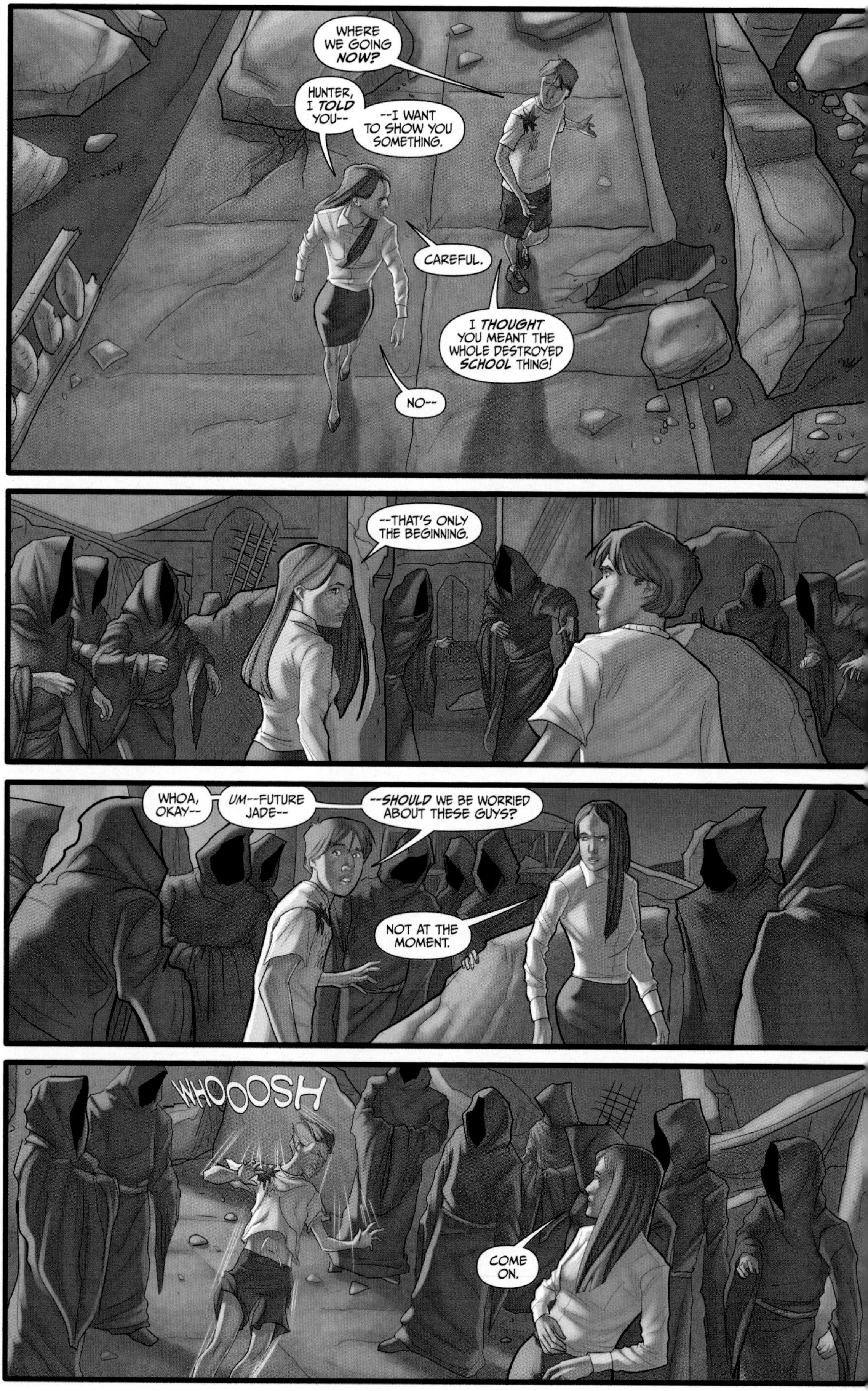
WHERE WE GOING NOW?
HUNTER, I TOLD YOU--
--I WANT TO SHOW YOU SOMETHING.
CAREFUL.
I THOUGHT YOU MEANT THE WHOLE DESTROYED SCHOOL THING!
NO--
--THAT'S ONLY THE BEGINNING.
WHOA, OKAY--
UM--FUTURE JADE--
--SHOULD WE BE WORRIED ABOUT THESE GUYS?
NOT AT THE MOMENT.
WHOOOSH
COME ON.

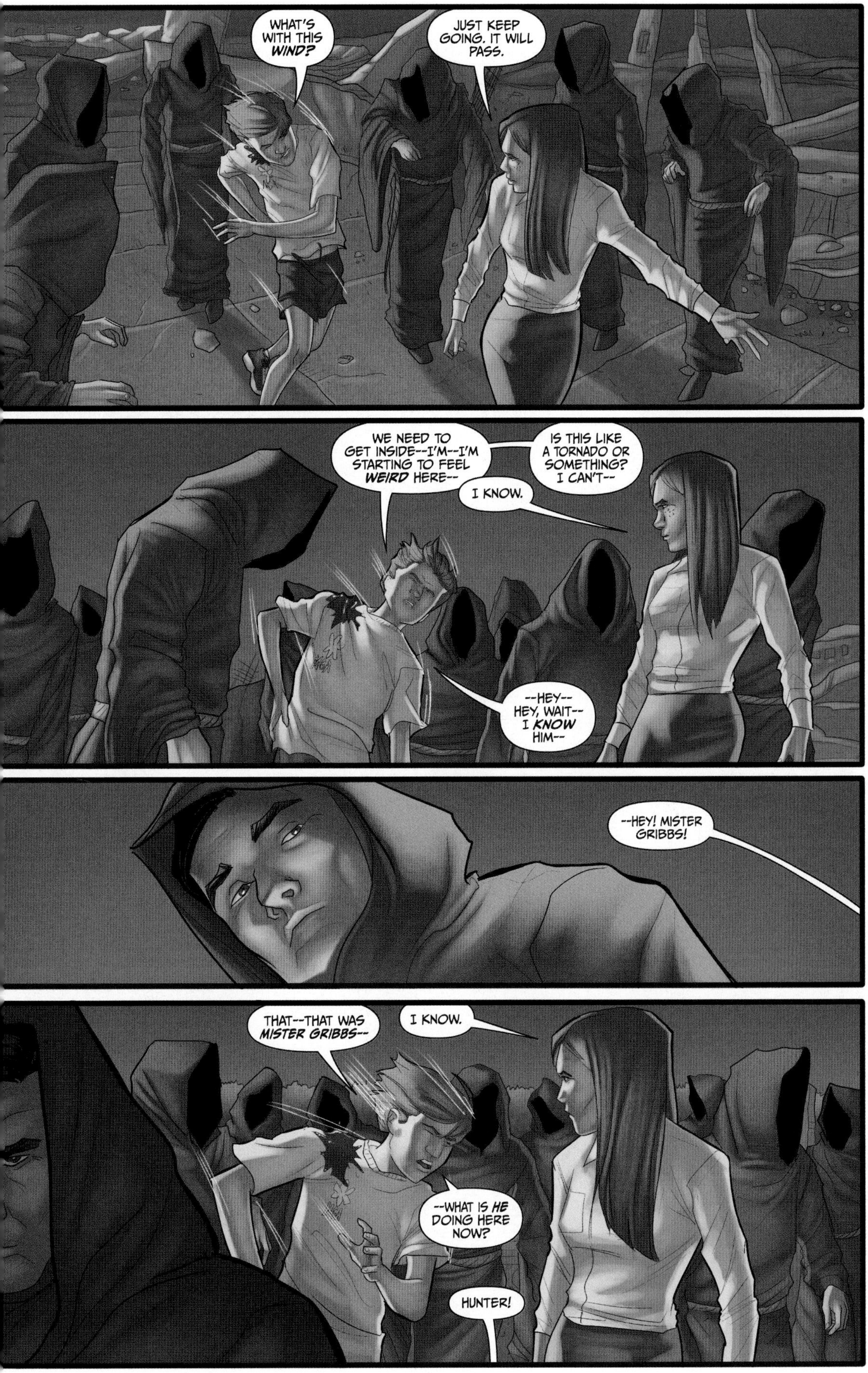
WHAT'S WITH THIS WIND?
JUST KEEP GOING. IT WILL PASS.
WE NEED TO GET INSIDE--I'M--I'M STARTING TO FEEL WEIRD HERE--
IS THIS LIKE A TORNADO OR SOMETHING? I CAN'T--
I KNOW.
--HEY-- HEY, WAIT-- I KNOW HIM--
--HEY! MISTER GRIBBS!
THAT--THAT WAS MISTER GRIBBS--
I KNOW.
--WHAT IS HE DOING HERE NOW?
HUNTER!

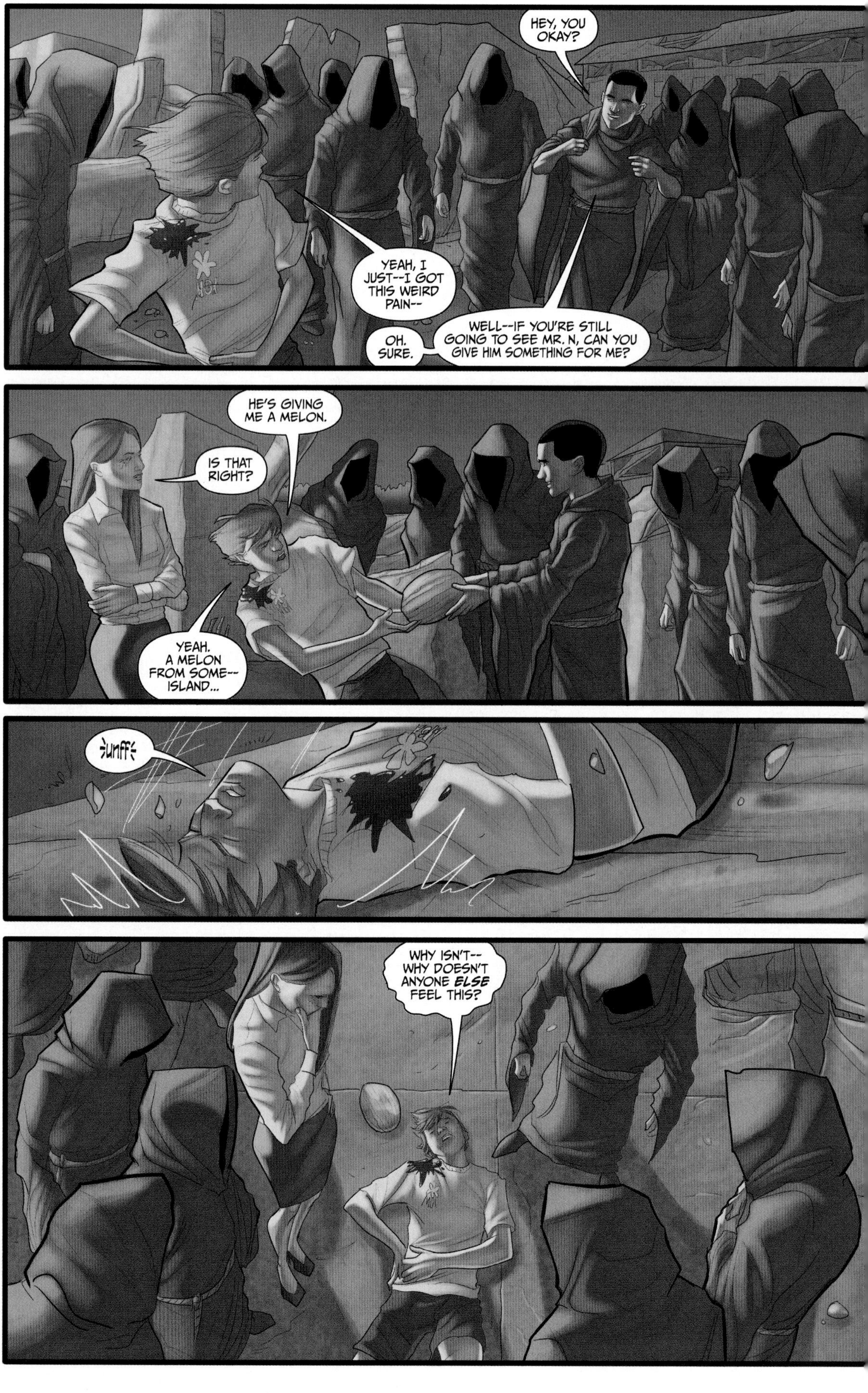
HEY, YOU OKAY?
YEAH, I JUST--I GOT THIS WEIRD PAIN--
WELL--IF YOU'RE STILL GOING TO SEE MR. N, CAN YOU GIVE HIM SOMETHING FOR ME?
OH. SURE.
HE'S GIVING ME A MELON.
IS THAT RIGHT?
YEAH. A MELON FROM SOME--ISLAND...
unff
WHY ISN'T--WHY DOESN'T ANYONE *ELSE* FEEL THIS?

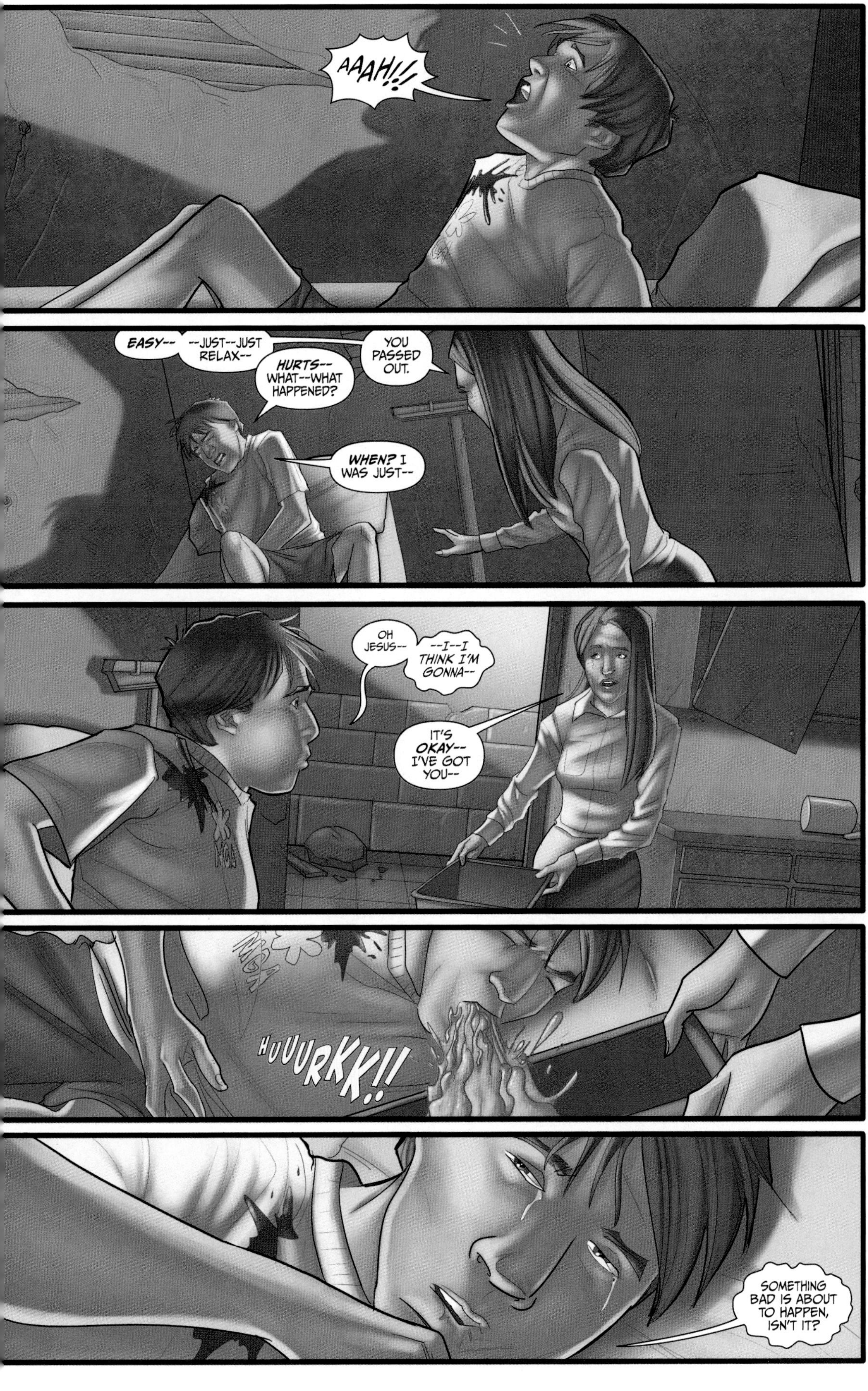
AAAH!!!
EASY--
--JUST--JUST RELAX--
HURTS-- WHAT--WHAT HAPPENED?
YOU PASSED OUT.
WHEN? I WAS JUST--
OH JESUS--
--I--I THINK I'M GONNA--
IT'S OKAY-- I'VE GOT YOU--
HUUURKK!!
SOMETHING BAD IS ABOUT TO HAPPEN, ISN'T IT?

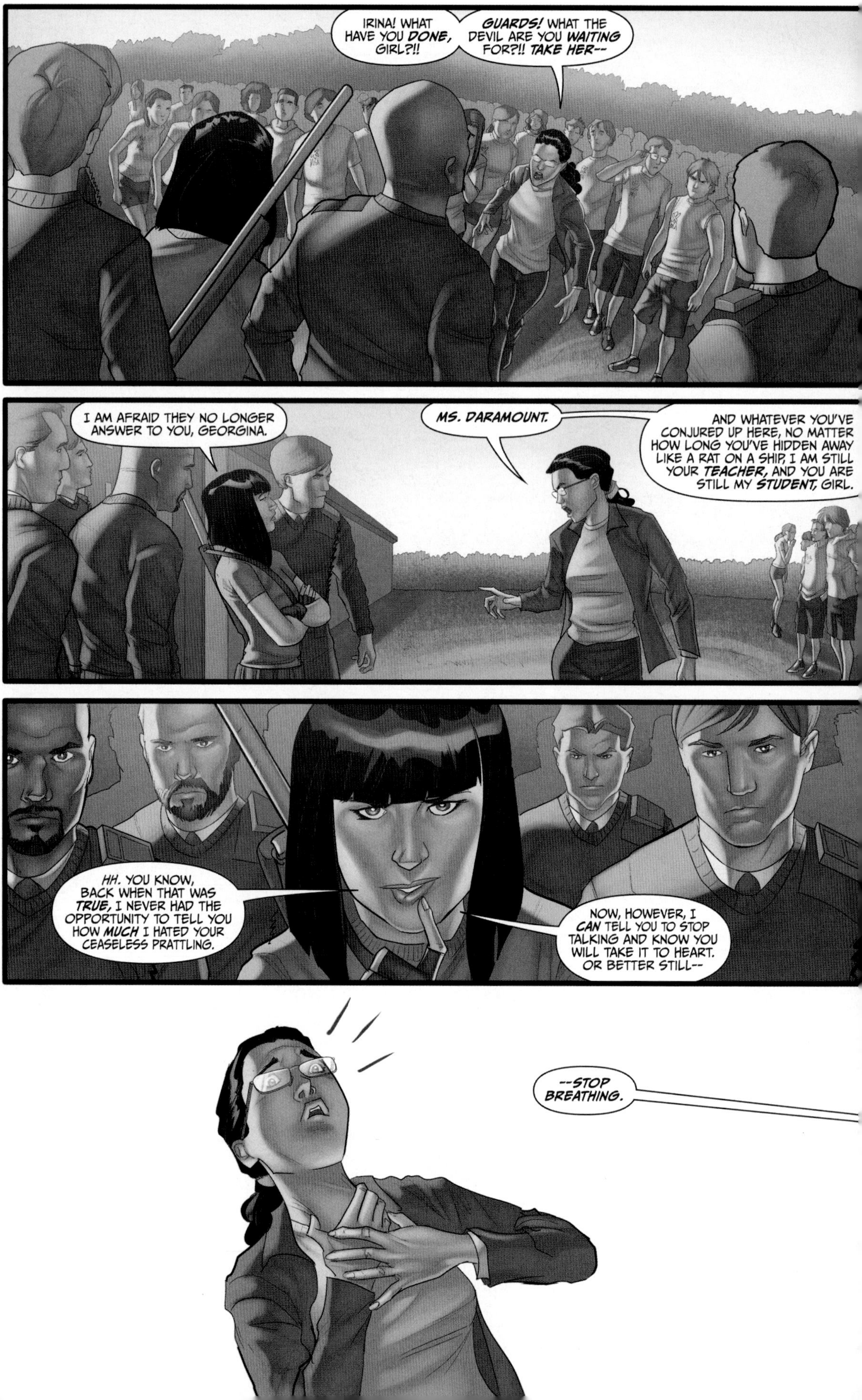

IRINA! WHAT HAVE YOU DONE, GIRL?!!
GUARDS! WHAT THE DEVIL ARE YOU WAITING FOR?!! TAKE HER--
I AM AFRAID THEY NO LONGER ANSWER TO YOU, GEORGINA.
MS. DARAMOUNT.
AND WHATEVER YOU'VE CONJURED UP HERE, NO MATTER HOW LONG YOU'VE HIDDEN AWAY LIKE A RAT ON A SHIP, I AM STILL YOUR TEACHER, AND YOU ARE STILL MY STUDENT, GIRL.
HH. YOU KNOW, BACK WHEN THAT WAS TRUE, I NEVER HAD THE OPPORTUNITY TO TELL YOU HOW MUCH I HATED YOUR CEASELESS PRATTLING.
NOW, HOWEVER, I CAN TELL YOU TO STOP TALKING AND KNOW YOU WILL TAKE IT TO HEART. OR BETTER STILL--
--STOP BREATHING.

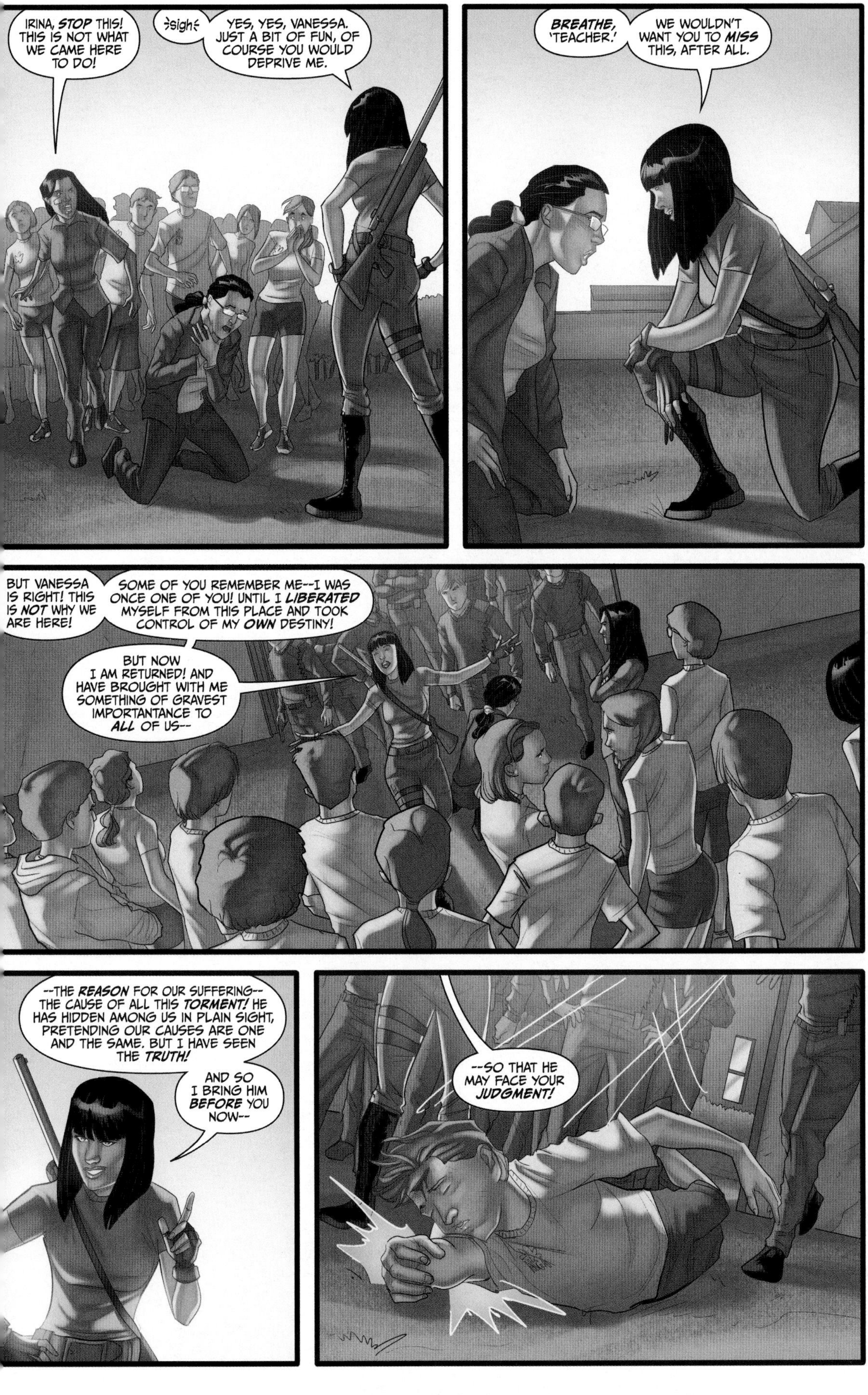
IRINA, STOP THIS! THIS IS NOT WHAT WE CAME HERE TO DO!
sigh
YES, YES, VANESSA. JUST A BIT OF FUN, OF COURSE YOU WOULD DEPRIVE ME.
BREATHE, 'TEACHER.'
WE WOULDN'T WANT YOU TO MISS THIS, AFTER ALL.
BUT VANESSA IS RIGHT! THIS IS NOT WHY WE ARE HERE!
SOME OF YOU REMEMBER ME--I WAS ONCE ONE OF YOU! UNTIL I LIBERATED MYSELF FROM THIS PLACE AND TOOK CONTROL OF MY OWN DESTINY!
BUT NOW I AM RETURNED! AND HAVE BROUGHT WITH ME SOMETHING OF GRAVEST IMPORTANTANCE TO ALL OF US--
--THE REASON FOR OUR SUFFERING-- THE CAUSE OF ALL THIS TORMENT! HE HAS HIDDEN AMONG US IN PLAIN SIGHT, PRETENDING OUR CAUSES ARE ONE AND THE SAME. BUT I HAVE SEEN THE TRUTH!
AND SO I BRING HIM BEFORE YOU NOW--
--SO THAT HE MAY FACE YOUR JUDGMENT!

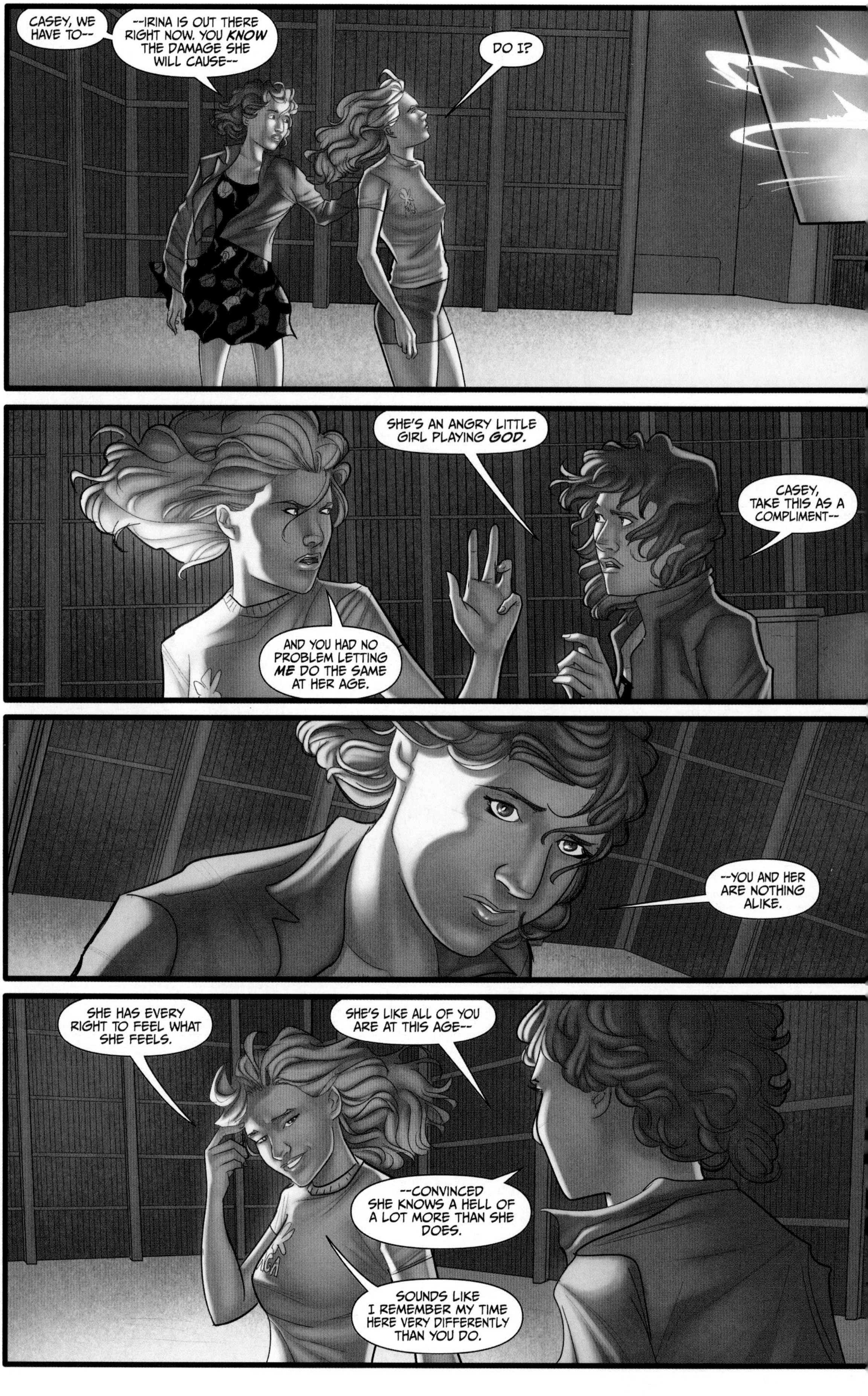
CASEY, WE HAVE TO--
--IRINA IS OUT THERE RIGHT NOW. YOU KNOW THE DAMAGE SHE WILL CAUSE--
DO I?
SHE'S AN ANGRY LITTLE GIRL PLAYING GOD.
AND YOU HAD NO PROBLEM LETTING ME DO THE SAME AT HER AGE.
CASEY, TAKE THIS AS A COMPLIMENT--
--YOU AND HER ARE NOTHING ALIKE.
SHE HAS EVERY RIGHT TO FEEL WHAT SHE FEELS.
SHE'S LIKE ALL OF YOU ARE AT THIS AGE--
--CONVINCED SHE KNOWS A HELL OF A LOT MORE THAN SHE DOES.
SOUNDS LIKE I REMEMBER MY TIME HERE VERY DIFFERENTLY THAN YOU DO.

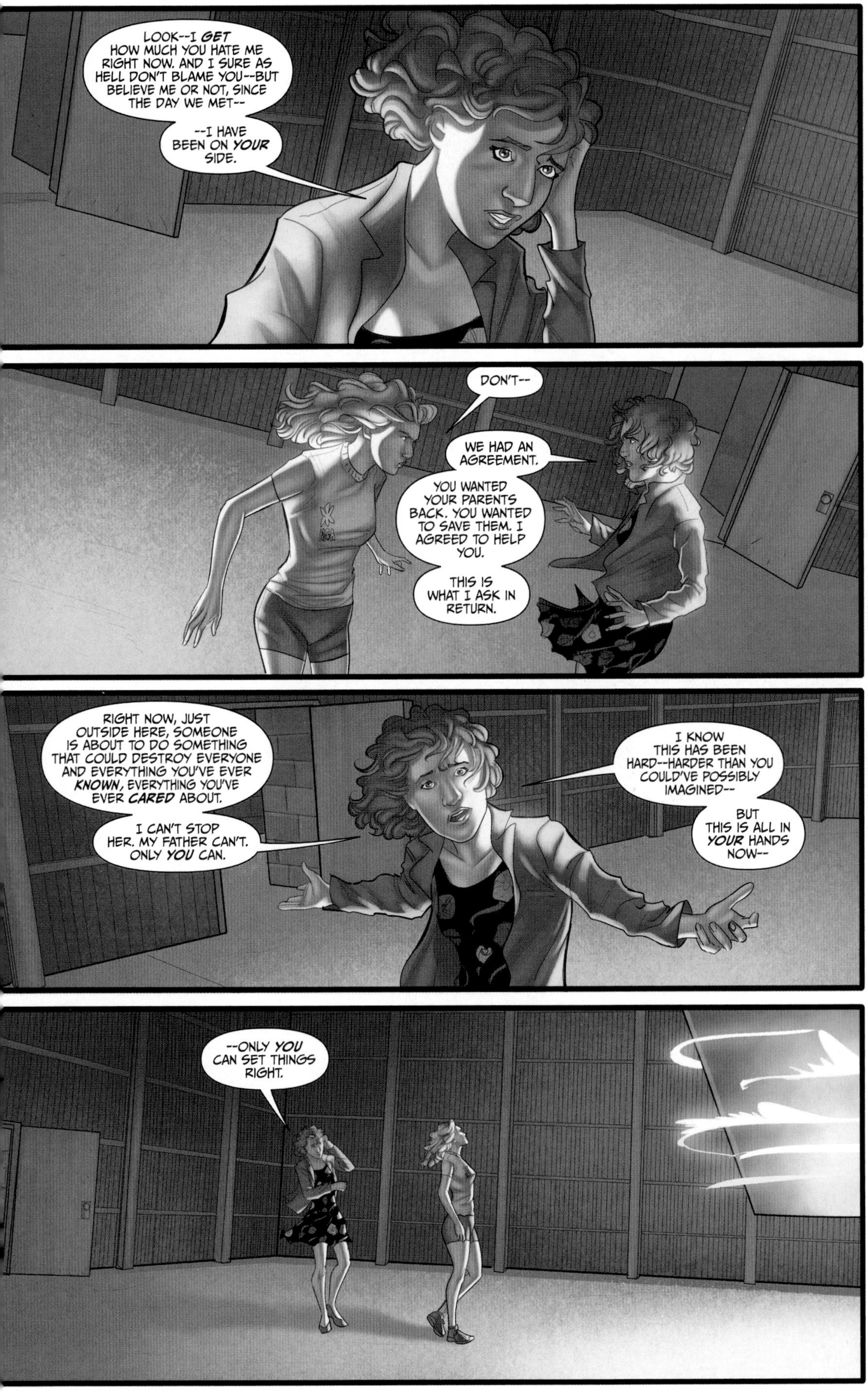
LOOK--I GET HOW MUCH YOU HATE ME RIGHT NOW. AND I SURE AS HELL DON'T BLAME YOU--BUT BELIEVE ME OR NOT, SINCE THE DAY WE MET--
--I HAVE BEEN ON YOUR SIDE.
DON'T--
WE HAD AN AGREEMENT.
YOU WANTED YOUR PARENTS BACK. YOU WANTED TO SAVE THEM. I AGREED TO HELP YOU.
THIS IS WHAT I ASK IN RETURN.
RIGHT NOW, JUST OUTSIDE HERE, SOMEONE IS ABOUT TO DO SOMETHING THAT COULD DESTROY EVERYONE AND EVERYTHING YOU'VE EVER KNOWN, EVERYTHING YOU'VE EVER CARED ABOUT.
I CAN'T STOP HER. MY FATHER CAN'T. ONLY YOU CAN.
I KNOW THIS HAS BEEN HARD--HARDER THAN YOU COULD'VE POSSIBLY IMAGINED--
BUT THIS IS ALL IN YOUR HANDS NOW--
--ONLY YOU CAN SET THINGS RIGHT.

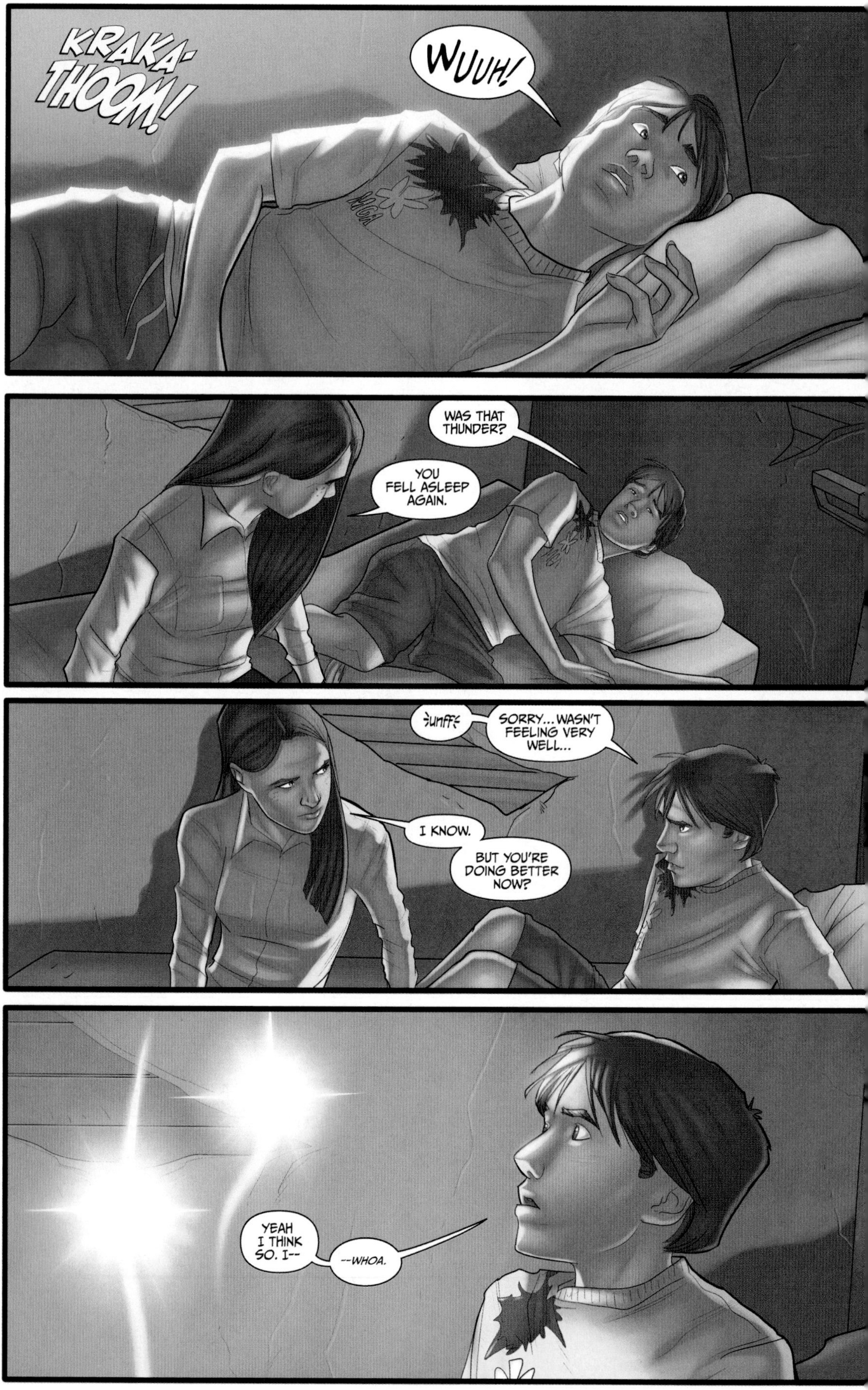
KRAKA-THOOM!
WUUH!
WAS THAT THUNDER?
YOU FELL ASLEEP AGAIN.
UNFF
SORRY... WASN'T FEELING VERY WELL...
I KNOW.
BUT YOU'RE DOING BETTER NOW?
YEAH I THINK SO. I--
--WHOA.

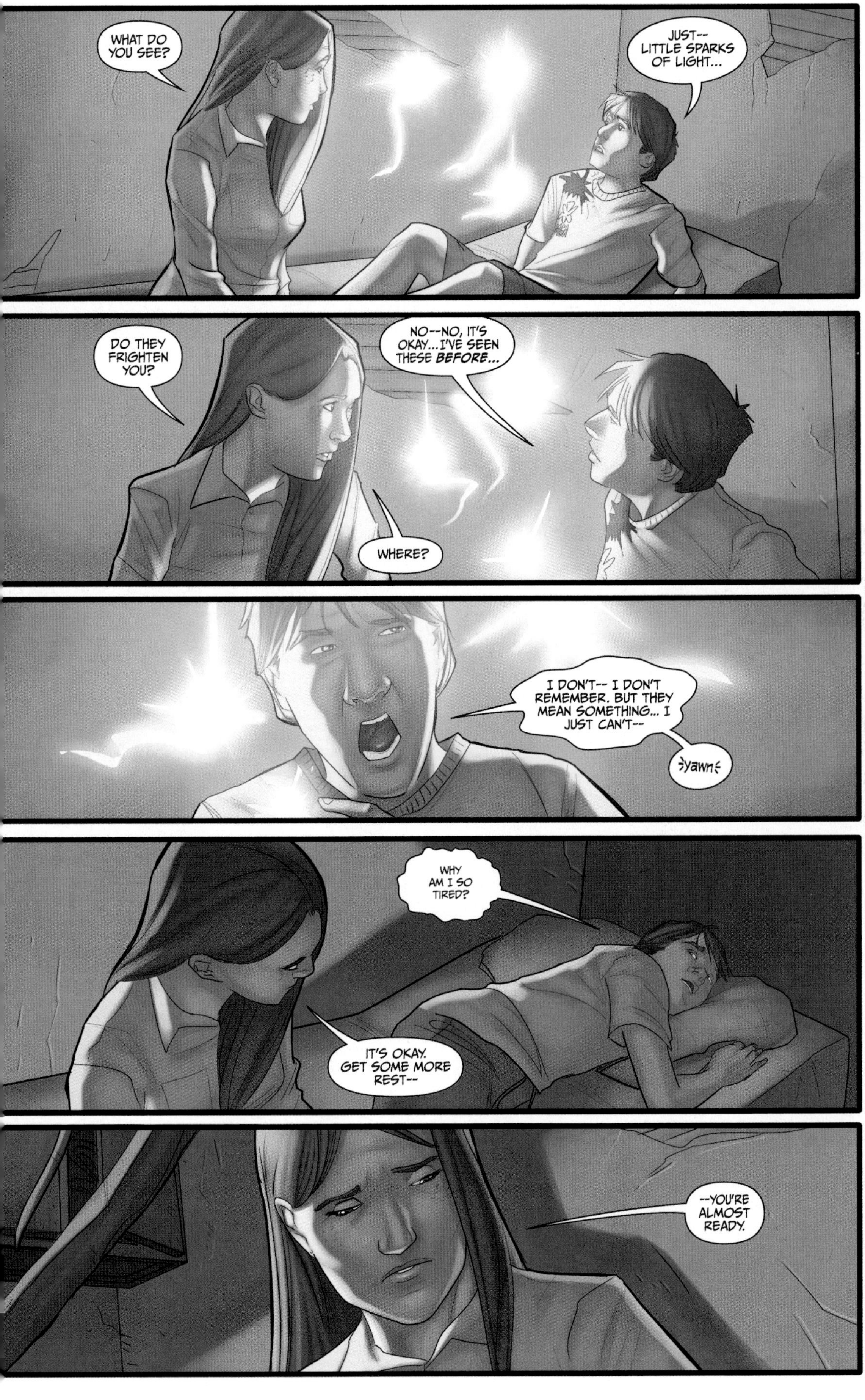
WHAT DO YOU SEE?
JUST-- LITTLE SPARKS OF LIGHT...
DO THEY FRIGHTEN YOU?
NO--NO, IT'S OKAY...I'VE SEEN THESE *BEFORE...*
WHERE?
I DON'T-- I DON'T REMEMBER. BUT THEY MEAN SOMETHING... I JUST CAN'T--
yawn
WHY AM I SO TIRED?
IT'S OKAY. GET SOME MORE REST--
--YOU'RE ALMOST READY.

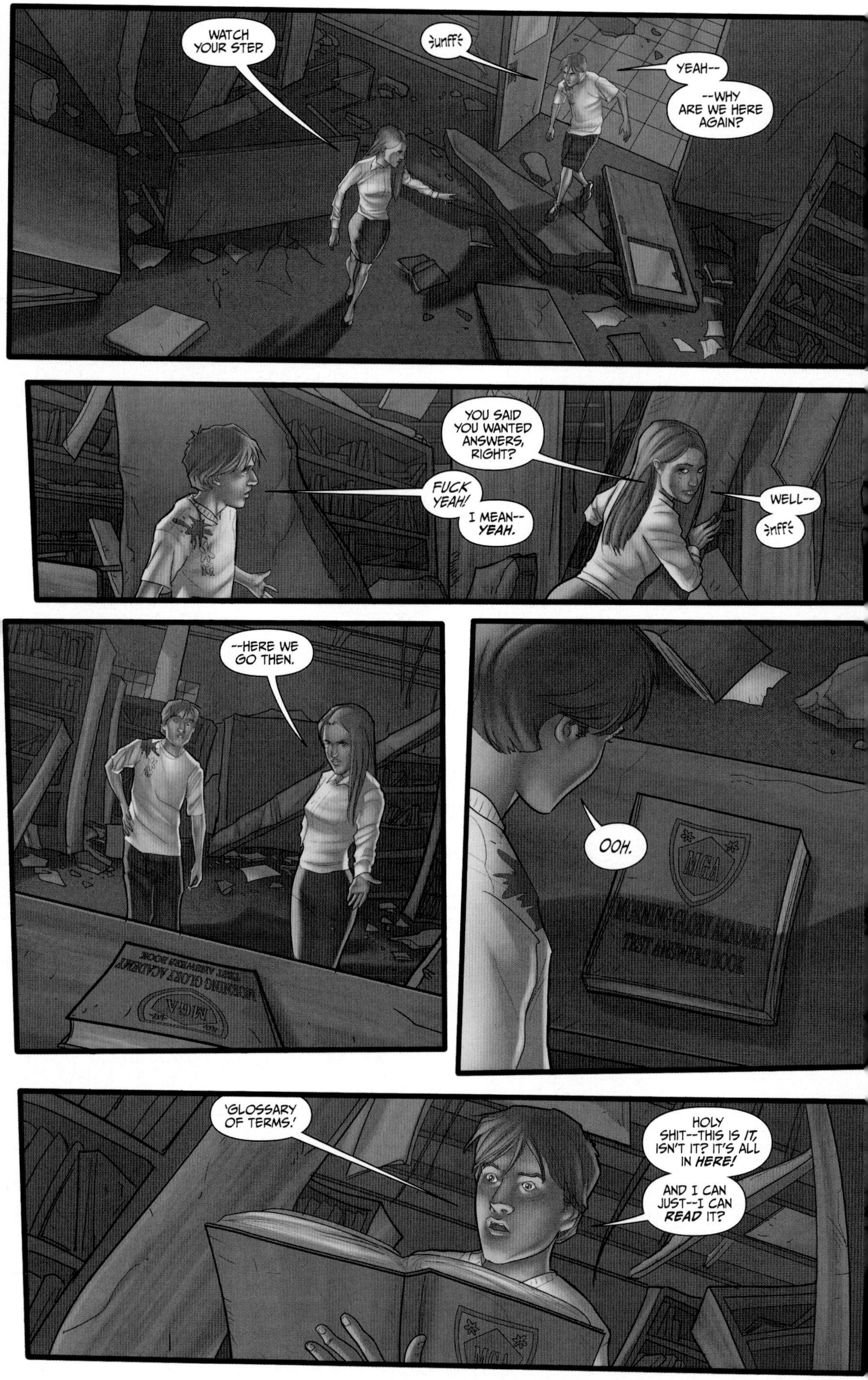
WATCH YOUR STEP.
unff
YEAH--
--WHY ARE WE HERE AGAIN?
YOU SAID YOU WANTED ANSWERS, RIGHT?
FUCK YEAH! I MEAN-- YEAH.
WELL--
nff
--HERE WE GO THEN.
MGA
MORNING GLORY ACADEMY
TEST ANSWERS BOOK
OOH.
MGA
MORNING GLORY ACADEMY
TEST ANSWERS BOOK
'GLOSSARY OF TERMS.'
HOLY SHIT--THIS IS IT, ISN'T IT? IT'S ALL IN HERE!
AND I CAN JUST--I CAN READ IT?
MGA

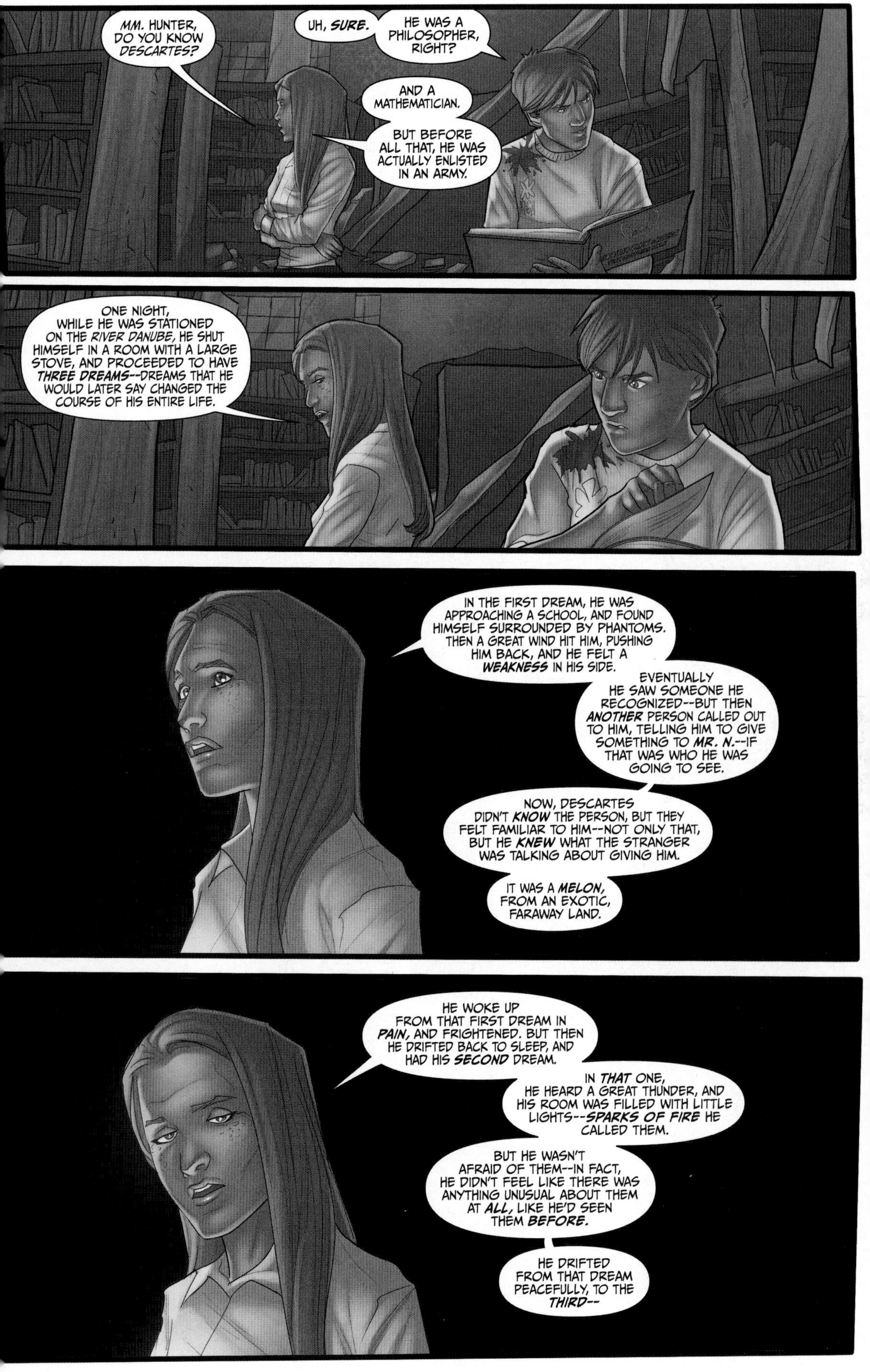
MM. HUNTER, DO YOU KNOW DESCARTES?
UH, SURE.
HE WAS A PHILOSOPHER, RIGHT?
AND A MATHEMATICIAN.
BUT BEFORE ALL THAT, HE WAS ACTUALLY ENLISTED IN AN ARMY.
ONE NIGHT, WHILE HE WAS STATIONED ON THE RIVER DANUBE, HE SHUT HIMSELF IN A ROOM WITH A LARGE STOVE, AND PROCEEDED TO HAVE THREE DREAMS--DREAMS THAT HE WOULD LATER SAY CHANGED THE COURSE OF HIS ENTIRE LIFE.
IN THE FIRST DREAM, HE WAS APPROACHING A SCHOOL, AND FOUND HIMSELF SURROUNDED BY PHANTOMS. THEN A GREAT WIND HIT HIM, PUSHING HIM BACK, AND HE FELT A WEAKNESS IN HIS SIDE.
EVENTUALLY HE SAW SOMEONE HE RECOGNIZED--BUT THEN ANOTHER PERSON CALLED OUT TO HIM, TELLING HIM TO GIVE SOMETHING TO MR. N.--IF THAT WAS WHO HE WAS GOING TO SEE.
NOW, DESCARTES DIDN'T KNOW THE PERSON, BUT THEY FELT FAMILIAR TO HIM--NOT ONLY THAT, BUT HE KNEW WHAT THE STRANGER WAS TALKING ABOUT GIVING HIM.
IT WAS A MELON, FROM AN EXOTIC, FARAWAY LAND.
HE WOKE UP FROM THAT FIRST DREAM IN PAIN, AND FRIGHTENED. BUT THEN HE DRIFTED BACK TO SLEEP, AND HAD HIS SECOND DREAM.
IN THAT ONE, HE HEARD A GREAT THUNDER, AND HIS ROOM WAS FILLED WITH LITTLE LIGHTS--SPARKS OF FIRE HE CALLED THEM.
BUT HE WASN'T AFRAID OF THEM--IN FACT, HE DIDN'T FEEL LIKE THERE WAS ANYTHING UNUSUAL ABOUT THEM AT ALL, LIKE HE'D SEEN THEM BEFORE.
HE DRIFTED FROM THAT DREAM PEACEFULLY, TO THE THIRD--

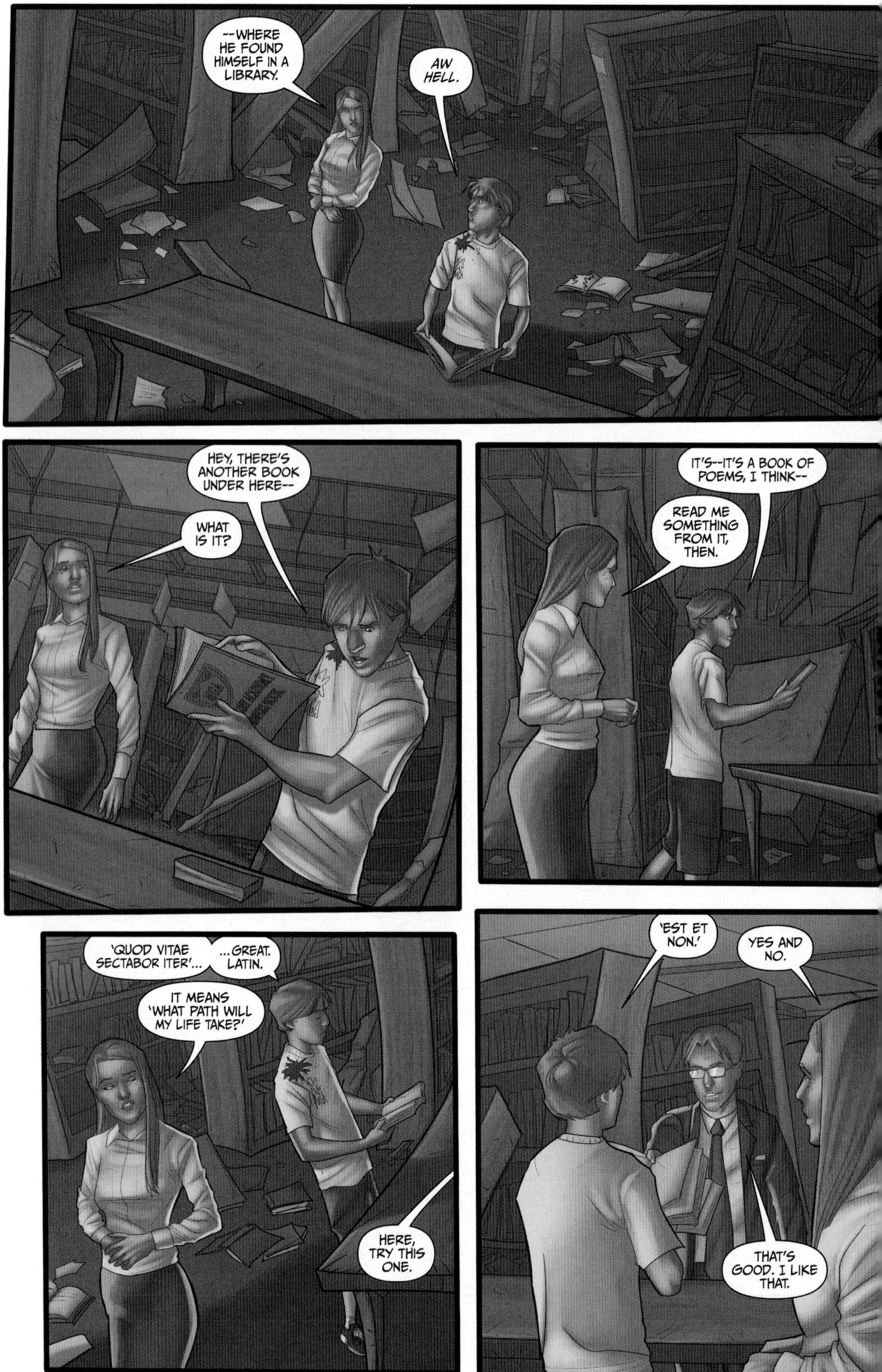
--WHERE HE FOUND HIMSELF IN A LIBRARY.
AW HELL.
HEY, THERE'S ANOTHER BOOK UNDER HERE--
WHAT IS IT?
IT'S--IT'S A BOOK OF POEMS, I THINK--
READ ME SOMETHING FROM IT, THEN.
'QUOD VITAE SECTABOR ITER'...
...GREAT. LATIN.
IT MEANS 'WHAT PATH WILL MY LIFE TAKE?'
HERE, TRY THIS ONE.
'EST ET NON.'
YES AND NO.
THAT'S GOOD. I LIKE THAT.

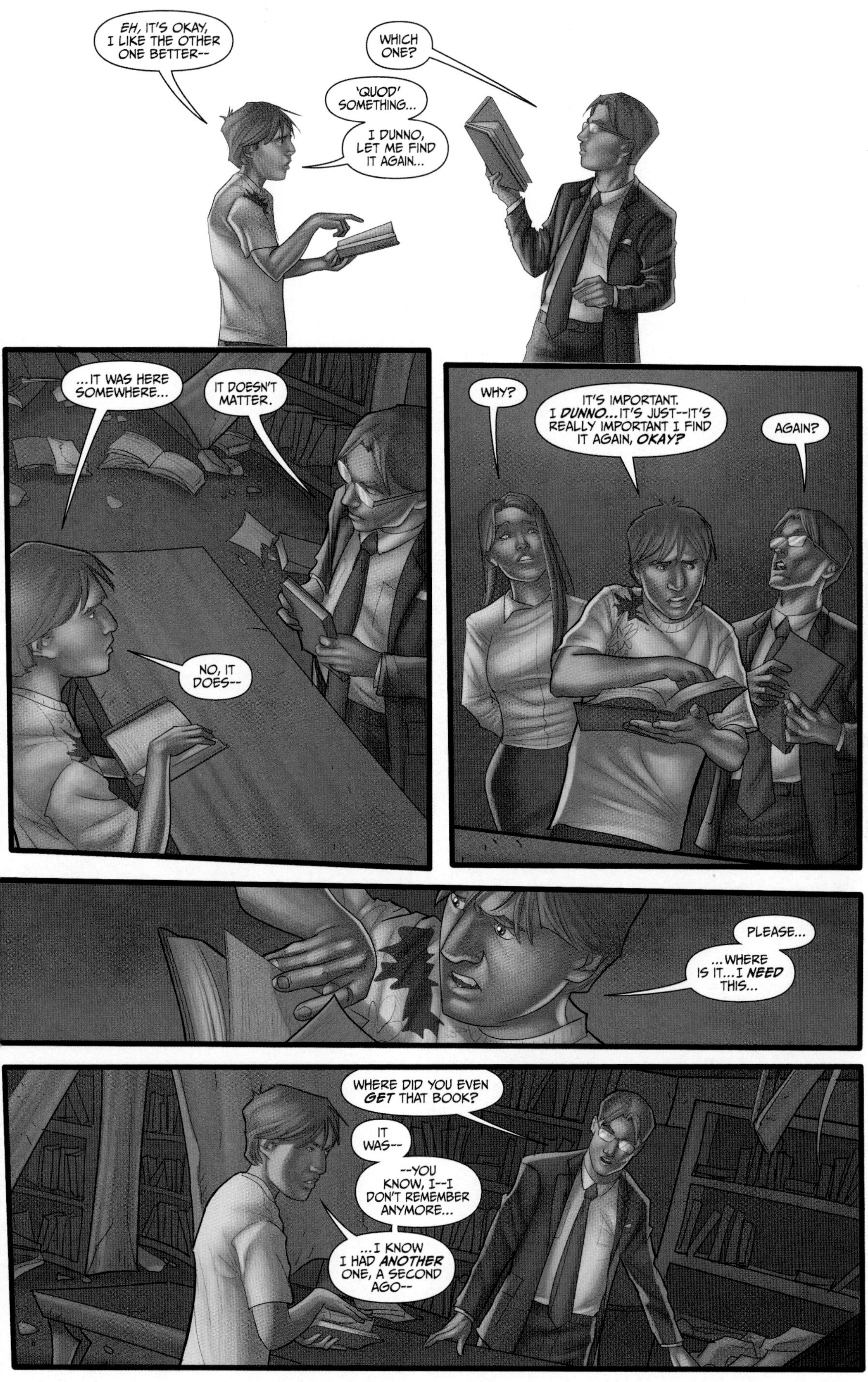
EH, IT'S OKAY, I LIKE THE OTHER ONE BETTER--
WHICH ONE?
'QUOD' SOMETHING...
I DUNNO, LET ME FIND IT AGAIN...
...IT WAS HERE SOMEWHERE...
IT DOESN'T MATTER.
NO, IT DOES--
WHY?
IT'S IMPORTANT. I DUNNO...IT'S JUST--IT'S REALLY IMPORTANT I FIND IT AGAIN, OKAY?
AGAIN?
PLEASE...
...WHERE IS IT...I NEED THIS...
WHERE DID YOU EVEN GET THAT BOOK?
IT WAS--
--YOU KNOW, I--I DON'T REMEMBER ANYMORE...
...I KNOW I HAD ANOTHER ONE, A SECOND AGO--

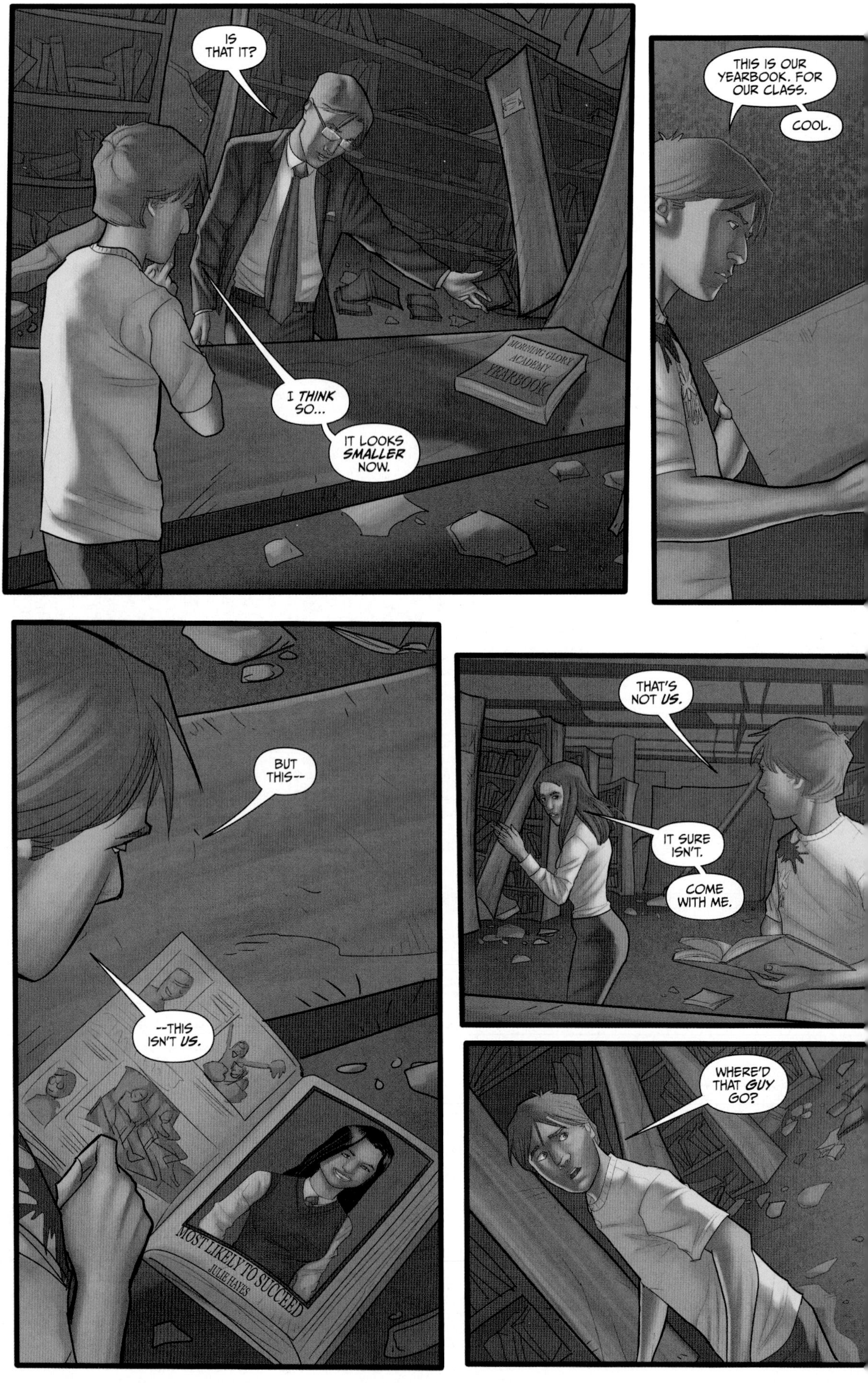
IS THAT IT?
I THINK SO...
IT LOOKS SMALLER NOW.
MORNING GLORY ACADEMY YEARBOOK
THIS IS OUR YEARBOOK. FOR OUR CLASS.
COOL.
BUT THIS--
--THIS ISN'T US.
MOST LIKELY TO SUCCEED
JULIE HAYES
THAT'S NOT US.
IT SURE ISN'T.
COME WITH ME.
WHERE'D THAT GUY GO?

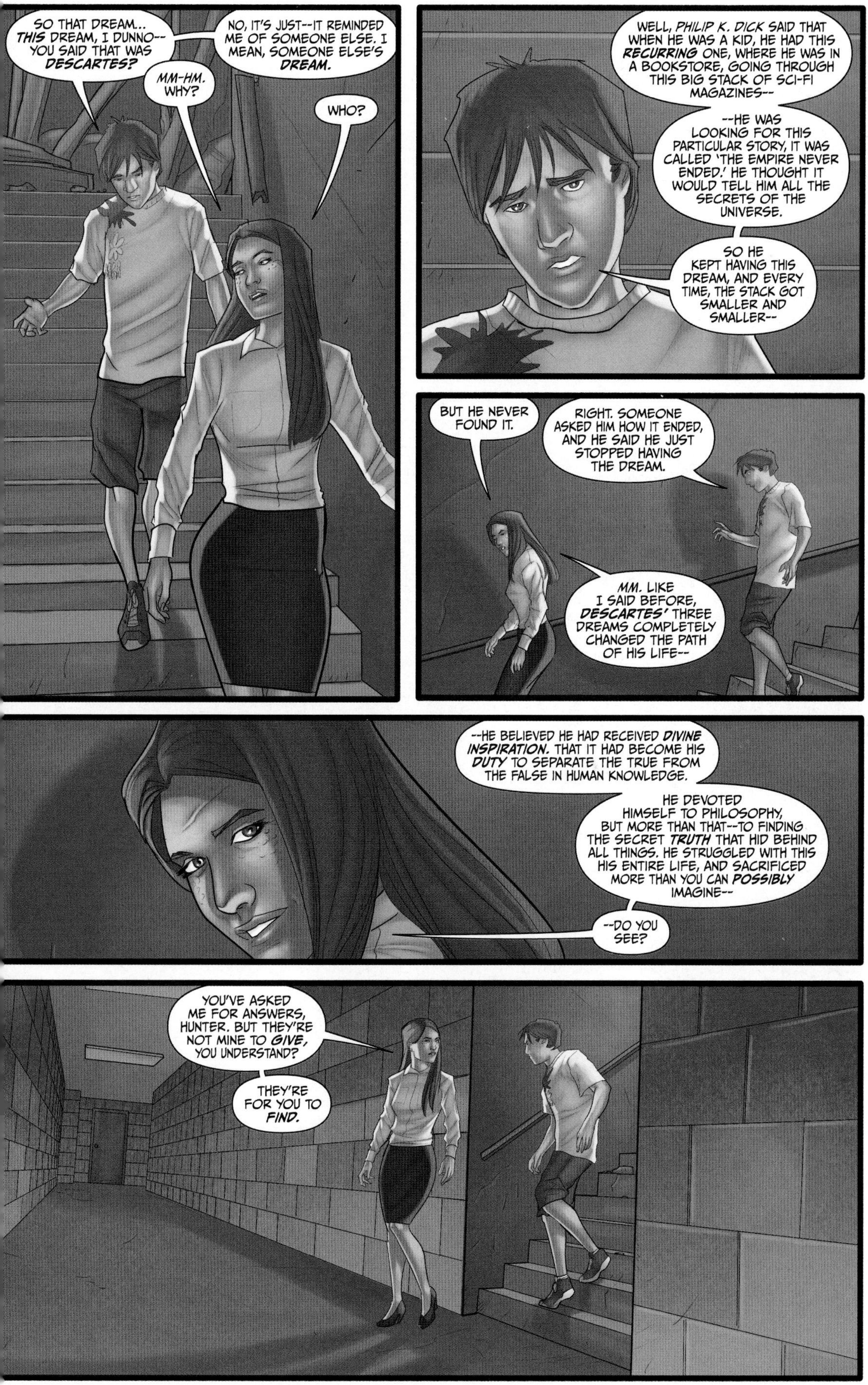

SO THAT DREAM... THIS DREAM, I DUNNO-- YOU SAID THAT WAS DESCARTES?
MM-HM. WHY?
NO, IT'S JUST--IT REMINDED ME OF SOMEONE ELSE. I MEAN, SOMEONE ELSE'S DREAM.
WHO?
WELL, PHILIP K. DICK SAID THAT WHEN HE WAS A KID, HE HAD THIS RECURRING ONE, WHERE HE WAS IN A BOOKSTORE, GOING THROUGH THIS BIG STACK OF SCI-FI MAGAZINES--
--HE WAS LOOKING FOR THIS PARTICULAR STORY, IT WAS CALLED 'THE EMPIRE NEVER ENDED.' HE THOUGHT IT WOULD TELL HIM ALL THE SECRETS OF THE UNIVERSE.
SO HE KEPT HAVING THIS DREAM, AND EVERY TIME, THE STACK GOT SMALLER AND SMALLER--
BUT HE NEVER FOUND IT.
RIGHT. SOMEONE ASKED HIM HOW IT ENDED, AND HE SAID HE JUST STOPPED HAVING THE DREAM.
MM. LIKE I SAID BEFORE, DESCARTES' THREE DREAMS COMPLETELY CHANGED THE PATH OF HIS LIFE--
--HE BELIEVED HE HAD RECEIVED DIVINE INSPIRATION. THAT IT HAD BECOME HIS DUTY TO SEPARATE THE TRUE FROM THE FALSE IN HUMAN KNOWLEDGE.
HE DEVOTED HIMSELF TO PHILOSOPHY, BUT MORE THAN THAT--TO FINDING THE SECRET TRUTH THAT HID BEHIND ALL THINGS. HE STRUGGLED WITH THIS HIS ENTIRE LIFE, AND SACRIFICED MORE THAN YOU CAN POSSIBLY IMAGINE--
--DO YOU SEE?
YOU'VE ASKED ME FOR ANSWERS, HUNTER. BUT THEY'RE NOT MINE TO GIVE, YOU UNDERSTAND?
THEY'RE FOR YOU TO FIND.

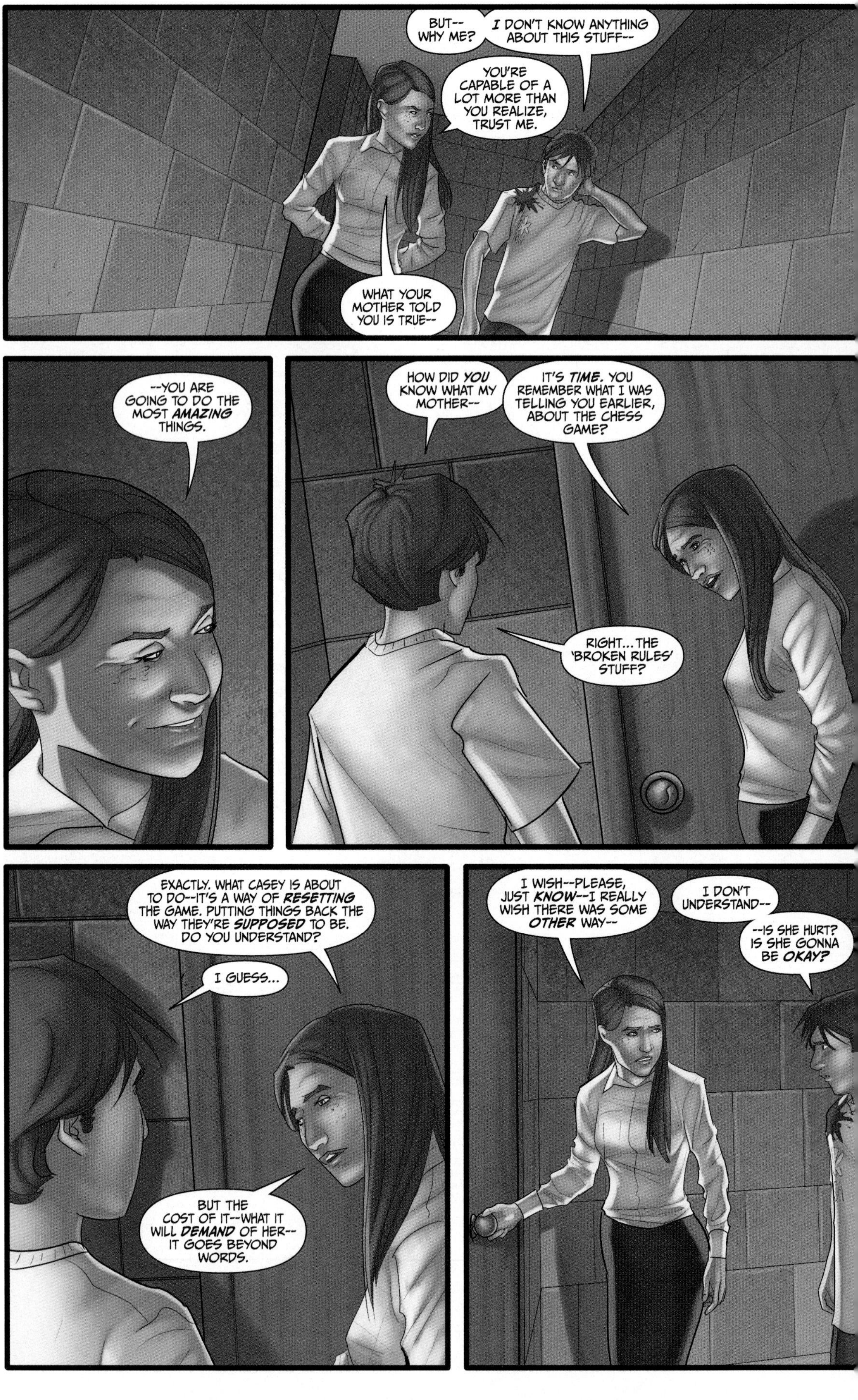
BUT-- WHY ME?
I DON'T KNOW ANYTHING ABOUT THIS STUFF--
YOU'RE CAPABLE OF A LOT MORE THAN YOU REALIZE, TRUST ME.
WHAT YOUR MOTHER TOLD YOU IS TRUE--
--YOU ARE GOING TO DO THE MOST AMAZING THINGS.
HOW DID YOU KNOW WHAT MY MOTHER--
IT'S TIME. YOU REMEMBER WHAT I WAS TELLING YOU EARLIER, ABOUT THE CHESS GAME?
RIGHT... THE 'BROKEN RULES' STUFF?
EXACTLY. WHAT CASEY IS ABOUT TO DO--IT'S A WAY OF RESETTING THE GAME. PUTTING THINGS BACK THE WAY THEY'RE SUPPOSED TO BE. DO YOU UNDERSTAND?
I GUESS...
BUT THE COST OF IT--WHAT IT WILL DEMAND OF HER-- IT GOES BEYOND WORDS.
I WISH--PLEASE, JUST KNOW--I REALLY WISH THERE WAS SOME OTHER WAY--
I DON'T UNDERSTAND--
--IS SHE HURT? IS SHE GONNA BE OKAY?

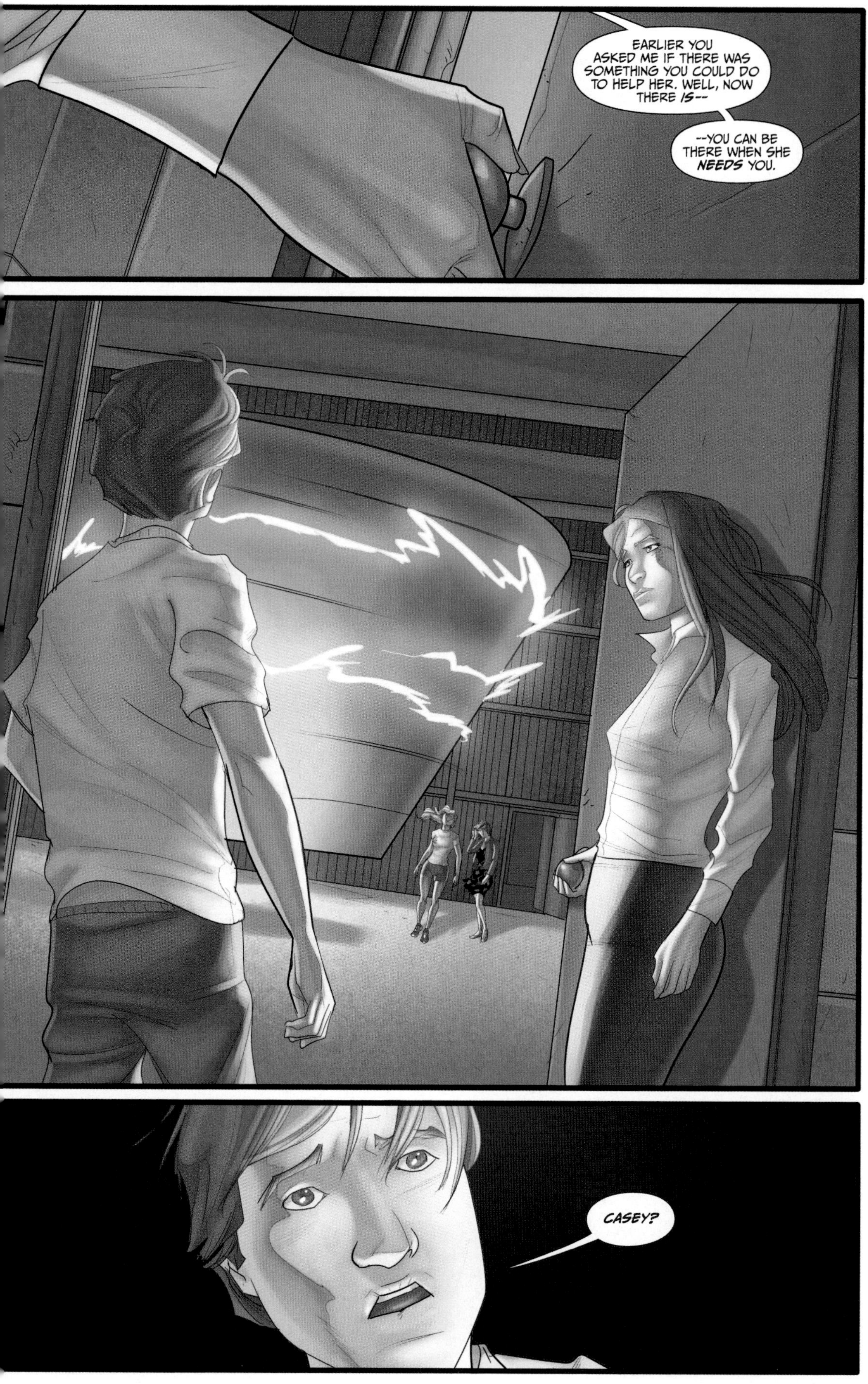

EARLIER YOU ASKED ME IF THERE WAS SOMETHING YOU COULD DO TO HELP HER. WELL, NOW THERE *IS*--
--YOU CAN BE THERE WHEN SHE ***NEEDS*** YOU.
CASEY?

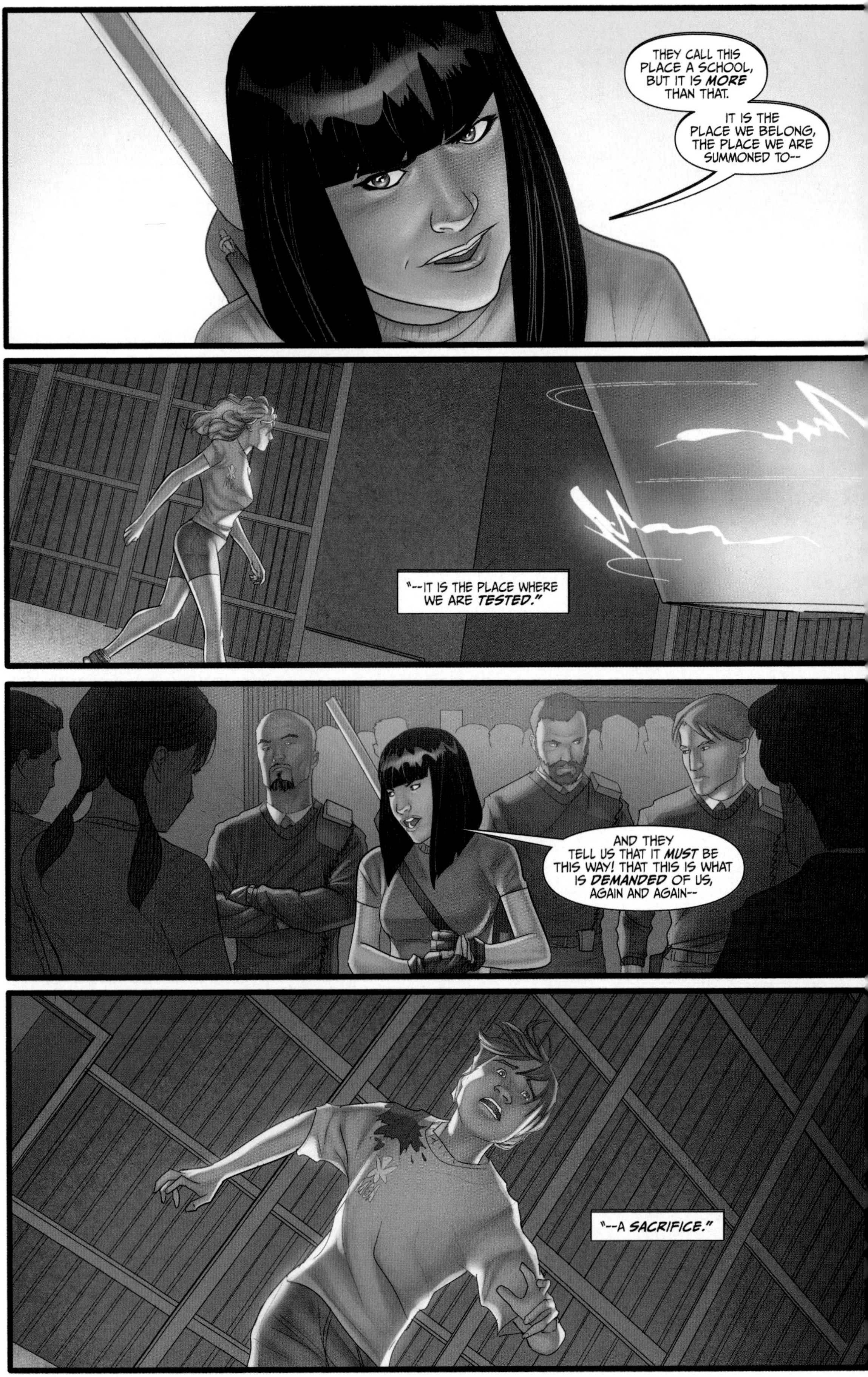
THEY CALL THIS PLACE A SCHOOL, BUT IT IS MORE THAN THAT.
IT IS THE PLACE WE BELONG, THE PLACE WE ARE SUMMONED TO--
"--IT IS THE PLACE WHERE WE ARE TESTED."
AND THEY TELL US THAT IT MUST BE THIS WAY! THAT THIS IS WHAT IS DEMANDED OF US, AGAIN AND AGAIN--
"--A SACRIFICE."

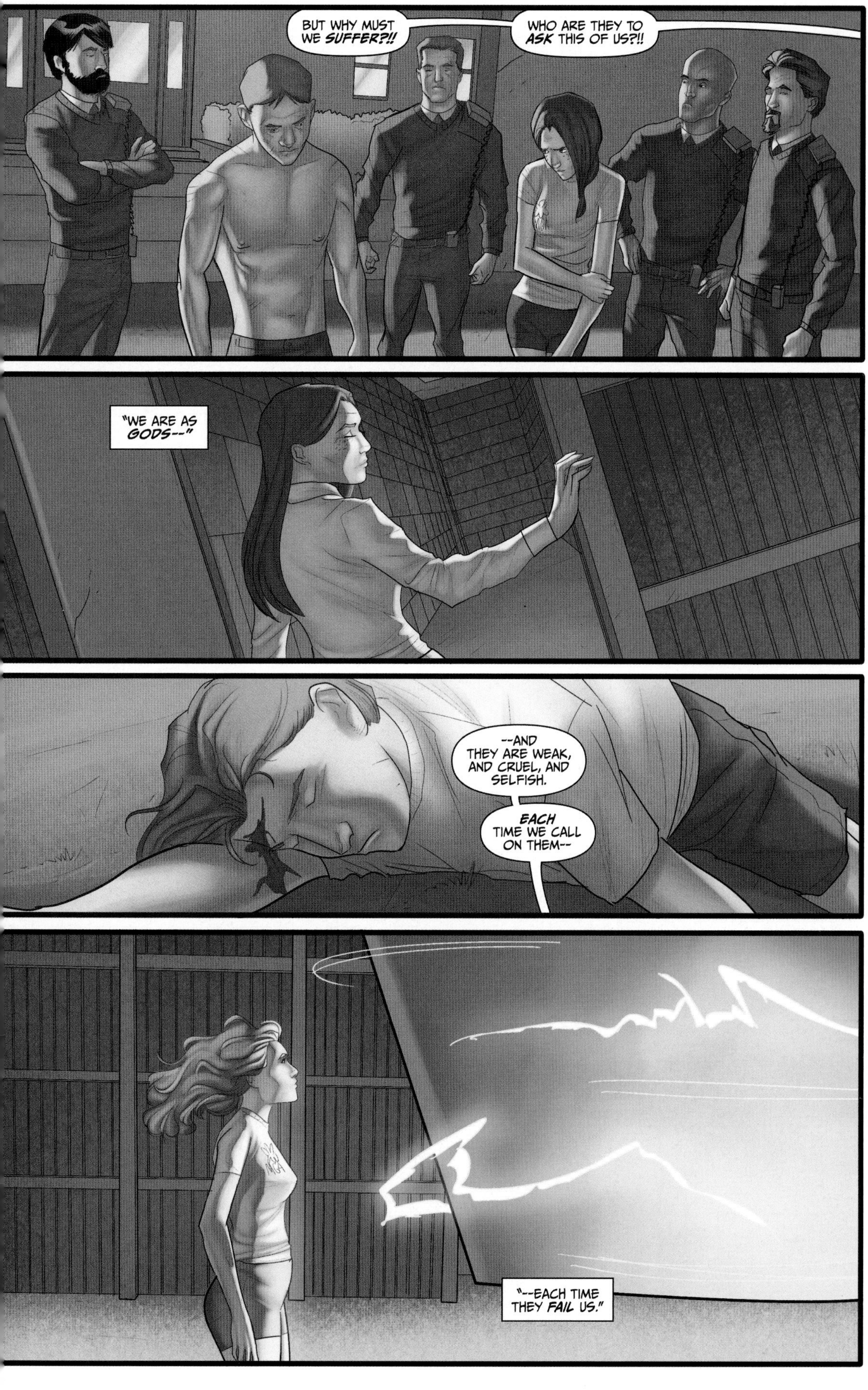
BUT WHY MUST WE SUFFER?!!
WHO ARE THEY TO ASK THIS OF US?!!
"WE ARE AS GODS--"
--AND THEY ARE WEAK, AND CRUEL, AND SELFISH.
EACH TIME WE CALL ON THEM--
"--EACH TIME THEY FAIL US."

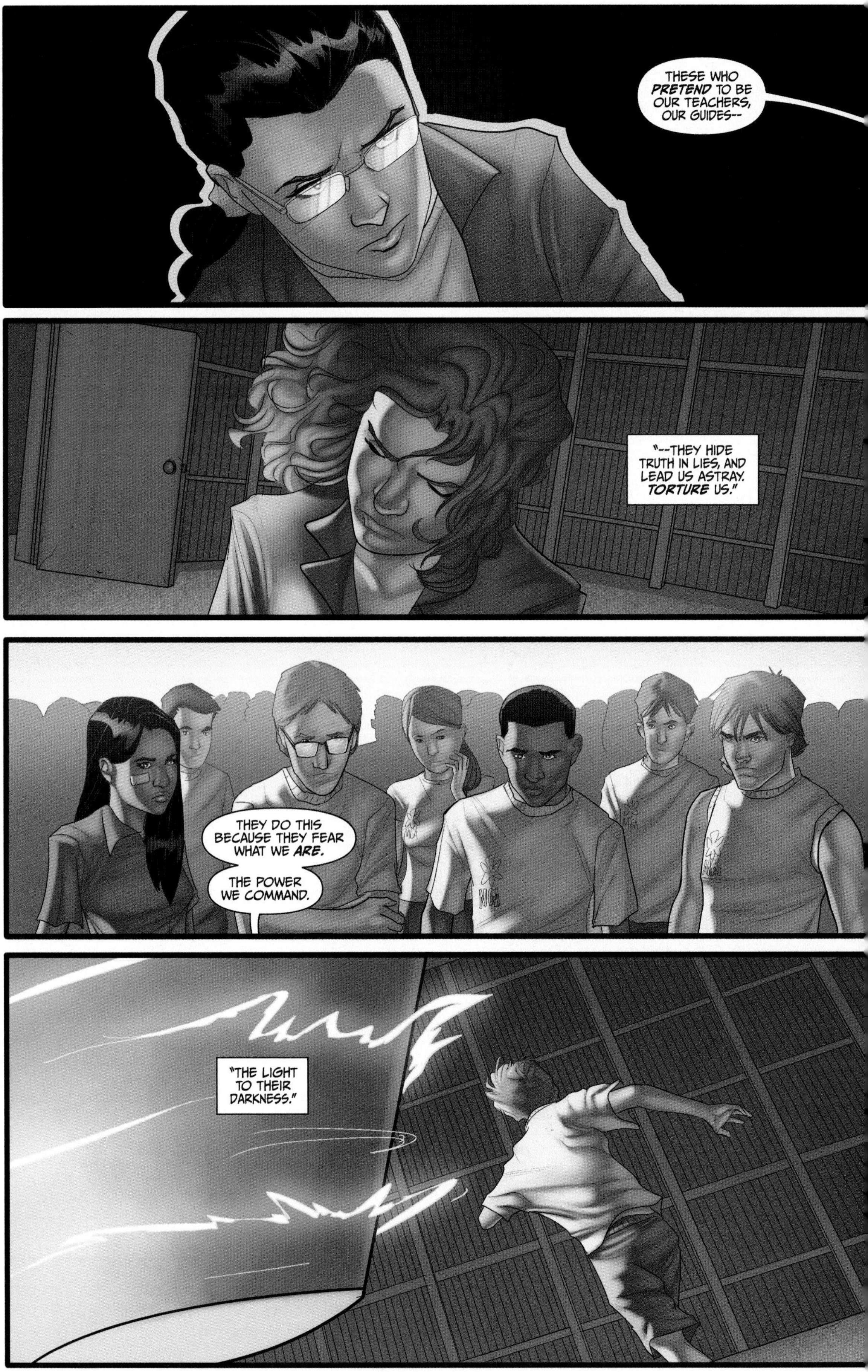
THESE WHO PRETEND TO BE OUR TEACHERS, OUR GUIDES--
"--THEY HIDE TRUTH IN LIES, AND LEAD US ASTRAY. TORTURE US."
THEY DO THIS BECAUSE THEY FEAR WHAT WE ARE.
THE POWER WE COMMAND.
"THE LIGHT TO THEIR DARKNESS."

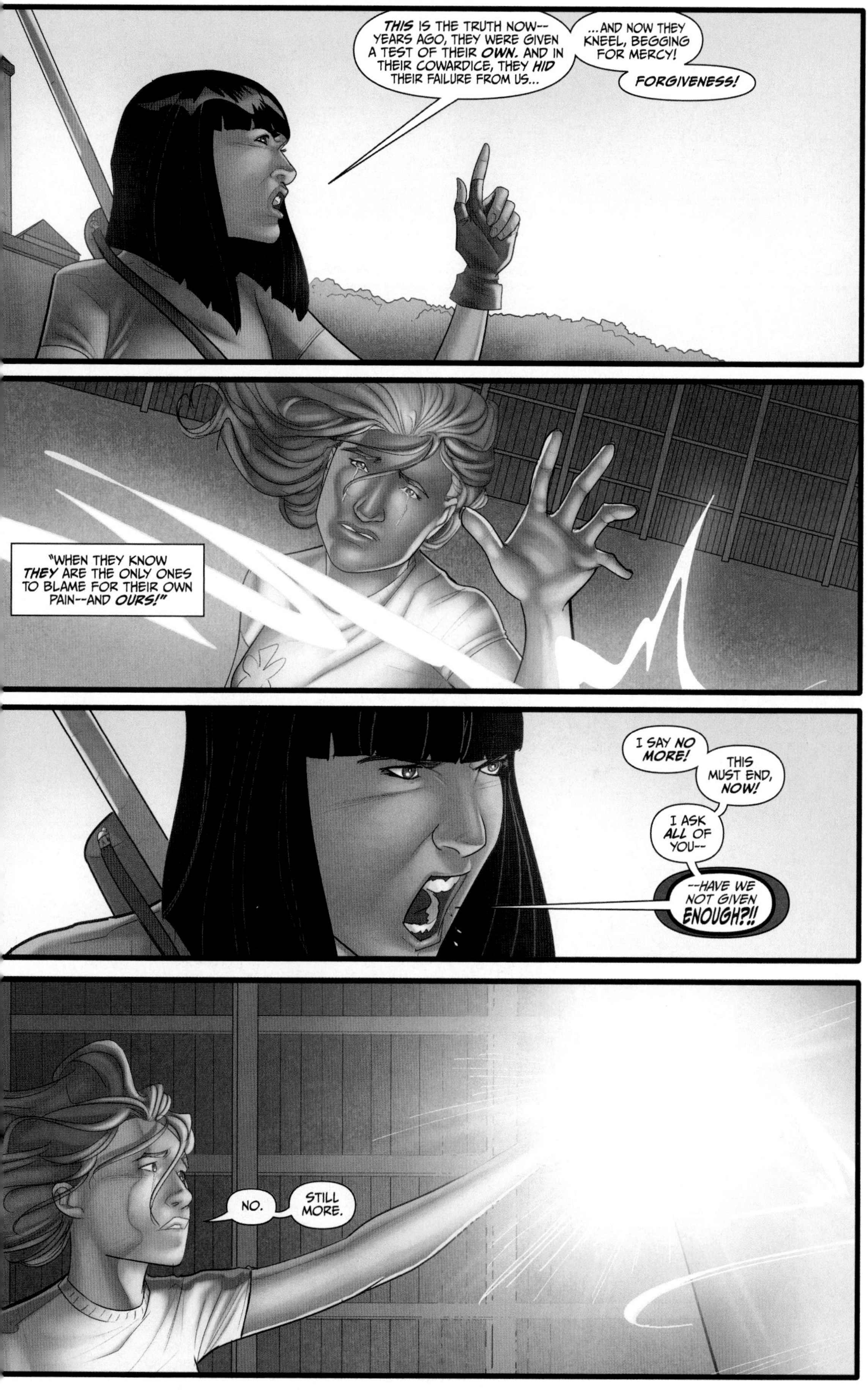
THIS IS THE TRUTH NOW-- YEARS AGO, THEY WERE GIVEN A TEST OF THEIR OWN. AND IN THEIR COWARDICE, THEY HID THEIR FAILURE FROM US...
...AND NOW THEY KNEEL, BEGGING FOR MERCY!
FORGIVENESS!
"WHEN THEY KNOW THEY ARE THE ONLY ONES TO BLAME FOR THEIR OWN PAIN--AND OURS!"
I SAY NO MORE!
THIS MUST END, NOW!
I ASK ALL OF YOU--
--HAVE WE NOT GIVEN ENOUGH?!!
NO.
STILL MORE.

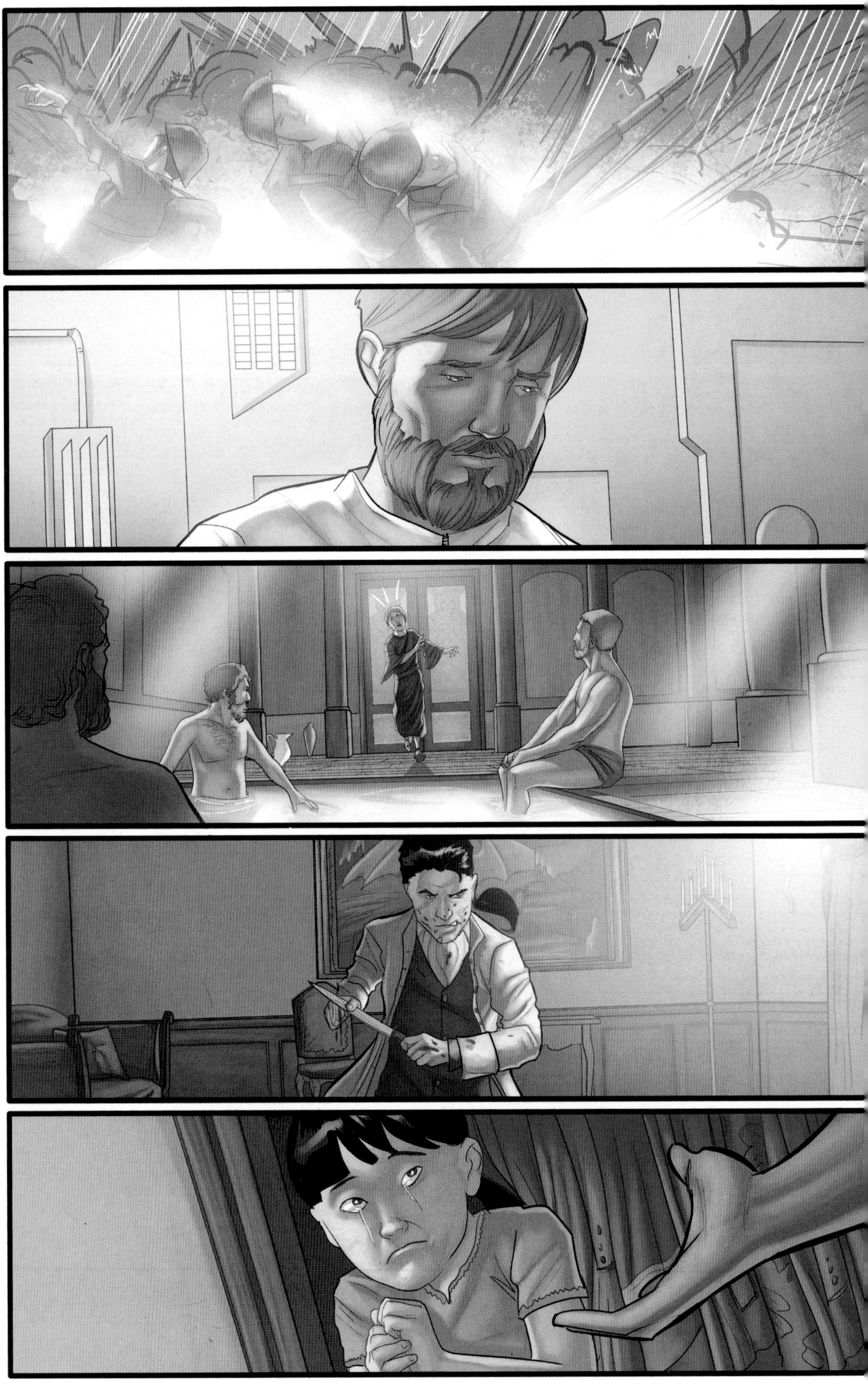

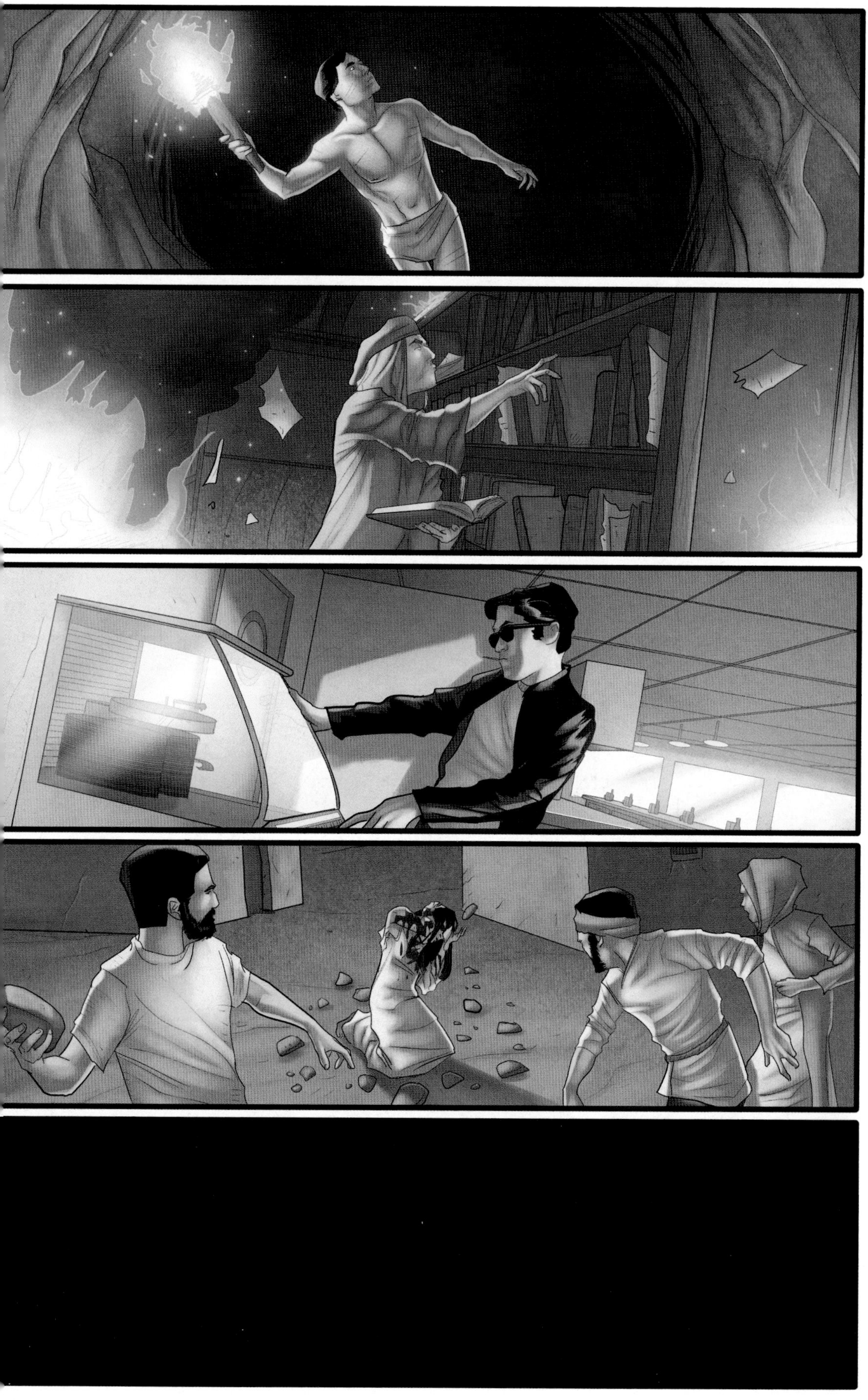

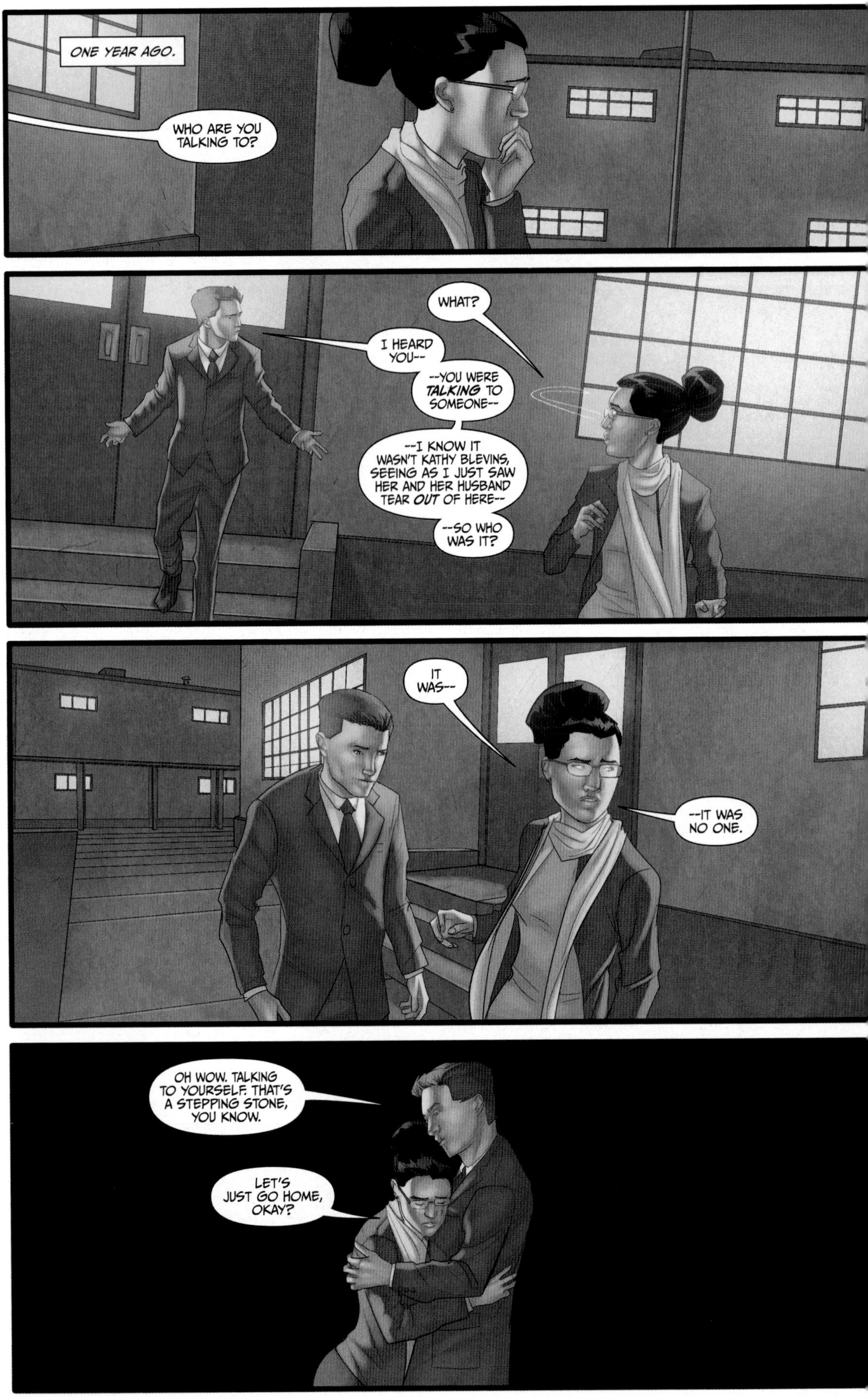
ONE YEAR AGO.
WHO ARE YOU TALKING TO?
WHAT?
I HEARD YOU--
--YOU WERE *TALKING* TO SOMEONE--
--I KNOW IT WASN'T KATHY BLEVINS, SEEING AS I JUST SAW HER AND HER HUSBAND TEAR *OUT* OF HERE--
--SO WHO WAS IT?
IT WAS--
--IT WAS NO ONE.
OH WOW. TALKING TO YOURSELF. THAT'S A STEPPING STONE, YOU KNOW.
LET'S JUST GO HOME, OKAY?

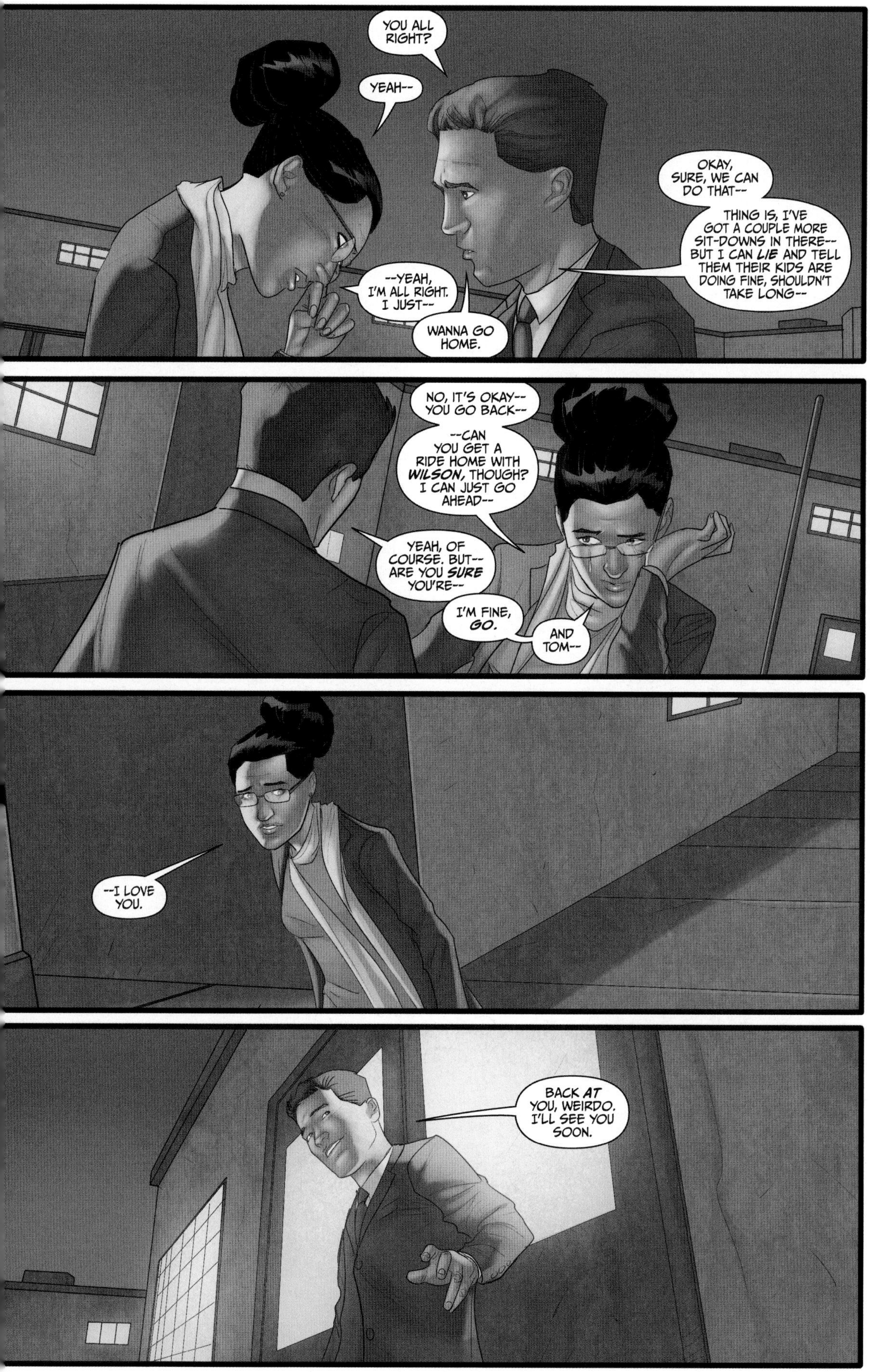
YOU ALL RIGHT?
YEAH--
OKAY, SURE, WE CAN DO THAT--
THING IS, I'VE GOT A COUPLE MORE SIT-DOWNS IN THERE-- BUT I CAN LIE AND TELL THEM THEIR KIDS ARE DOING FINE, SHOULDN'T TAKE LONG--
--YEAH, I'M ALL RIGHT. I JUST--
WANNA GO HOME.
NO, IT'S OKAY-- YOU GO BACK--
--CAN YOU GET A RIDE HOME WITH WILSON, THOUGH? I CAN JUST GO AHEAD--
YEAH, OF COURSE. BUT-- ARE YOU SURE YOU'RE--
I'M FINE, GO.
AND TOM--
--I LOVE YOU.
BACK AT YOU, WEIRDO. I'LL SEE YOU SOON.

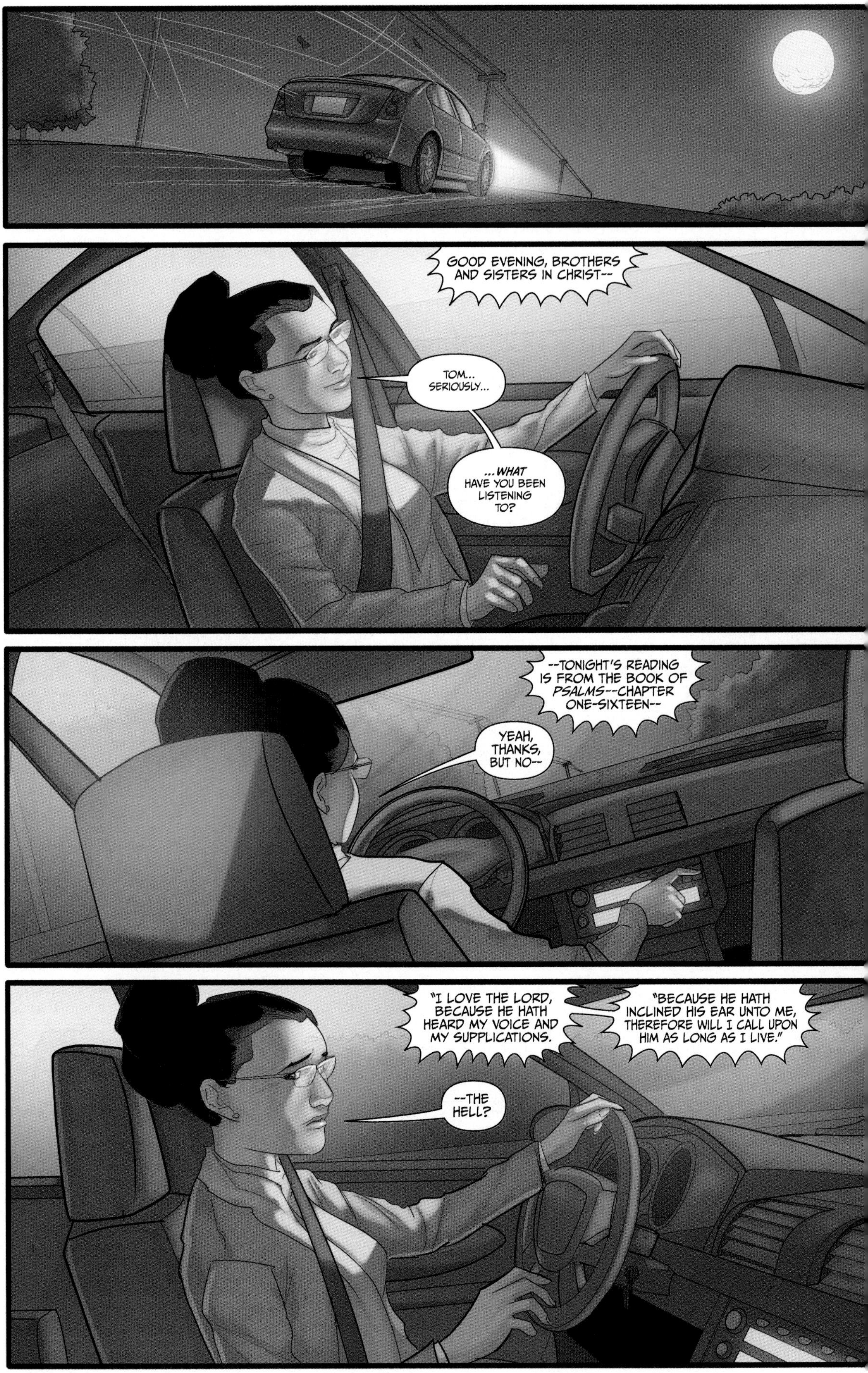
GOOD EVENING, BROTHERS AND SISTERS IN CHRIST--
TOM... SERIOUSLY...
...WHAT HAVE YOU BEEN LISTENING TO?
--TONIGHT'S READING IS FROM THE BOOK OF PSALMS--CHAPTER ONE-SIXTEEN--
YEAH, THANKS, BUT NO--
"I LOVE THE LORD, BECAUSE HE HATH HEARD MY VOICE AND MY SUPPLICATIONS.
"BECAUSE HE HATH INCLINED HIS EAR UNTO ME, THEREFORE WILL I CALL UPON HIM AS LONG AS I LIVE."
--THE HELL?

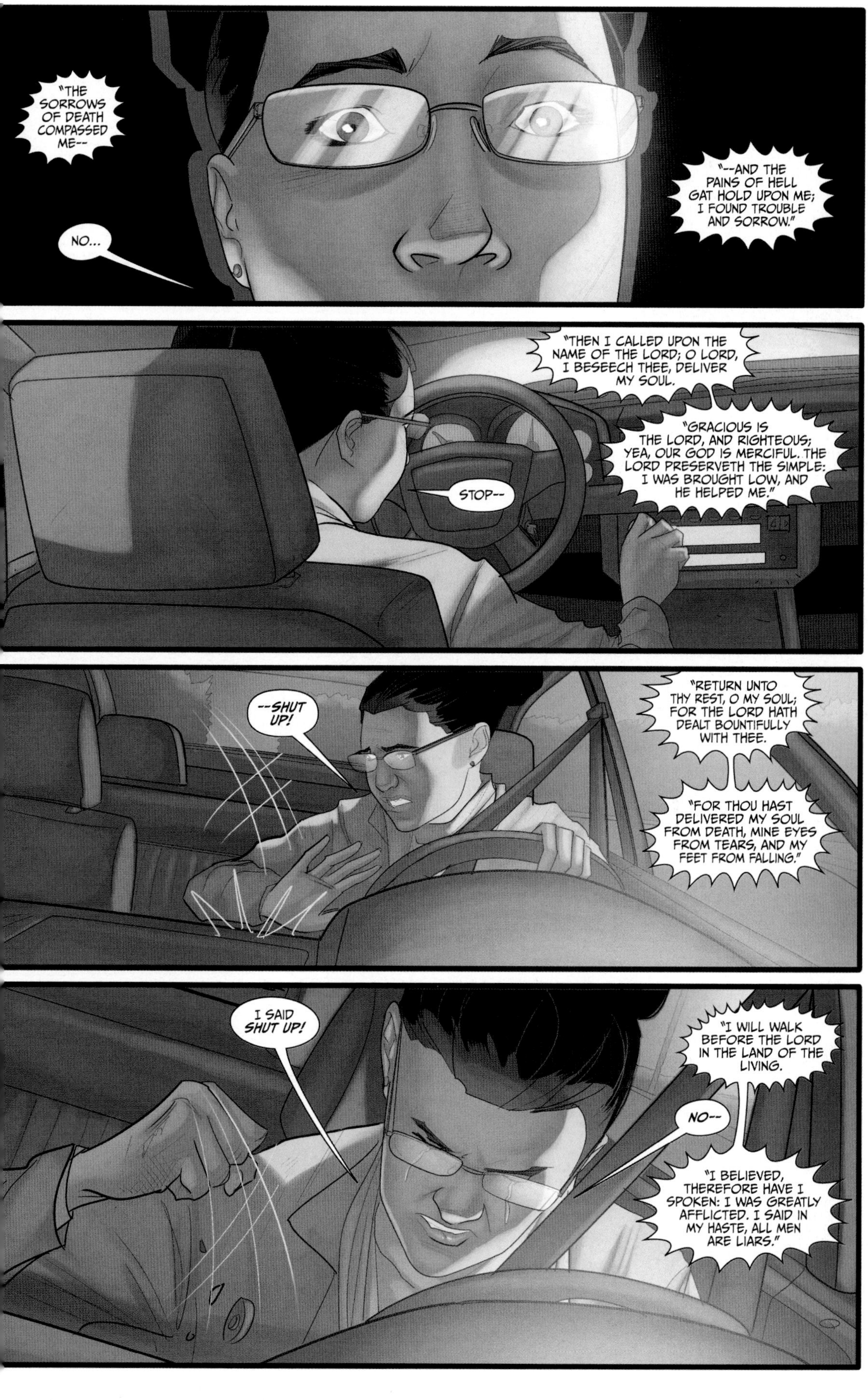
"THE SORROWS OF DEATH COMPASSED ME--
NO...
"--AND THE PAINS OF HELL GAT HOLD UPON ME; I FOUND TROUBLE AND SORROW."
"THEN I CALLED UPON THE NAME OF THE LORD; O LORD, I BESEECH THEE, DELIVER MY SOUL.
"GRACIOUS IS THE LORD, AND RIGHTEOUS; YEA, OUR GOD IS MERCIFUL. THE LORD PRESERVETH THE SIMPLE: I WAS BROUGHT LOW, AND HE HELPED ME."
STOP--
--SHUT UP!
"RETURN UNTO THY REST, O MY SOUL; FOR THE LORD HATH DEALT BOUNTIFULLY WITH THEE.
"FOR THOU HAST DELIVERED MY SOUL FROM DEATH, MINE EYES FROM TEARS, AND MY FEET FROM FALLING."
I SAID SHUT UP!
"I WILL WALK BEFORE THE LORD IN THE LAND OF THE LIVING.
NO--
"I BELIEVED, THEREFORE HAVE I SPOKEN: I WAS GREATLY AFFLICTED. I SAID IN MY HASTE, ALL MEN ARE LIARS."

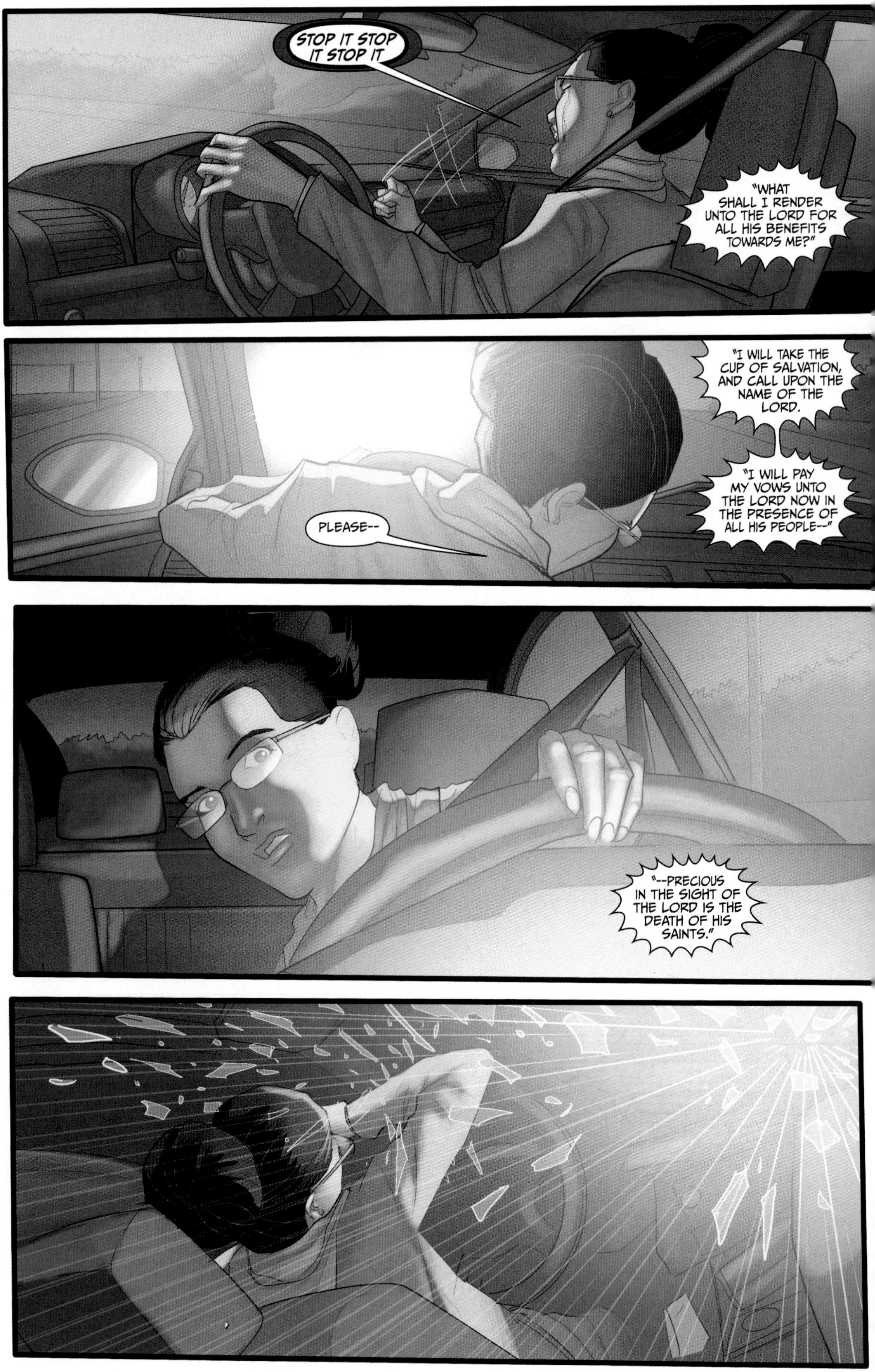
STOP IT STOP IT STOP IT
"WHAT SHALL I RENDER UNTO THE LORD FOR ALL HIS BENEFITS TOWARDS ME?"
"I WILL TAKE THE CUP OF SALVATION, AND CALL UPON THE NAME OF THE LORD.
PLEASE--
"I WILL PAY MY VOWS UNTO THE LORD NOW IN THE PRESENCE OF ALL HIS PEOPLE--"
"--PRECIOUS IN THE SIGHT OF THE LORD IS THE DEATH OF HIS SAINTS."

twenty**nine**

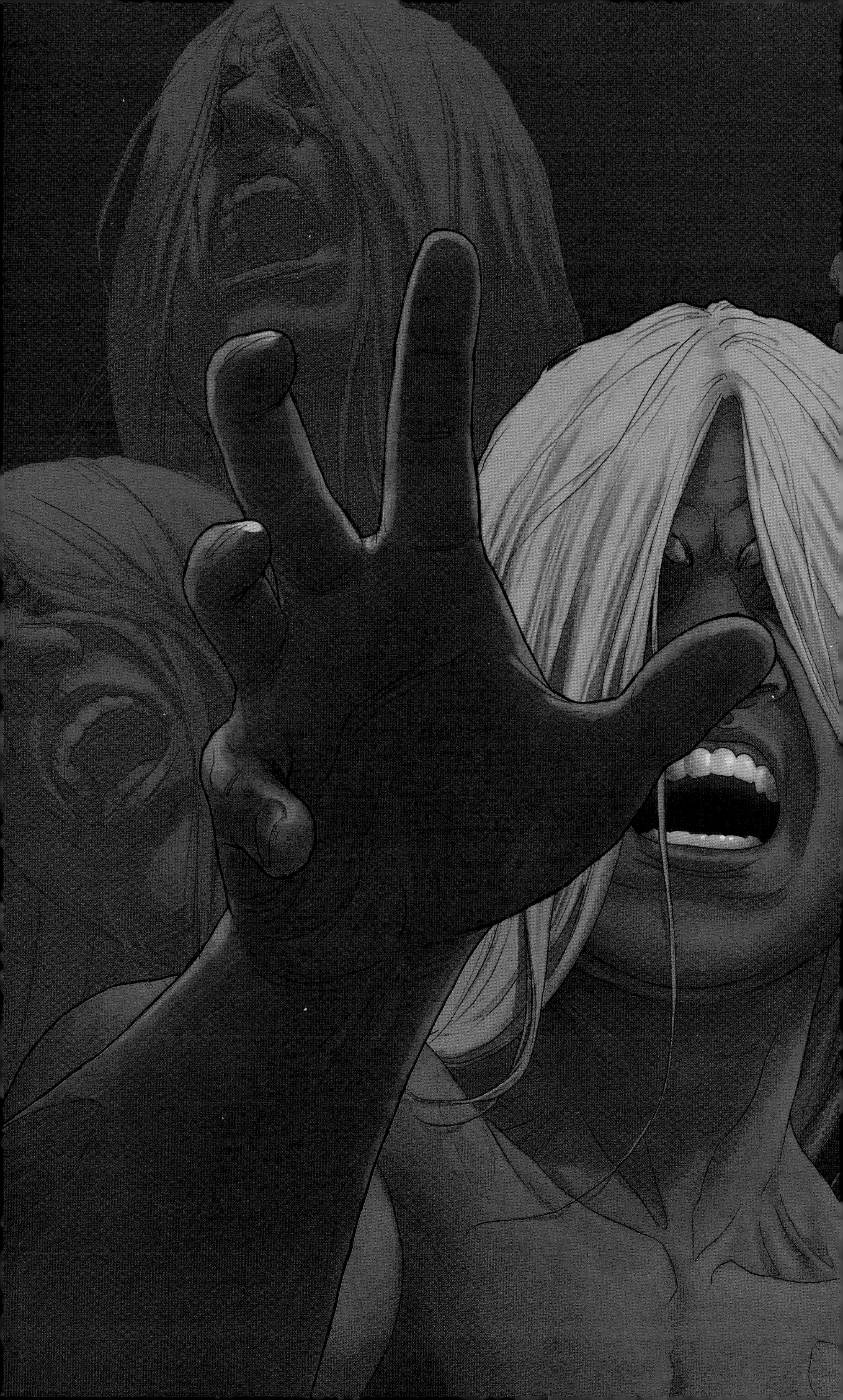

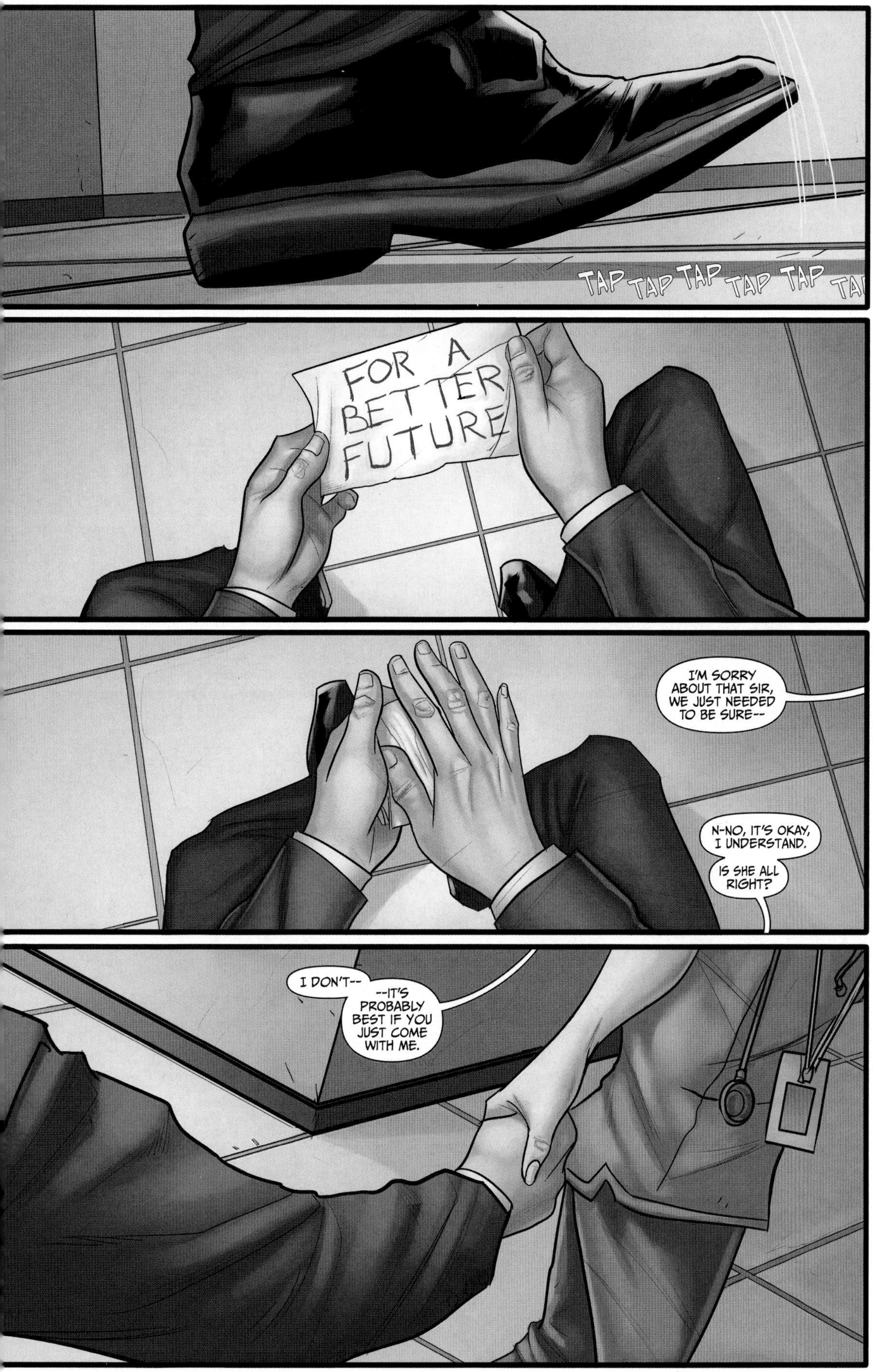
TAP TAP TAP TAP TAP
FOR A BETTER FUTURE
I'M SORRY ABOUT THAT SIR, WE JUST NEEDED TO BE SURE--
N-NO, IT'S OKAY, I UNDERSTAND.
IS SHE ALL RIGHT?
I DON'T--
--IT'S PROBABLY BEST IF YOU JUST COME WITH ME.

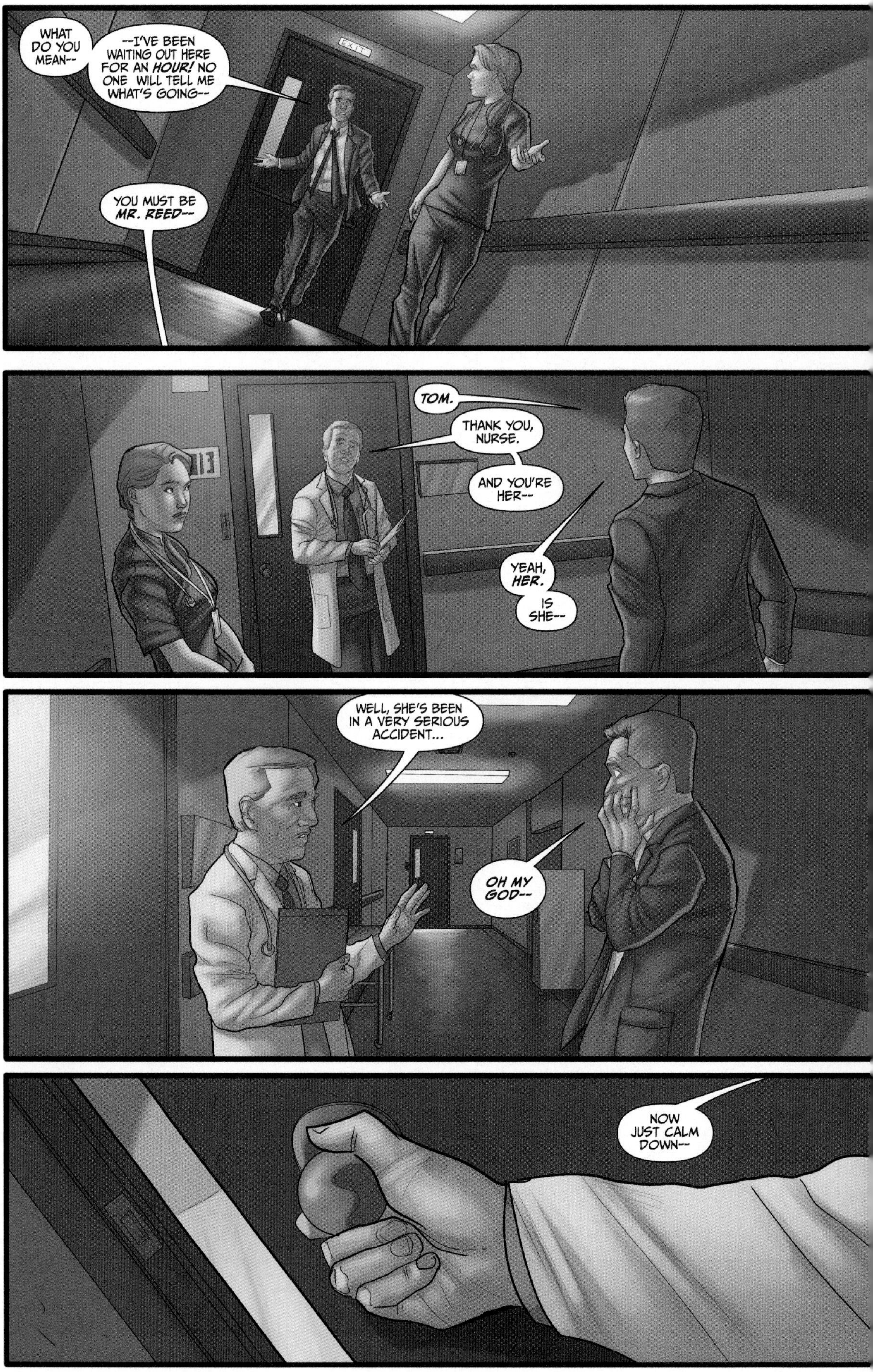
WHAT DO YOU MEAN--
--I'VE BEEN WAITING OUT HERE FOR AN *HOUR!* NO ONE WILL TELL ME WHAT'S GOING--
YOU MUST BE *MR. REED--*
TOM.
THANK YOU, NURSE.
AND YOU'RE HER--
YEAH, *HER.*
IS SHE--
WELL, SHE'S BEEN IN A VERY SERIOUS ACCIDENT...
OH MY GOD--
NOW JUST CALM DOWN--

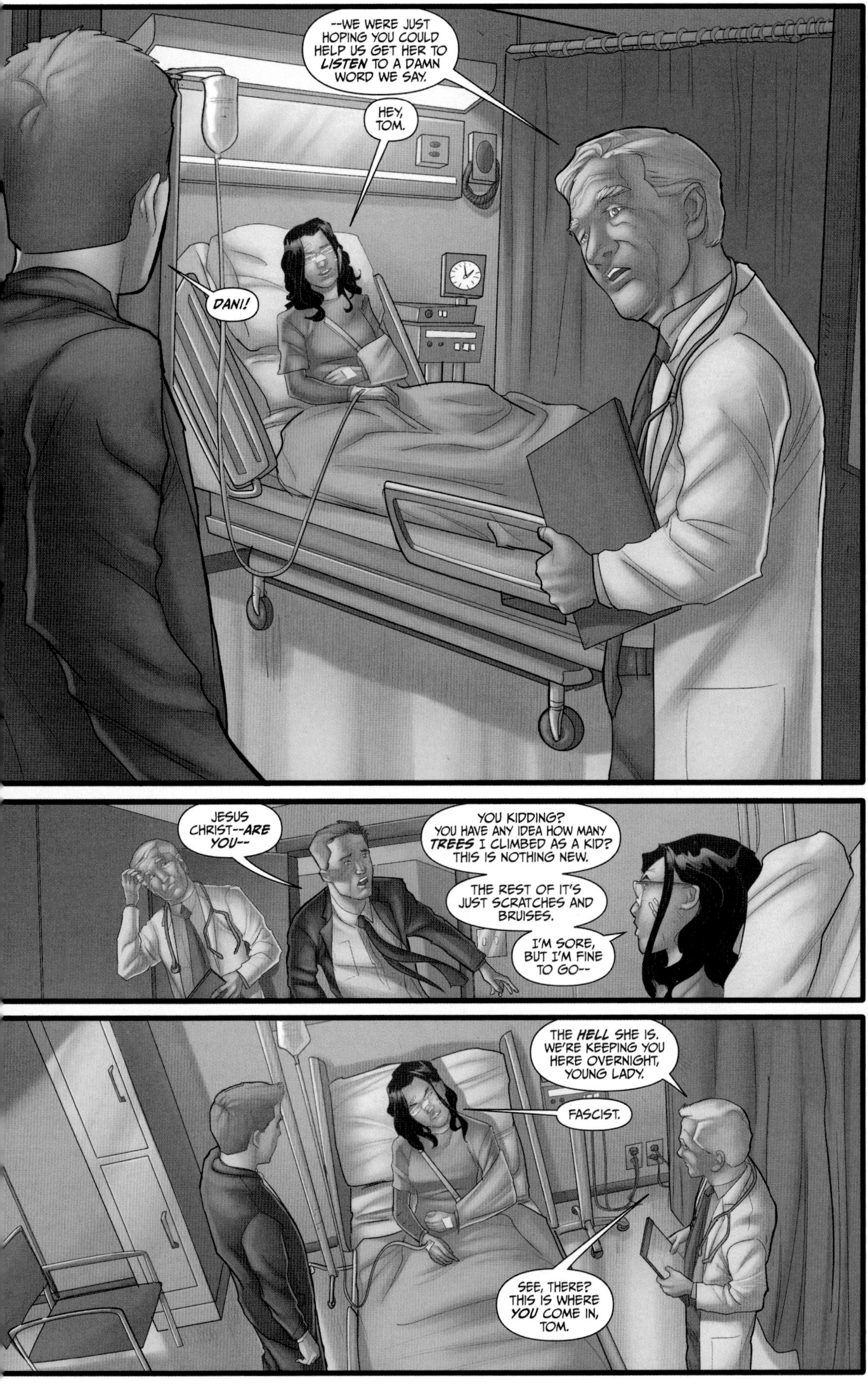
--WE WERE JUST HOPING YOU COULD HELP US GET HER TO LISTEN TO A DAMN WORD WE SAY.
HEY, TOM.
DANI!
JESUS CHRIST--ARE YOU--
YOU KIDDING? YOU HAVE ANY IDEA HOW MANY TREES I CLIMBED AS A KID? THIS IS NOTHING NEW.
THE REST OF IT'S JUST SCRATCHES AND BRUISES.
I'M SORE, BUT I'M FINE TO GO--
THE HELL SHE IS. WE'RE KEEPING YOU HERE OVERNIGHT, YOUNG LADY.
FASCIST.
SEE, THERE? THIS IS WHERE YOU COME IN, TOM.

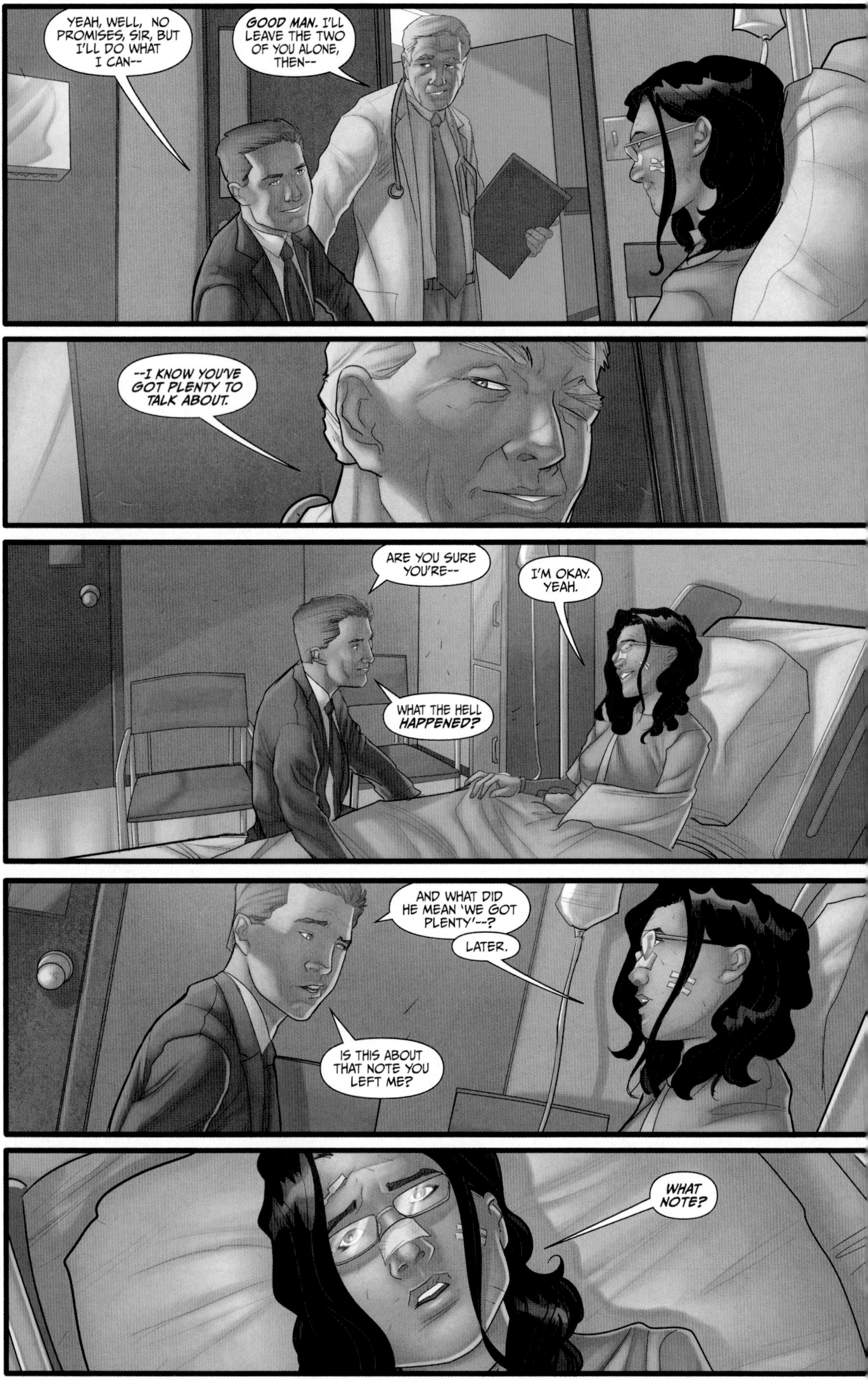
YEAH, WELL, NO PROMISES, SIR, BUT I'LL DO WHAT I CAN--
GOOD MAN. I'LL LEAVE THE TWO OF YOU ALONE, THEN--
--I KNOW YOU'VE GOT PLENTY TO TALK ABOUT.
ARE YOU SURE YOU'RE--
I'M OKAY. YEAH.
WHAT THE HELL HAPPENED?
AND WHAT DID HE MEAN 'WE GOT PLENTY'--?
LATER.
IS THIS ABOUT THAT NOTE YOU LEFT ME?
WHAT NOTE?

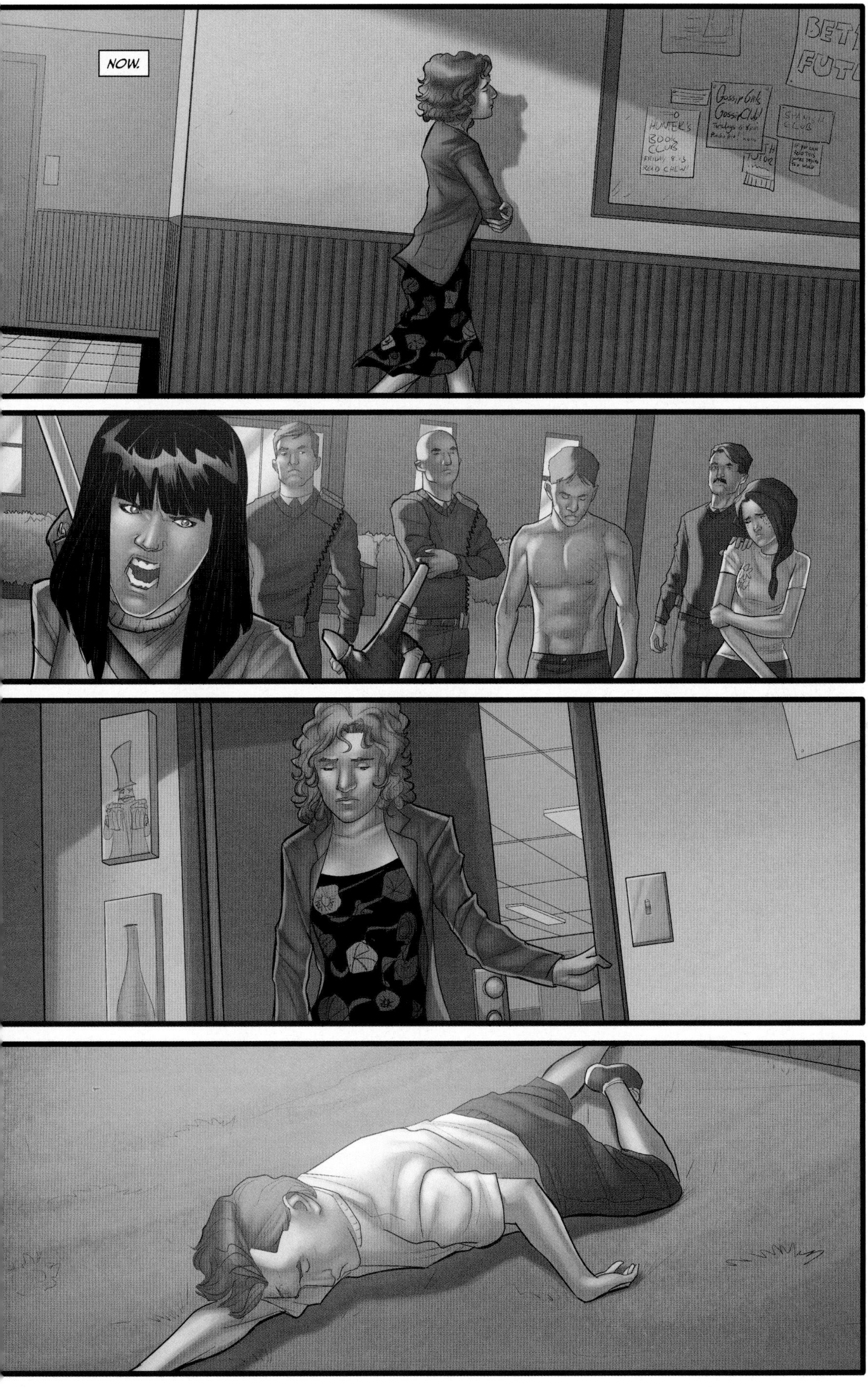

NOW.
Gossip Girls Gossip Club!
HUNTER'S BOOK CLUB
READ CHEW!

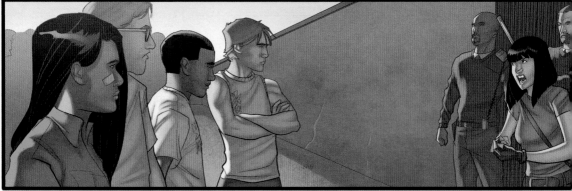

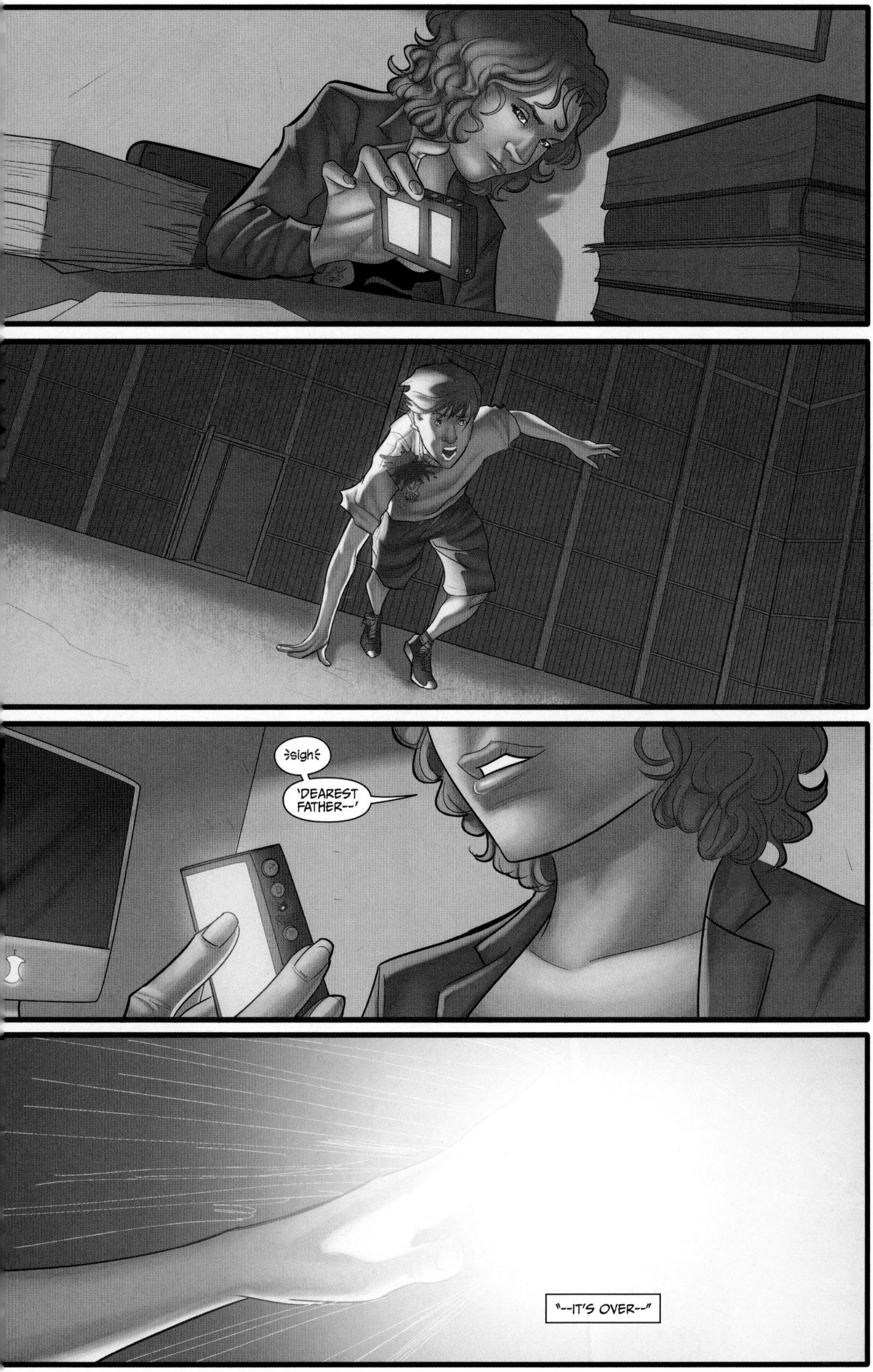

sigh
'DEAREST FATHER--'
"--IT'S OVER--"

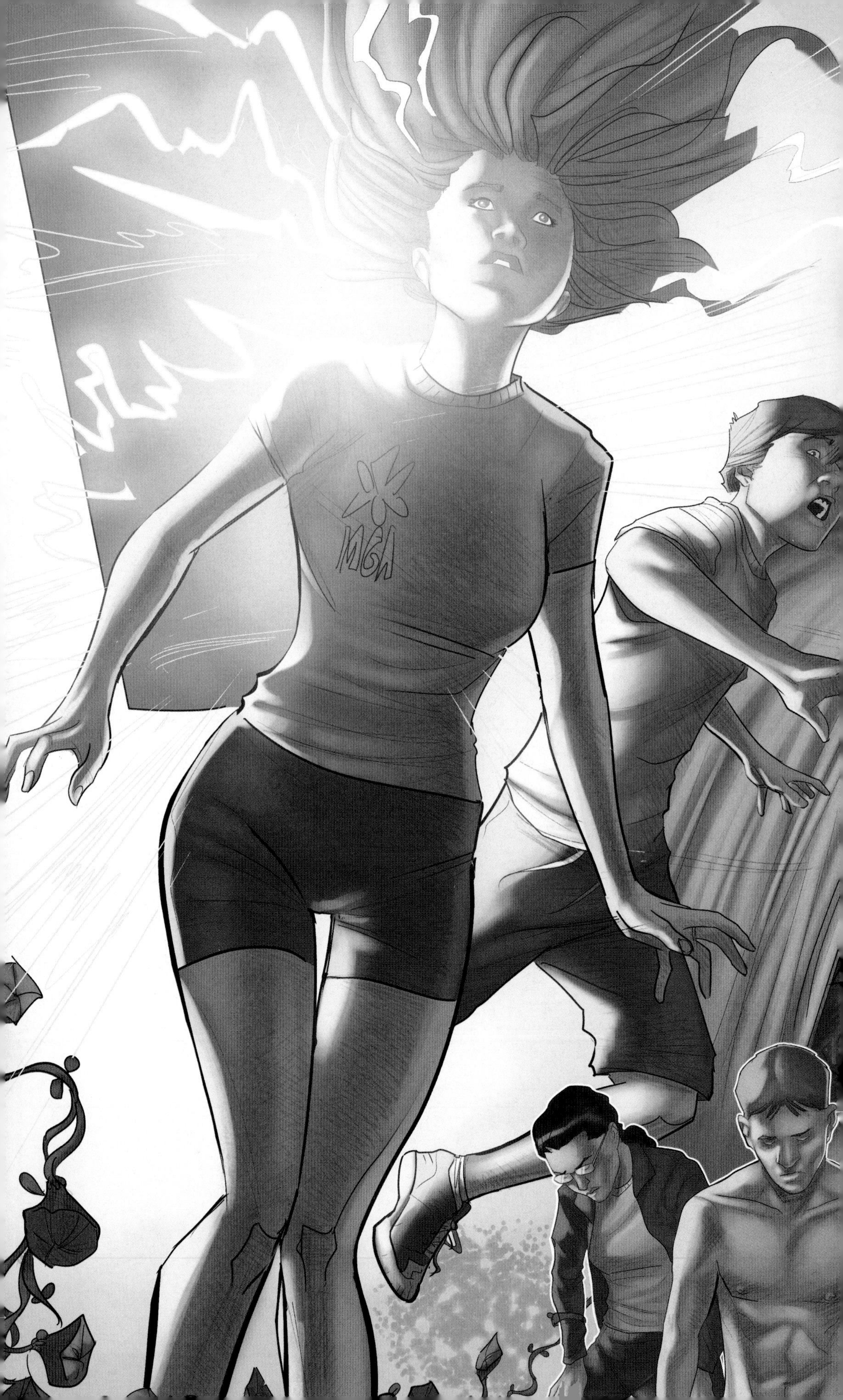
MGA

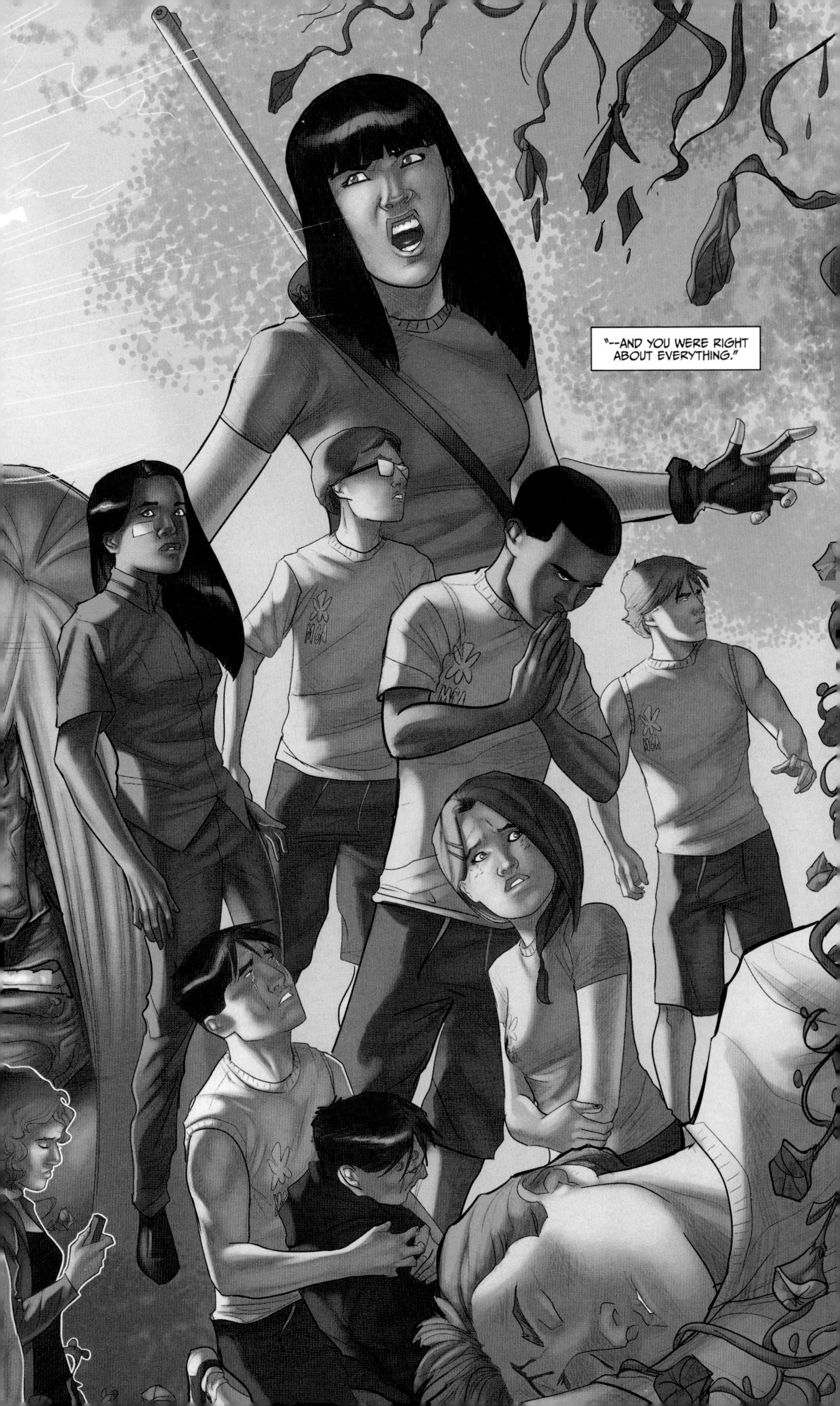
"--AND YOU WERE RIGHT
ABOUT EVERYTHING."

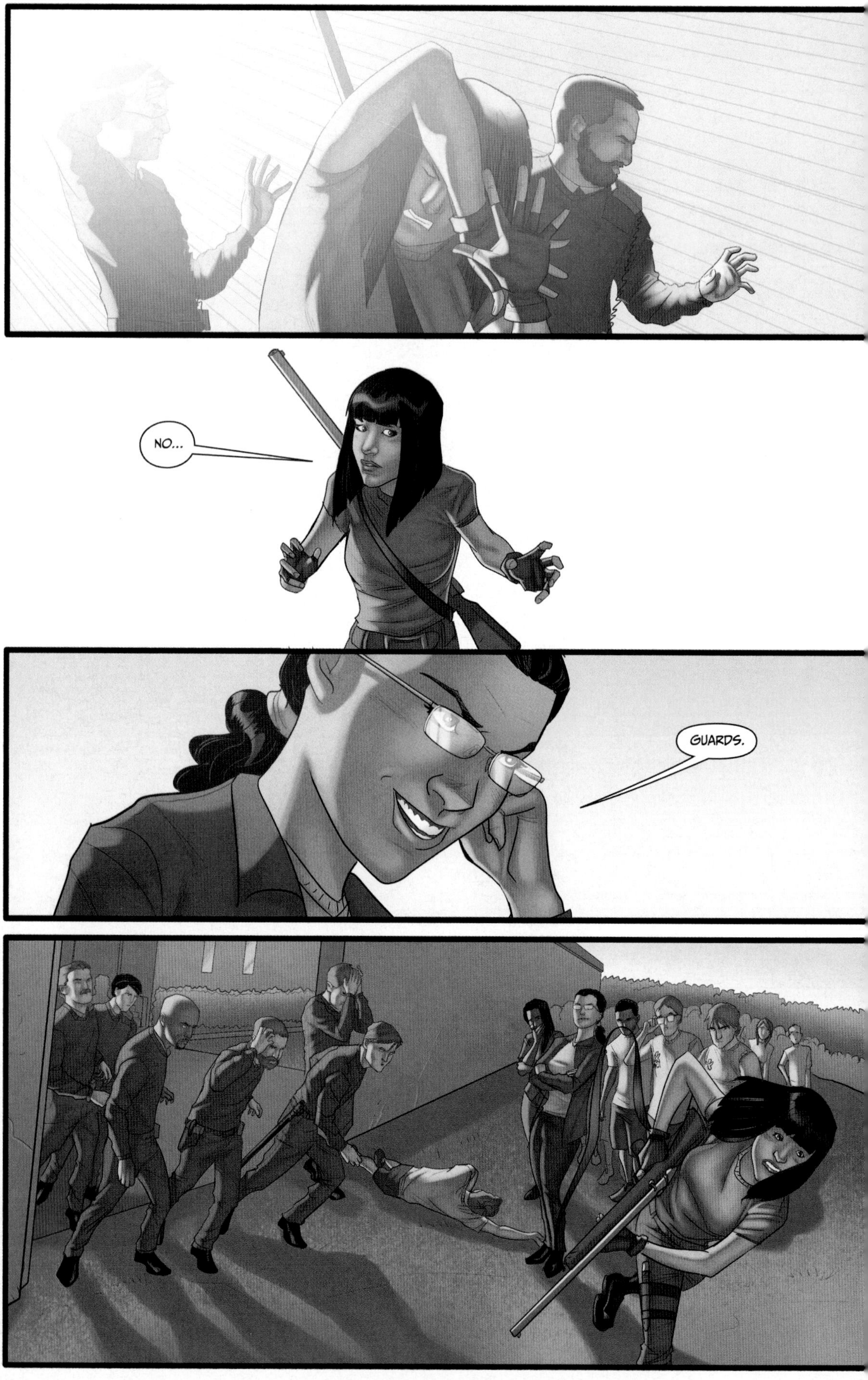
NO...
GUARDS.

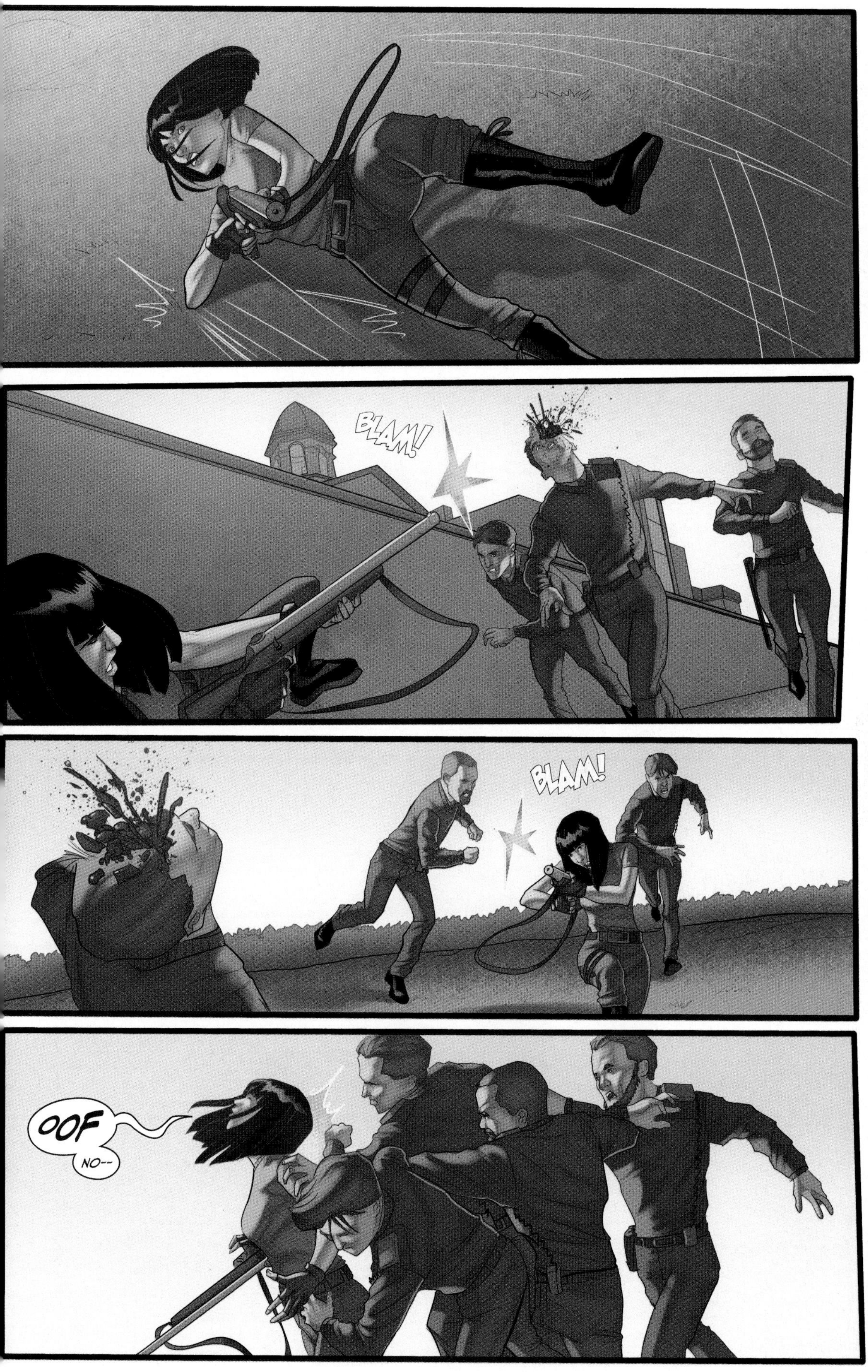
BLAM!
BLAM!
OOF
NO--

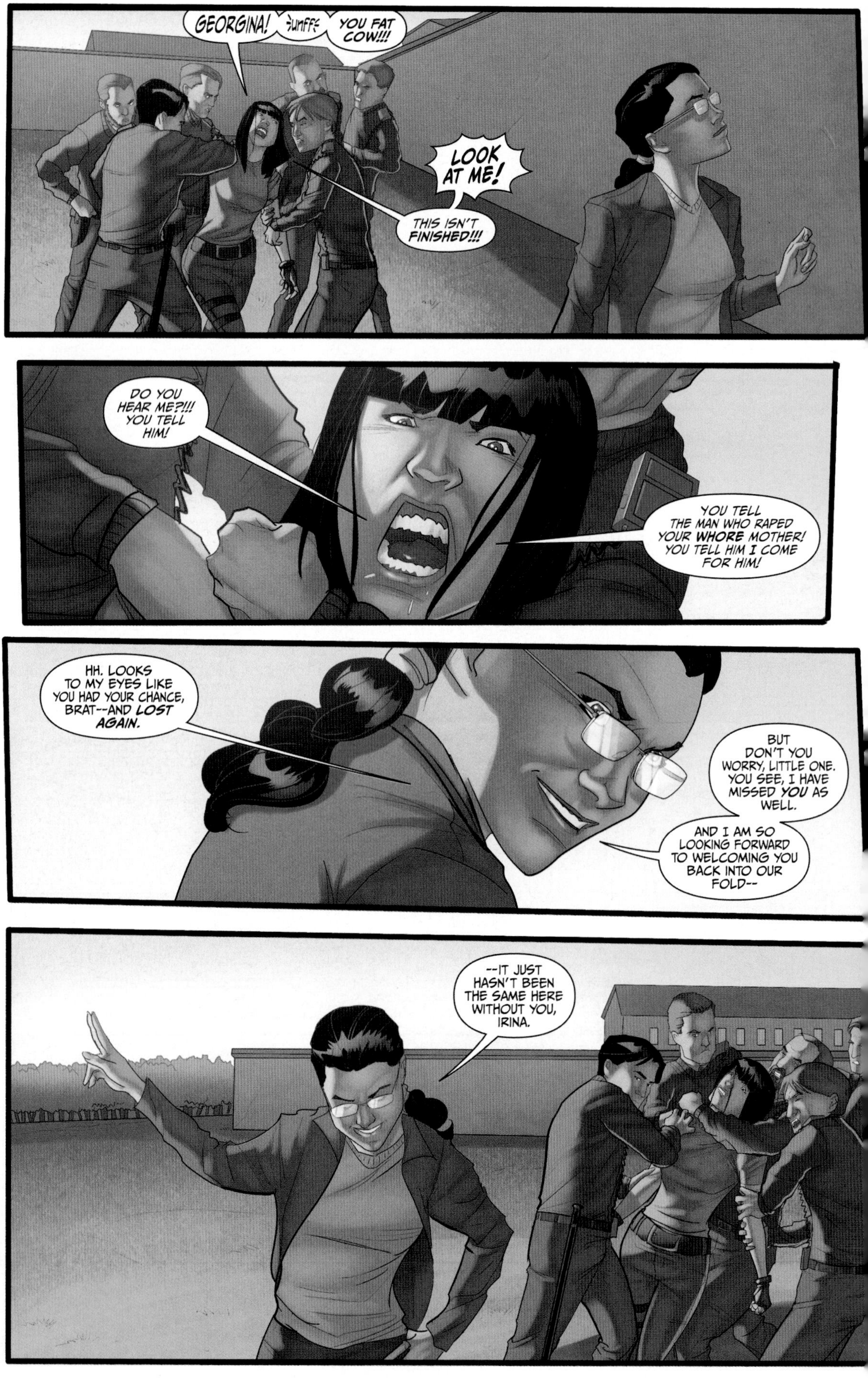
GEORGINA!
unff
YOU FAT COW!!!
LOOK AT ME!
THIS ISN'T FINISHED!!!
DO YOU HEAR ME?!!! YOU TELL HIM!
YOU TELL THE MAN WHO RAPED YOUR WHORE MOTHER! YOU TELL HIM I COME FOR HIM!
HH. LOOKS TO MY EYES LIKE YOU HAD YOUR CHANCE, BRAT--AND LOST AGAIN.
BUT DON'T YOU WORRY, LITTLE ONE. YOU SEE, I HAVE MISSED YOU AS WELL.
AND I AM SO LOOKING FORWARD TO WELCOMING YOU BACK INTO OUR FOLD--
--IT JUST HASN'T BEEN THE SAME HERE WITHOUT YOU, IRINA.

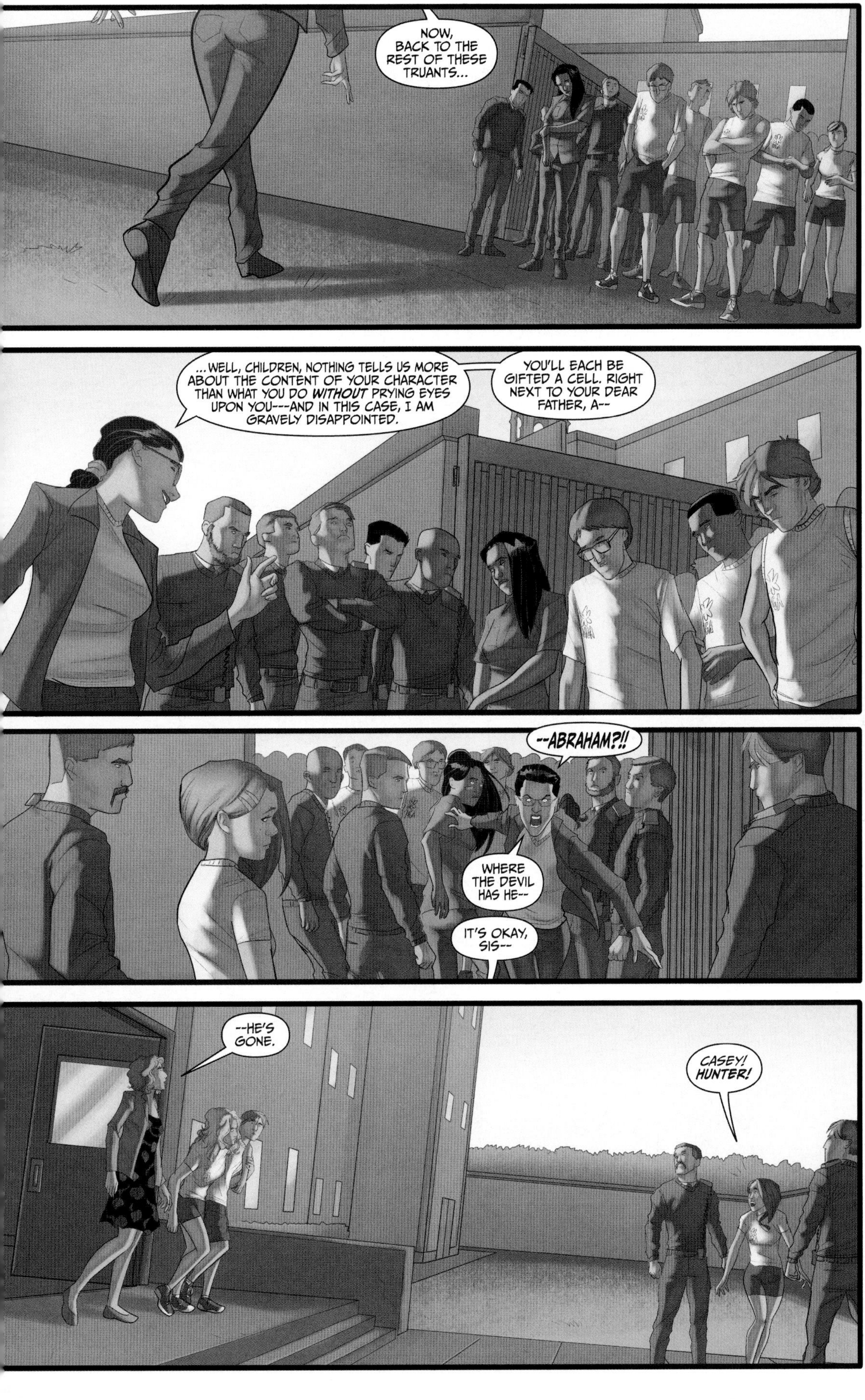
NOW, BACK TO THE REST OF THESE TRUANTS...
...WELL, CHILDREN, NOTHING TELLS US MORE ABOUT THE CONTENT OF YOUR CHARACTER THAN WHAT YOU DO *WITHOUT* PRYING EYES UPON YOU---AND IN THIS CASE, I AM GRAVELY DISAPPOINTED.
YOU'LL EACH BE GIFTED A CELL. RIGHT NEXT TO YOUR DEAR FATHER, A--
--ABRAHAM?!!
WHERE THE DEVIL HAS HE--
IT'S OKAY, SIS--
--HE'S GONE.
CASEY! *HUNTER!*

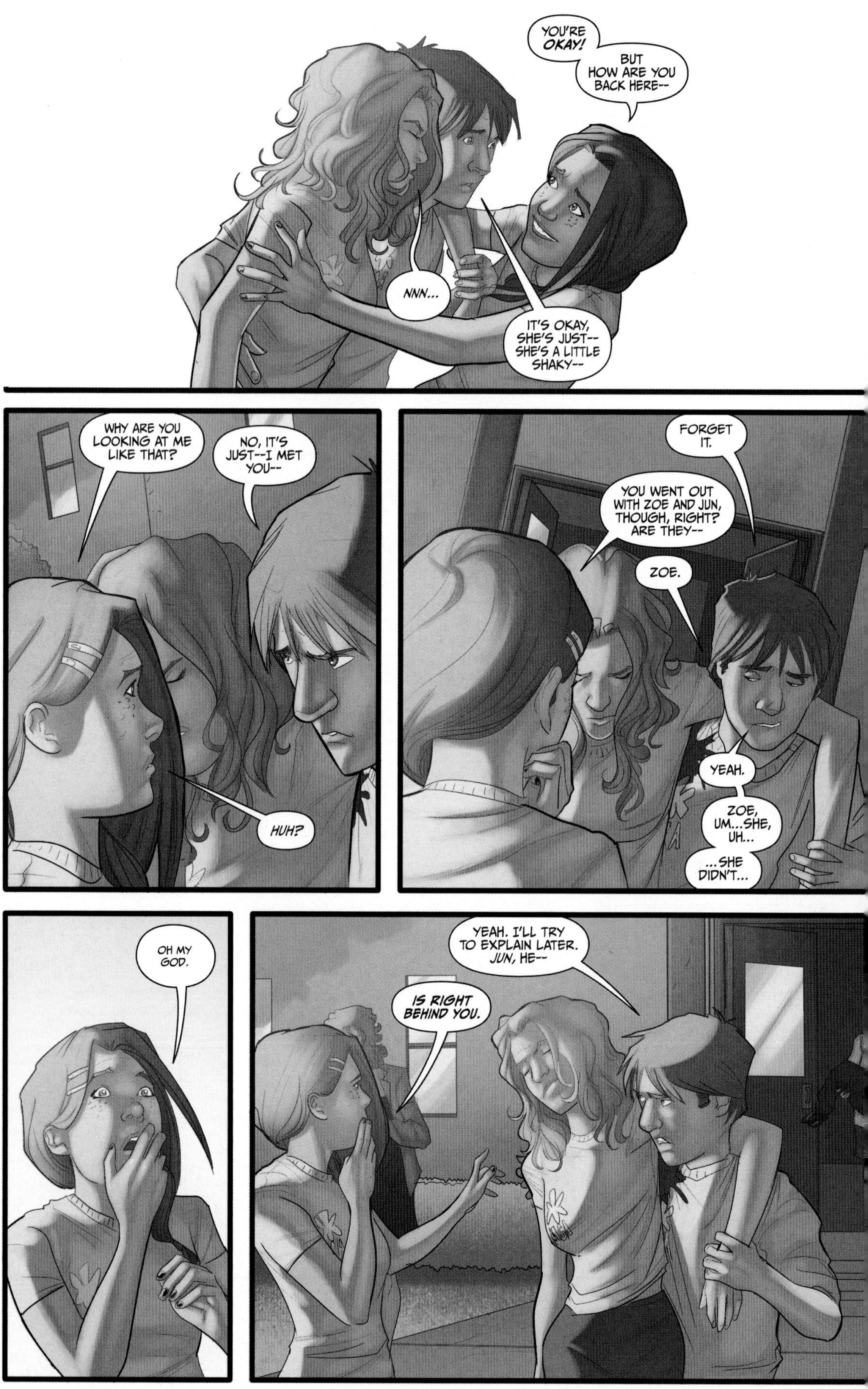
YOU'RE OKAY!
BUT HOW ARE YOU BACK HERE--
NNN...
IT'S OKAY, SHE'S JUST-- SHE'S A LITTLE SHAKY--
WHY ARE YOU LOOKING AT ME LIKE THAT?
NO, IT'S JUST--I MET YOU--
HUH?
FORGET IT.
YOU WENT OUT WITH ZOE AND JUN, THOUGH, RIGHT? ARE THEY--
ZOE.
YEAH.
ZOE, UM...SHE, UH...
...SHE DIDN'T...
OH MY GOD.
YEAH. I'LL TRY TO EXPLAIN LATER. JUN, HE--
IS RIGHT BEHIND YOU.

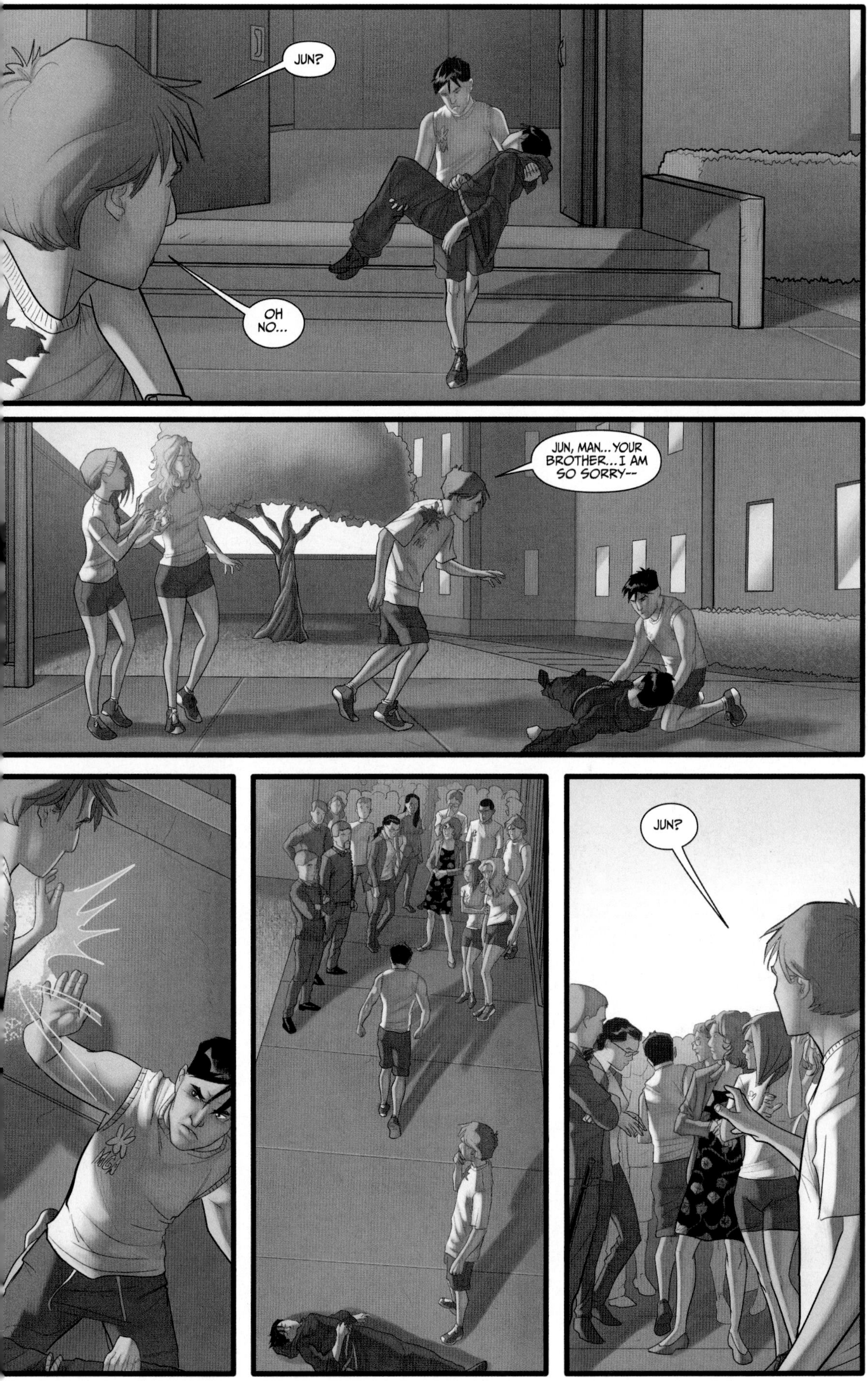
JUN?
OH NO...
JUN, MAN...YOUR BROTHER...I AM SO SORRY--
JUN?

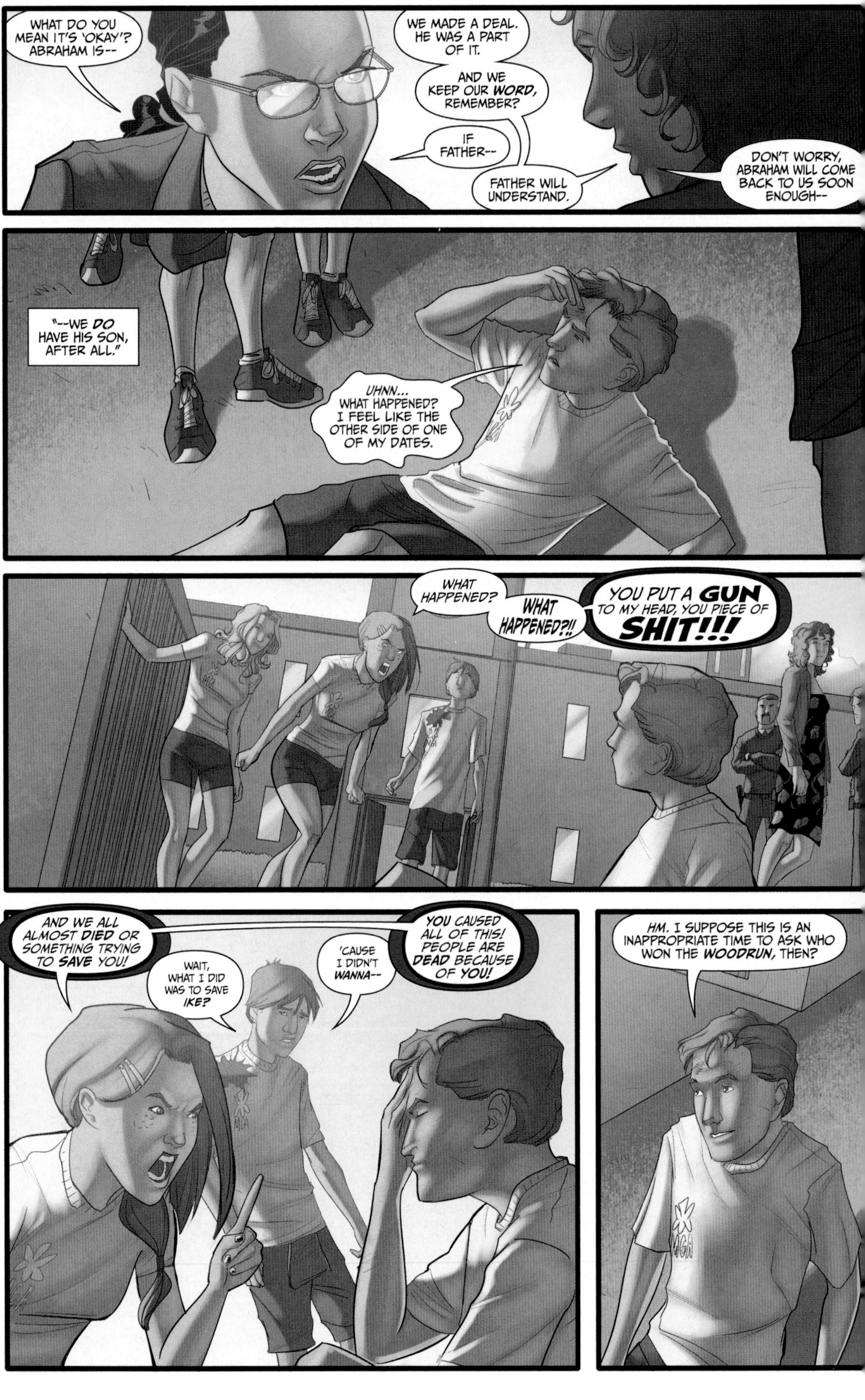

WHAT DO YOU MEAN IT'S 'OKAY'? ABRAHAM IS--
WE MADE A DEAL. HE WAS A PART OF IT.
AND WE KEEP OUR WORD, REMEMBER?
IF FATHER--
FATHER WILL UNDERSTAND.
DON'T WORRY, ABRAHAM WILL COME BACK TO US SOON ENOUGH--
"--WE DO HAVE HIS SON, AFTER ALL."
UHNN... WHAT HAPPENED? I FEEL LIKE THE OTHER SIDE OF ONE OF MY DATES.
WHAT HAPPENED?
WHAT HAPPENED?!!
YOU PUT A GUN TO MY HEAD, YOU PIECE OF SHIT!!!
AND WE ALL ALMOST DIED OR SOMETHING TRYING TO SAVE YOU!
YOU CAUSED ALL OF THIS! PEOPLE ARE DEAD BECAUSE OF YOU!
WAIT, WHAT I DID WAS TO SAVE IKE?
'CAUSE I DIDN'T WANNA--
HM. I SUPPOSE THIS IS AN INAPPROPRIATE TIME TO ASK WHO WON THE WOODRUN, THEN?

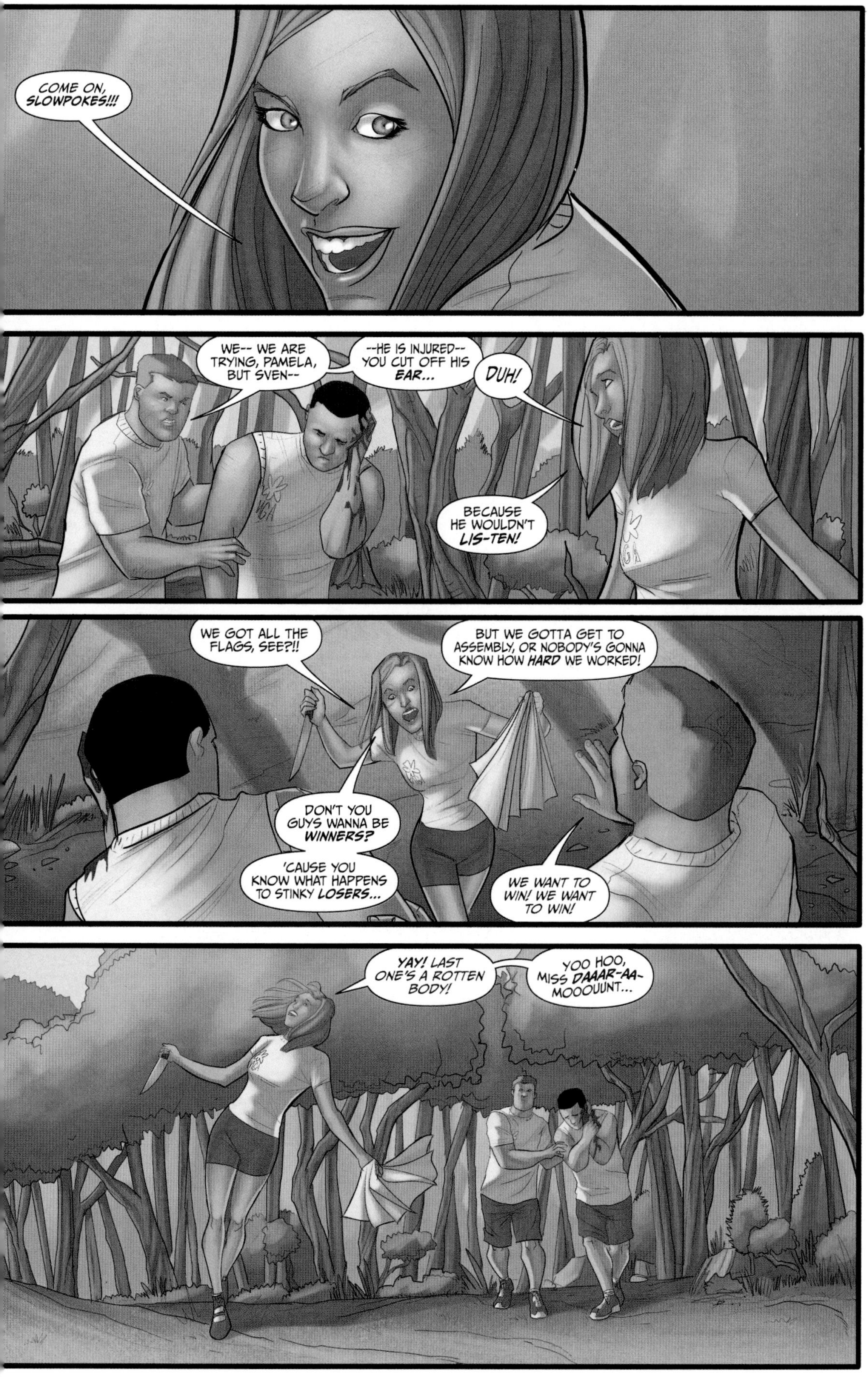

COME ON, SLOWPOKES!!!
WE-- WE ARE TRYING, PAMELA, BUT SVEN--
--HE IS INJURED-- YOU CUT OFF HIS EAR...
DUH!
BECAUSE HE WOULDN'T LIS-TEN!
WE GOT ALL THE FLAGS, SEE?!!
BUT WE GOTTA GET TO ASSEMBLY, OR NOBODY'S GONNA KNOW HOW HARD WE WORKED!
DON'T YOU GUYS WANNA BE WINNERS?
'CAUSE YOU KNOW WHAT HAPPENS TO STINKY LOSERS...
WE WANT TO WIN! WE WANT TO WIN!
YAY! LAST ONE'S A ROTTEN BODY!
YOO HOO, MISS DAAAR-AA-MOOOUUNT...

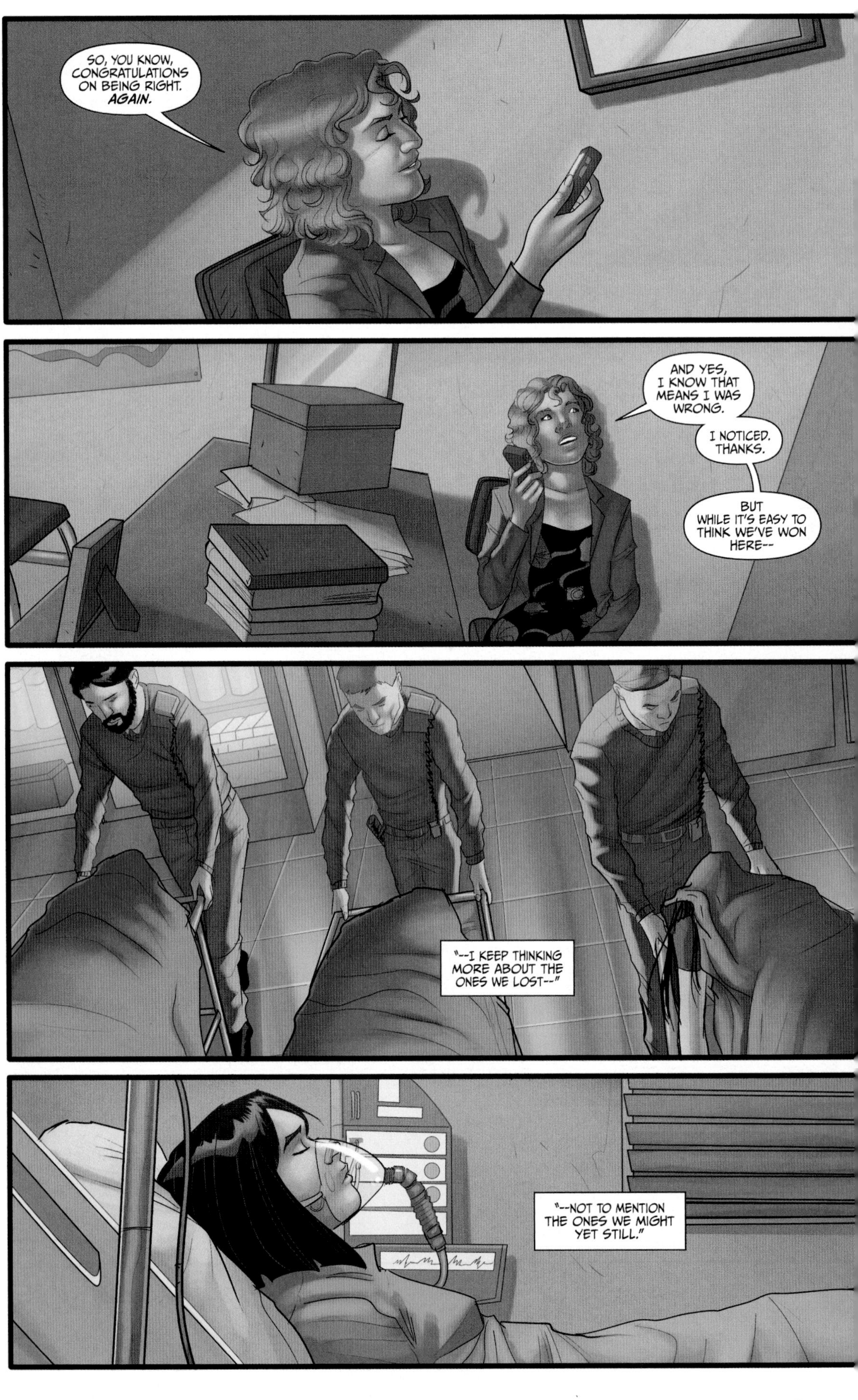
SO, YOU KNOW, CONGRATULATIONS ON BEING RIGHT. *AGAIN.*
AND YES, I KNOW THAT MEANS I WAS WRONG.
I NOTICED. THANKS.
BUT WHILE IT'S EASY TO THINK WE'VE WON HERE--
"--I KEEP THINKING MORE ABOUT THE ONES WE LOST--"
"--NOT TO MENTION THE ONES WE MIGHT YET STILL."

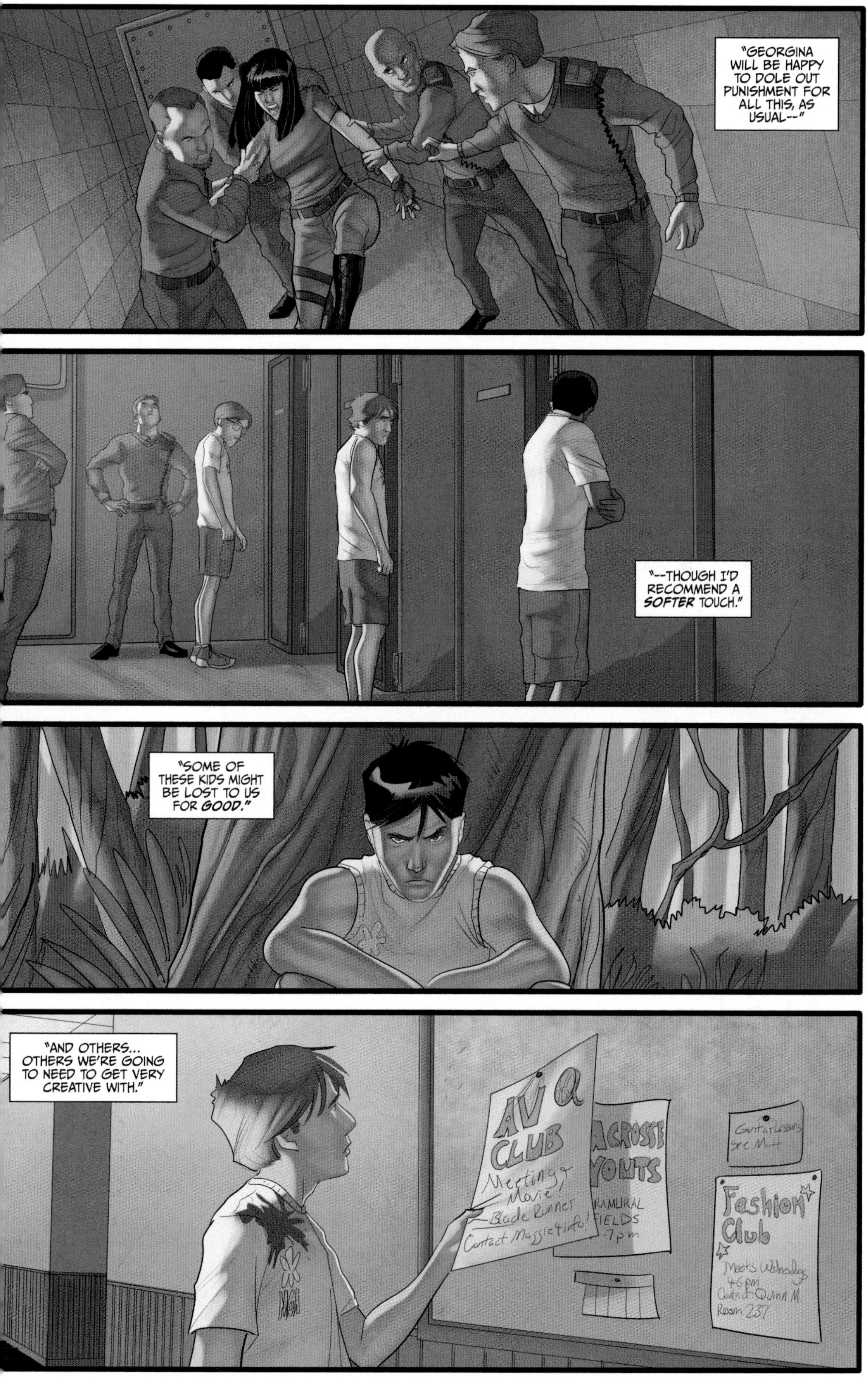

"GEORGINA WILL BE HAPPY TO DOLE OUT PUNISHMENT FOR ALL THIS, AS USUAL--"
"--THOUGH I'D RECOMMEND A *SOFTER* TOUCH."
"SOME OF THESE KIDS MIGHT BE LOST TO US FOR *GOOD.*"
"AND OTHERS... OTHERS WE'RE GOING TO NEED TO GET VERY CREATIVE WITH."
AV CLUB
Meeting & Movie!
Blade Runner
Contact Maggie 4 info!
ACROSSE
YOUTS
RAMURAL FIELDS
-7pm
Guitar Lessons see Matt
Fashion Club
Meets Wednesdays 4-6pm
Contact Quinn M.
Room 237

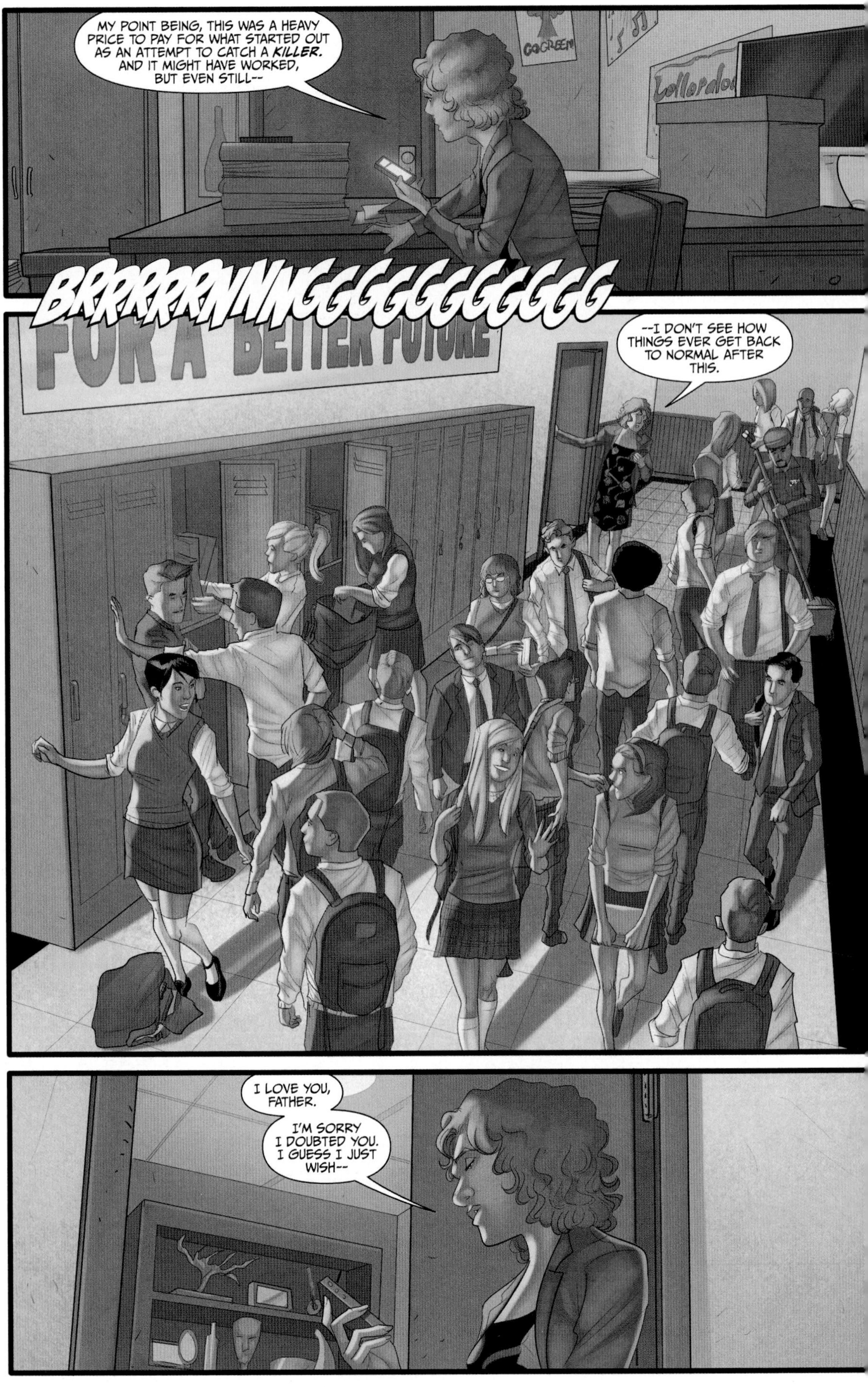
MY POINT BEING, THIS WAS A HEAVY PRICE TO PAY FOR WHAT STARTED OUT AS AN ATTEMPT TO CATCH A KILLER. AND IT MIGHT HAVE WORKED, BUT EVEN STILL--
GO GREEN
BRRRRRNNNGGGGGGGGGG
FOR A BETTER FUTURE
--I DON'T SEE HOW THINGS EVER GET BACK TO NORMAL AFTER THIS.
I LOVE YOU, FATHER.
I'M SORRY I DOUBTED YOU. I GUESS I JUST WISH--

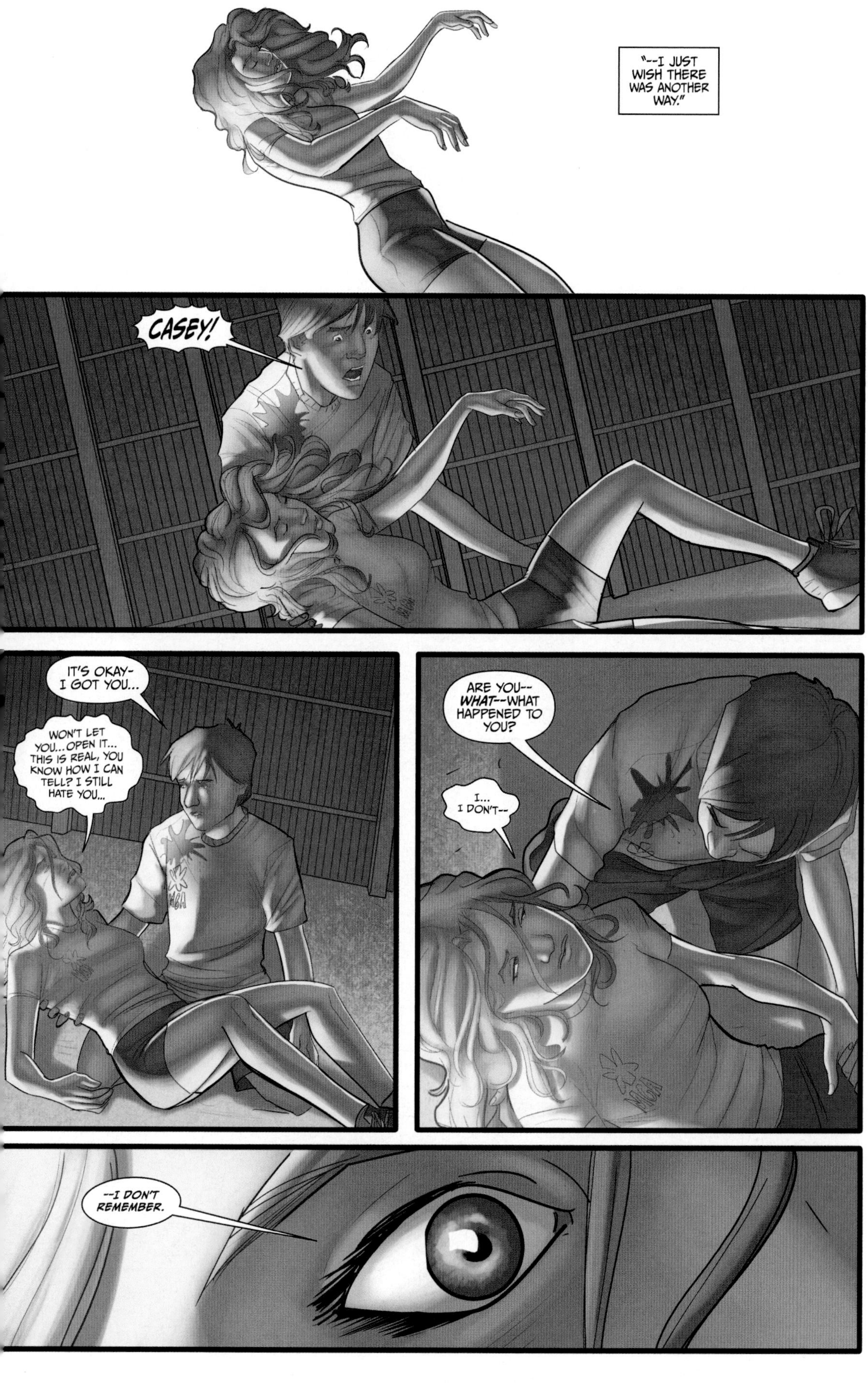
"--I JUST WISH THERE WAS ANOTHER WAY."
CASEY!
IT'S OKAY- I GOT YOU...
WON'T LET YOU...OPEN IT... THIS IS REAL, YOU KNOW HOW I CAN TELL? I STILL HATE YOU...
ARE YOU-- WHAT--WHAT HAPPENED TO YOU?
I... I DON'T--
--I DON'T REMEMBER.

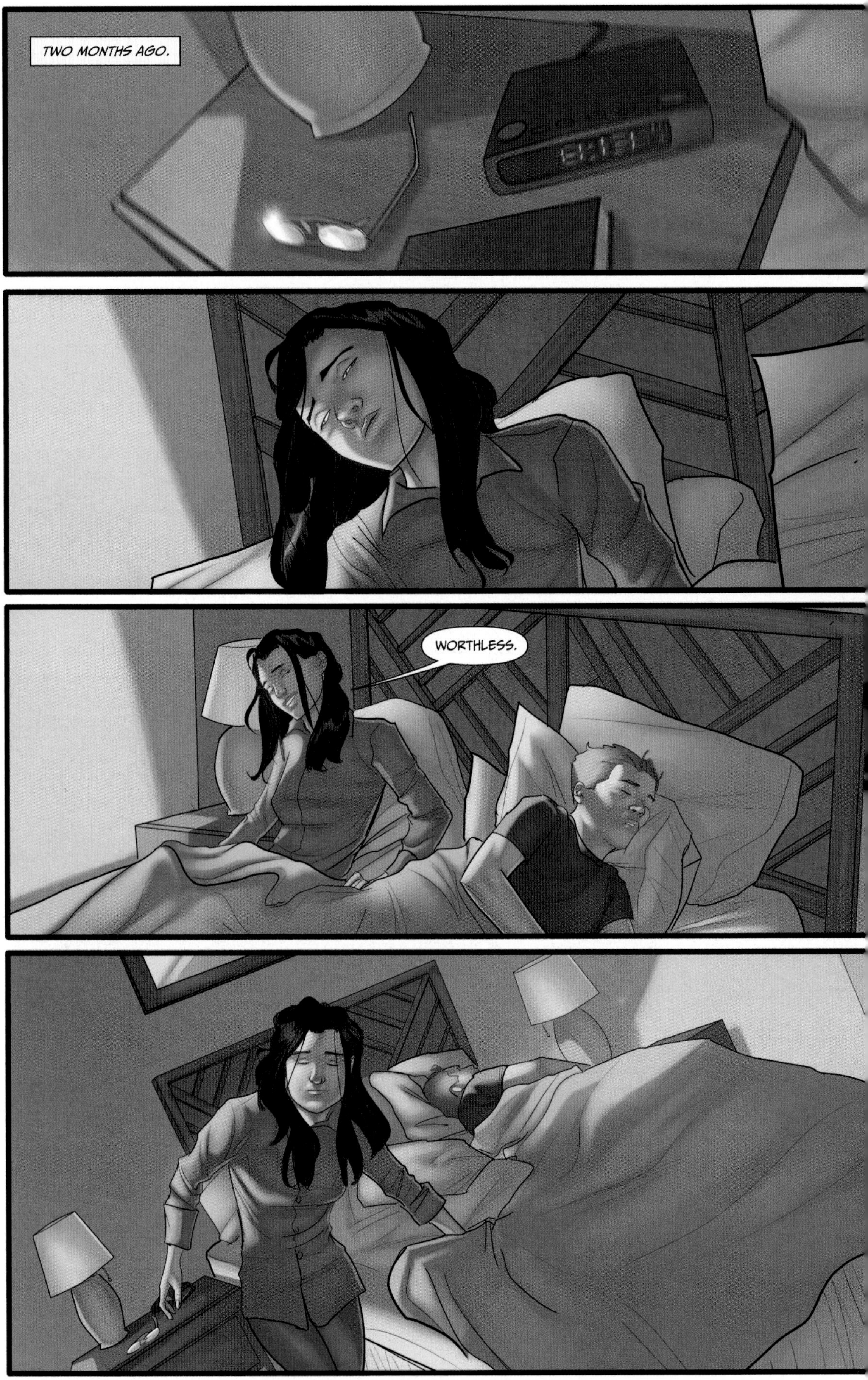
TWO MONTHS AGO.
WORTHLESS.

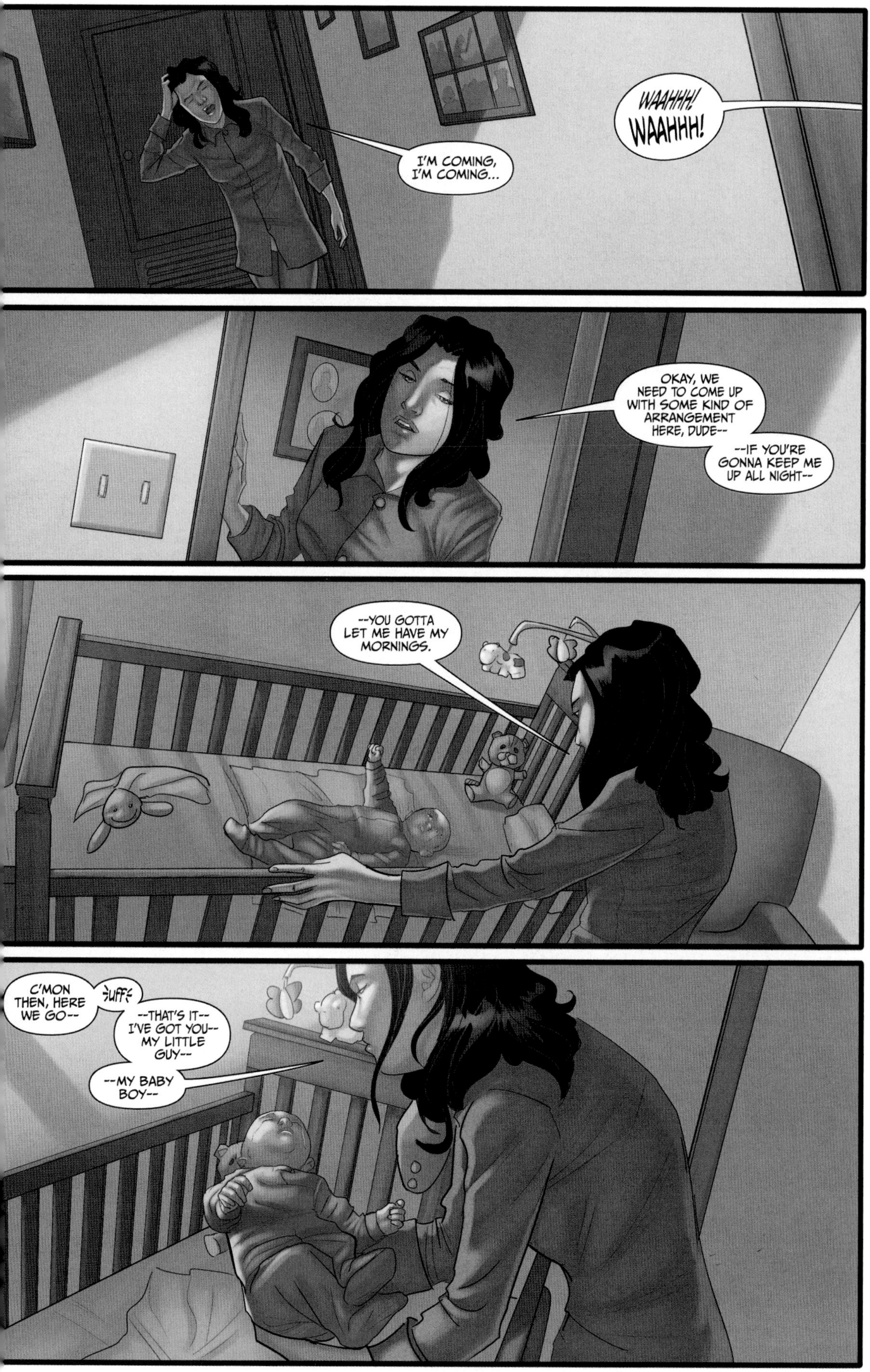
WAAHHH! WAAHHH!
I'M COMING, I'M COMING...
OKAY, WE NEED TO COME UP WITH SOME KIND OF ARRANGEMENT HERE, DUDE--
--IF YOU'RE GONNA KEEP ME UP ALL NIGHT--
--YOU GOTTA LET ME HAVE MY MORNINGS.
C'MON THEN, HERE WE GO--
UFF
--THAT'S IT-- I'VE GOT YOU-- MY LITTLE GUY--
--MY BABY BOY--

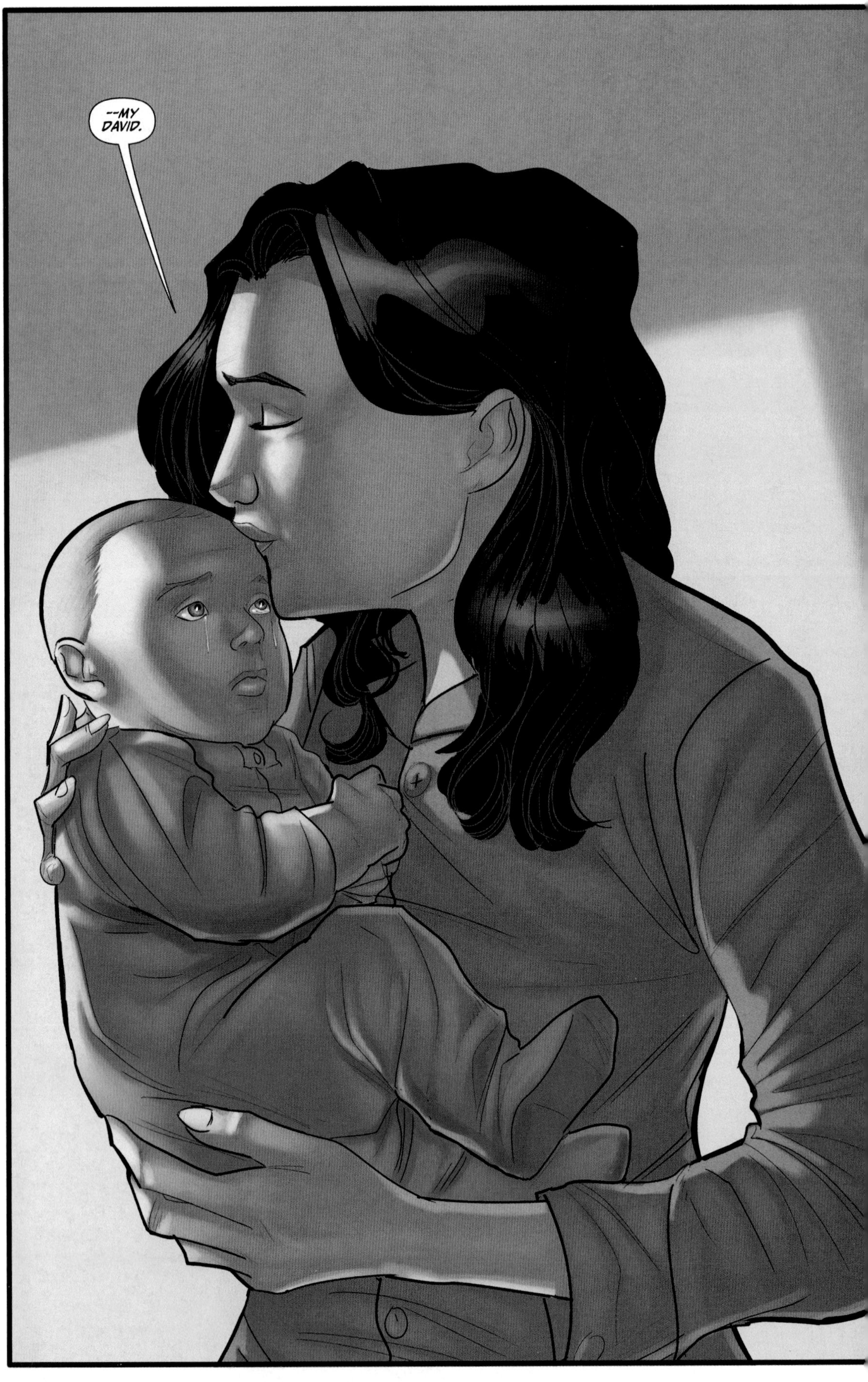
--MY DAVID.